THE TAIL WAGS THE DOG

⌐ WAGS
⌐⌐ DOG

International Politics and the Middle East

Efraim Karsh

B L O O M S B U R Y

NEW YORK • LONDON • OXFORD • NEW DELHI • SYDNEY

Bloomsbury USA
An imprint of Bloomsbury Publishing Plc

1385 Broadway	50 Bedford Square
New York	London
NY 10018	WC1B 3DP
USA	UK

www.bloomsbury.com

BLOOMSBURY and the Diana logo are trademarks of Bloomsbury Publishing Plc

First published in Great Britain 2015
First U.S. edition 2015

ISBN: HB: 978-1-63286-118-4
        ePub: 978-1-63286-119-1

Library of Congress Cataloging-in-Publication Data has been applied for.

2 4 6 8 10 9 7 5 3 1

Typeset by Integra Software Services Pvt. Ltd.
Printed and bound in the U.S.A. by Thomson-Shore Inc., Dexter, Michigan

To find out more about our authors and books visit www.bloomsbury.com.
Here you will find extracts, author interviews, details of forthcoming events,
and the option to sign up for our newsletters.

Bloomsbury books may be purchased for business or promotional use.
For information on bulk purchases please contact Macmillan Corporate and
Premium Sales Department at specialmarkets@macmillan.com.

In memory of Fred Halliday

CONTENTS

INTRODUCTION

In the morning hours of Tuesday, 22 July 2014, US Secretary of State John Kerry arrived at the presidential palace in Cairo for a meeting with Abdel Fattah Sisi. Israel and the 'Islamic Resistance Movement' (better known by its Arabic acronym Hamas) were in the midst of their third war in five years and the US administration sought to convince the newly inaugurated president to desist from his mediation attempts and endorse a ceasefire proposal by Turkey and Qatar – Hamas's foremost patrons.

Engaged in a mortal fight against Egypt's Muslim Brotherhood, Hamas's parent organization, which he had removed from power the previous year, Sisi had no intention of helping its Gaza offspring and he lost no time indicating his view of the American initiative. Rather than spirit Kerry to his appointment, as is the common practice on such occasions, Sisi required the secretary of state and his entourage to undergo a thorough metal detector screening – in full view of the world media. And while the State Department shrugged off the incident as a glitch by an overzealous employee, the Egyptian press and social media applauded it as a courageous snub of the world's 'only remaining superpower' (as the United States has been commonly known since the collapse of its Soviet nemesis).[1]

However extraordinary, the image of America's top diplomat manhandled by security guards of a client state in receipt of tens of billions in US economic and military aid was just the latest (if the most striking) of a long series of foreign policy humiliations endured by the Obama administration in the Middle East. At the end of June 2014 the White House's plea for revocation of the prison sentencing of three Al Jazeera journalists on concocted security charges was flatly rejected by Sisi, while four months later Vice President Joe Biden was forced to publicly apologize to Turkish Prime Minister Recep Tayyip Erdoğan for having (correctly) criticized Ankara's blanket permission to foreign jihadists to cross into Syria.[2]

More significantly, when in October 2013 Washington suspended weapons supplies to the Egyptian army in retribution for its overthrow of the country's Muslim Brotherhood regime a few months earlier, Cairo hosted the Russian foreign and defence ministers on a state visit – the first of its kind since changing its orientation from East to West four decades earlier – and in February 2014 then-Minister of Defence Sisi, already Egypt's effective ruler, visited Moscow, where he met with President Putin and signed a large arms deal in return for the restoration of the port services enjoyed by the Russian navy until the mid-1970s. Having apparently got the message, on 10 June a humbler Barack Obama called Sisi to congratulate him on his electoral victory and to reaffirm 'the strategic partnership between the United States and Egypt'. Three weeks later Kerry travelled to Cairo to voice strong support for the new president and to express the administration's eagerness to repair its strategic relationship with Egypt, beginning with the resumption of arms transfers.[3] Which didn't prevent Sisi from hosting Putin for a historic visit to Cairo in February 2015, at the height of Washington's bitterest confrontation with Moscow since the end of the Cold War.

While these incidents offer a sad testament to the freefall of America's regional standing and prestige during the Obama years – even in comparison to the George W. Bush administration's darkest moments[4] – they are by no means an exception to the overall pattern of Middle Eastern great power relations during the past two centuries. For, contrary to the common perception of regional affairs as an offshoot of global power politics, modern Middle Eastern history has been the culmination of long-existing indigenous trends, passions and patterns of behaviour; contrary to their treatment as hapless objects lacking an internal, autonomous dynamic of their own, Middle Easterners have been active and enterprising free agents doggedly pursuing their national interests and swaying the region pretty much in their desired direction, often in disregard of great-power wishes. External influences, however potent, have played a secondary role, constituting neither the primary force behind the region's political development nor the main cause of its notorious volatility.

Of course, the British Empire destroyed its Ottoman counterpart during World War I, occupied Iran together with the Soviet Union during World War II, and co-engineered a coup d'état in Tehran a few years later; while

Moscow overthrew the Afghan government in December 1979, a feat repeated 22 years later by Washington, which proceeded to topple the Iraqi regime in the spring of 2003.

Yet these were all extreme exceptions that underscored the farthest limits of external interference rather than its endemic pervasiveness. None of the interventions represented a deliberate design on the region; all were grudging responses to undesirable developments that could have readily been averted by the local actors, which would in turn come to have a decisive, if not the final, say in these interventions' ultimate outcomes. Just as the Soviets were squeezed out of Afghanistan after a decade of bitter fighting only to see the ascent of a worse regime than the one they had toppled, so 14 years after its overthrow by a US-led international coalition the Taliban is poised to return to power in Kabul despite the massive military, economic and political resources expended to prevent this eventuality. Likewise, not only did the US-led intervention fail to reconstitute Iraq as a modern-day stable democracy despite the expenditure of thousands of lives and over a trillion dollars, but the country's eight-year-long occupation unleashed violent centrifugal forces, hitherto checked by Saddam Hussein's brutal regime, which have brought it to the verge of disintegration. No less seriously, the Iraq intervention has boosted Tehran's regional influence and reduced Washington's ability and readiness to contain its dogged quest for nuclear weapons – the foremost threat to regional security in the coming years.

More broadly, the destruction of the Ottoman Empire, on whose ruins the contemporary Middle Eastern state system arose, was a corollary of a global conflict that saw the fall of far more powerful European empires and set in train a process of national self-determination that was to end the worldwide imperial epoch before too long. Within this larger order of things, the Ottoman Empire was *not* the hapless victim of secret diplomacy bent on carving up its territories but a casualty of its own catastrophic decision to join the war on the losing side. This was by far the most important decision in the history of the modern Middle East, and it was anything but inevitable. Had Istanbul stayed out of the conflict, as pleaded by the Anglo-French-Russian Triple Entente, it would have readily weathered the storm and the region's future development might well have taken a different course.

Indeed, even after the Ottoman entry into the war London was reluctant to divert the necessary resources for its defeat from the European war theatre and for months remained wedded to the Muslim empire's continued existence, leaving it to a local Meccan potentate – Sharif Hussein ibn Ali of the Hashemite family – to push the idea of its destruction. Impressed by Hussein's (false) promises to raise the Ottoman Empire's Arabic-speaking subjects in revolt against their Muslim suzerain, the British accepted his main territorial demands, albeit in a highly equivocal fashion, then persuaded their French and Russian allies to endorse them in what came to be known as the May 1916 Sykes–Picot Agreement (named after its two main negotiators – Sir Marc Sykes and François Georges-Picot). And while Hussein never came close to fulfilling his end of the bargain, and the Sykes–Picot Agreement never saw the light of day (in contravention of its lasting denigration as the source of all evil), the sharif's false pretences would have a considerable impact on the future shape of the Middle East: the emirate of Transjordan (later to be known as the Kingdom of Jordan) was established in 1921 to satisfy the ambitions of his second son Abdullah, while in the same year the modern state of Iraq was created at the instigation of Abdullah's younger brother Faisal. Hussein himself became King of the Hijaz, Islam's birthplace, only to be evicted a few years later by a fellow Arabian potentiate, Abdul Aziz ibn Saud, founding father of Saudi Arabia.

If at the weakest point in their modern history, during World War I and its immediate aftermath, the local Middle Eastern actors managed to be decisive in the restructuring of their region, it was hardly surprising that their bargaining power was substantially enhanced during the cold war era, when global polarization and the nuclear balance of terror constrained great-power manoeuvrability. For all their exertions, neither the United States nor the Soviet Union, the two powers that had supplanted the traditional European empires after World War II, had a decisive say in their smaller allies' grand strategies. Time and again they were powerless to contain undesirable regional developments – be it the fall of Iraq's pro-Western Hashemite dynasty (in 1958), Egypt's defection to the Soviet camp in the mid-1950s and its shift to the American fold two decades later, the building of Israeli settlements in the territories occupied during the 1967 war, or the 1979 Islamic revolution in Iran – and were forced to acquiesce in actions with which they were in total disagreement. Just as Israel went to war in June 1967 and destroyed Iraq's nuclear weapons program 14 years later without Washington's blessing when it deemed its existence threatened, so Egypt's war of attrition (1969–70) and the October 1973 war, Syria's military intervention in Lebanon (1976) and the Iraqi invasions of Iran (1980) and Kuwait (1990) took place against Soviet wishes and advice. Only in terminating hostilities did superpower intervention seem to carry any weight, if of a very limited kind and mostly where Israel was concerned. The Soviets failed to convince Egyptian President Anwar Sadat to accept a ceasefire on the first day of the October 1973 war, or to force Syrian President Hafez Assad to stop his offensive against the PLO in the summer of 1976; and neither superpower managed to bring Tehran and Baghdad to end their eight-year war.

This is not to say that the US and the USSR slavishly followed the wishes of their junior partners, or that their impact was not critical at times. Rather, whatever success they had was largely due to the convergence of their own wishes with indigenous trends. It was the trauma of the October 1973 war that made Israelis painfully aware of their vulnerability and allowed the US administration to mediate the Egyptian-Israeli disengagement agreement of 1975, just as it was the determination of Sadat and Israeli Prime Minister Menachem Begin to end the longstanding enmity between their peoples that rendered American mediation effective. But when the Carter administration attempted to sustain the momentum and bring the Palestinians into the picture, it ran into the brick wall of PLO rejectionism.

Twenty-one years later, PLO Chairman Yasser Arafat aborted two more presidential attempts to mediate peace with Israel by rejecting, in July and December 2000, President Bill Clinton's proposals (accepted by Israel) for the creation of an independent Palestinian state in 95 per cent of the West Bank and the entire Gaza Strip, with east Jerusalem as its capital. Even after Israel had confined him to his Ramallah compound following the launch of his war of terror in September 2000 (shrewdly euphemized as the 'al-Aqsa intifada' after the mosque in Jerusalem), and even after President Bush had urged the Palestinians to substitute a new and democratic leadership for Arafat's corrupt and oppressive regime, there was little Washington could do to enforce this vision; the US president was forced to watch helplessly as his own preferred candidate, Mahmoud Abbas (Abu Mazen), was unceremoniously subverted by Arafat. A decade later Barack Obama would be similarly snubbed when his predecessor's would-be Palestinian leader ostentatiously left the US-sponsored peace talks with Israel in favour of an imposed solution on Palestinian terms.

By now the Cold War had long ended and the Soviet Union had disintegrated, along with its Communist bloc, leaving the United States 'the only remaining superpower'. Yet notwithstanding the initial euphoria attending these developments, their impact on the Middle East has been rather negligible. For one thing, the fundamental asymmetry inherent in great-power/small-state relations, whereby the latter's parochial outlook and localized interests make it better tuned to the threats and opportunities in its immediate environment than its larger counterpart, whose global range of interests precludes full and lasting concentration on specific regional problems, has been unaffected by the changes in the international system. For another, the void left by the diminution in superpower rivalry was quickly filled by a host of concerns, from greater American preoccupation with domestic problems to the expansion and integration of the European Union, to the economic and sociopolitical restructuring of the former Communist regimes. With great-power attention vacillating between these competing calls on their resources, local actors have largely retained their political and strategic manoeuvrability.

Thus, for example, for all its unprecedented global preeminence the United States failed to deter Saddam Hussein from invading Kuwait or to induce him to withdraw peacefully from the emirate, and was forced to go to war to this end; and while the war ended in a resounding victory, its very occurrence, let alone Saddam's survival for another 12 years, underscored the limits of great-power influence in the 'New World Order'. Indeed, Washington's ability to wage the war in the first place hinged on Saudi Arabia's permission to use its territory for this purpose as well as Egyptian, Syrian and Gulf states' support for the move – stemming as it did from local self-interest rather than US pressure.

Nor did the United States succeed in preventing the creation of the al-Qaeda terror organization and its launch of a worldwide jihad culminating in the 9/11 attacks – the most devastating assault ever on the American homeland; and though the 'war on terror' triggered by the attacks degraded al-Qaeda's military capabilities and decimated its leadership, it failed to destroy it altogether as the organization morphed into a loose coalition of no less lethal terror groups, some of which have subsequently assumed disparate lives of their own, notably the Islamic State (IS) that managed to conquer substantial parts of Syria and Iraq and to proclaim the restoration of the millenarian caliphate.

And yet, without discounting the Obama administration's foreign policy blunders – from wilfully ignoring the surge of militant Islamism to mishandling the 'Arab Spring' (as the upheavals sweeping across the region since December 2010 were initially misnamed), to failing to contain Tehran's dogged quest for the Bomb – there are limits to Washington's ability to influence regional dynamics. Just as no foreign surgeon could have saved the 'Sick Man of Europe' (as the Ottoman Empire was famously known) unless he helped himself, so no 'only remaining superpower' can fix the Middle East's endemic malaise. Only when the region is a place where religion does not trump all sociopolitical loyalties; where citizenship is not synonymous with submission; where political, ethnic and religious differences are not settled by internecine strife and murder; and where individuals and societies take responsibility for their actions rather than blame others for their misfortunes, will its inhabitants at last be able to look forward to a real 'spring'.

1. THE MAKING OF THE MODERN MIDDLE EAST

It is a commonplace to view the modern Middle East as an artificial creation of the West. According to this conventional wisdom, which is adhered to across the political spectrum, the record goes something like this: the European powers, having 'slowly picked the Ottoman Empire to pieces' during the eighteenth and nineteenth centuries,[1] drove it into World War I so as to expedite its demise and gobble up its lands. They did so by duping the naive Arab nationalist movement into a revolt against its Ottoman suzerain, and then cheated it of its fruits by carving the region into artificial states in complete disregard of local yearnings for political unity, thereby sowing the seeds of the region's future turmoil.[2]

While there is no denying the thesis's widespread appeal, there is also no way around the fact that, in almost every particular, it is not only demonstrably wrong but the inverse of the truth: the Ottoman Empire was not a hapless victim of European imperialism but an active participant in the great-power game; the destruction of this empire was predominantly self-inflicted; there was no Arab yearning for regional unity; the European powers did not break the Middle East's political unity but rather over-unified the region; Britain neither misled its Arab allies nor made simultaneous contradictory promises regarding the post-war settlement in the Middle East; and the creation of the post-Ottoman regional order was no less of the making of the local actors than of the great powers.[3]

The Eastern Question Revisited

Far from setting their sights on Ottoman lands, the European powers shored up the ailing Muslim empire during the protracted era preceding its collapse, or the Eastern Question as it is commonly known.[4] In the 1830s, these powers saved Istanbul from assured destruction by its ambitious subject – Egypt's governor Muhammad Ali. Similarly, Britain and France, later joined by Sardinia, bailed out the Ottomans from their ill-conceived holy war (*jihad*) against Russia, triggering in the process what came to be known as the Crimean War of 1854–5. When in the 1870s the Ottomans were confronted with a general revolt in their Balkan provinces that culminated in a fully fledged war with Russia, it was yet again the great powers that redressed their setbacks and kept the almost moribund Muslim empire alive. The same scenario repeated itself as late as 1913, when Istanbul was about to be overrun by a coalition of Balkan states, only this time Russia played the lead role in salvaging the Ottoman existence.

This pattern of outside powers saving the Ottomans resulted not from luck but from political acumen. The Ottoman Empire might have been the 'Sick Man of Europe', to use Tsar Nicholas I's famous metaphor, but it would not just lie down and die. Instead it did whatever it took to survive, be that skilfully pitting its enemies against one another or using European support to arrest domestic disintegration and external decline; and notwithstanding its internal weakness and marked inferiority to its European counterparts, the Ottoman Empire managed to stay in this intricate game of great-power politics for a surprisingly long period of time, and even to outlive (if only by a slim margin) its two formidable rivals, the Russian and the Austro-Hungarian empires.

Another source of Ottoman success relates to European imperial solidarity. Those were the high days of imperialism; the Ottomans were an empire among empires and, apart from their strategic, economic, and political interest in Ottoman survival, the European powers were loath to knock a fellow empire out of existence lest they rock the Continental imperial order. This solidarity had its limits, of course, and the Europeans did occasionally encroach on Ottoman territories (as they did on each other's lands), notably with the French occupation of Algeria (1830) and Tunisia (1881) and the Italian conquest of Libya (1911–12). But these were nibbles at the fringes of empire that had little effect on the Ottoman edifice.

The only substantial great-power infringement on Ottoman territorial integrity – the British occupation of Egypt – was born of chance, not design. Unaware of the brewing crisis in Egypt (where disgruntled military officers challenged the authority of the Ottoman viceroy, or *khedive*) until it reached boiling point, policymakers in London found themselves sliding down a slippery slope. At the end of June 1882, London declined the sultan's plea to take over Egypt;[5] two months later, after the sultan refused to participate in an international effort to defuse the Egyptian crisis, it was sufficiently alarmed by the deteriorating situation in the country to do precisely that without his formal approval. Yet even before the invading forces completed their mission the British ambassador to Istanbul informed the sultan that 'Her Majesty's Government contemplated shortly commencing the withdrawal of the British troops from Egypt', while the foreign secretary promised to withdraw from Egypt 'as soon as the state of the country, and the organization of proper means for the maintenance of the Khedive's authority, will admit of it'. This promise was to be repeated sixty-six times between 1882 and the end of World War I, only to be aborted time and again by Ottoman policies.[6] As such, contrary to the conventional wisdom, the British invasion of Egypt was *not* an imperialist feat of conquest and colonization[7] but a demonstration of great-power entanglement in an undesirable regional crisis that it had done little to create and over which it exercised little control: had the sultan not mismanaged the Egyptian situation on a grand scale, British intervention would have been readily averted; had he responded to London's post-invasion overtures, a quick British withdrawal from Egypt might well have ensued.[8]

Despite extensive external support, the Ottoman Empire steadily contracted due to internal fragmentation and decay. However adept in manipulating European interests to their advantage, the Ottomans could not perform miracles. Like their imperialist peers they never developed an adequate response to the ultimate empire-buster of modern times: the rise of nationalism. Nationalism had wrested Greece from Ottoman domination already in the 1820s and thereafter relentlessly squeezed them out of their European provinces, resulting in the independent states of Romania, Bulgaria, Serbia, Montenegro and Albania.

And it was the desire to redress these setbacks that largely accounted for the Ottoman decision to enter World War I. Istanbul was neither forced into the war in a last-ditch bid for survival, nor 'driven into an alliance with Germany and Austro-Hungary – the Central Powers – against the Triple Entente of Russia, Britain, and France'.[9] Rather it was in the highly enviable position of being courted by both warring camps: the Central Powers wished for its participation and the Entente hoped for its abstention. As early as 18 August 1914, less than a month after the outbreak of hostilities, the British, French and Russian ambassadors assured the grand vizier of the empire's continued survival were it to stay out of the war, while the British

Foreign Secretary, Edward Grey, told the Ottoman ambassador to London that his empire's territorial integrity 'would be preserved in any conditions of peace which affected the Near East, provided she preserved a real neutrality during the war'. Five days later, at Ottoman request, the three powers put down this pledge in writing.[10]

That the Ottoman leaders chose to ignore this guarantee of imperial survival reflected their determination to reverse centuries of decline and reassert their empire's lost glory. This in turn meant the liberation of Egypt and Cyprus from British occupation; the recovery of Turkey's lost territories in Europe, first and foremost Macedonia and Western Thrace; and, above all, the destruction of Russian power as overtly stated in the Ottoman proclamation of war: 'Our participation in the world war represents the vindication of our national ideal. The ideal of our nation and people leads us toward the destruction of our Muscovite enemy to obtain a natural frontier to our empire, which should include and unite all branches of our race.'[11] As late as the autumn of 1916, more than two years after the outbreak of the Great War, Ottoman officers in the Levant were still talking openly of an intended march on India via Iran and Afghanistan.[12] This terrible miscalculation led in the short run to the destruction of Turkey-in-Asia by the British army during World War I. In the long run, it led to the century of flux and instability that has caused so much misery to so many.

Not the Great Arab Revolt

Just as the chain of events culminating in the fall of the Ottoman Empire was set in train by Istanbul's supremely reckless decision to side with the losing war coalition, so it was *not* the British government but Sharif Hussein of Mecca, perpetrator of the 'Great Arab Revolt' against the Ottoman Empire, who provided the initial impetus for the creation of the modern Middle East by manoeuvring the largest empire on earth to extend itself well beyond its original plans for the post-war era.

The key turn took place in the second half of 1915. As late as June of that year, British policymakers were still amenable to the continued existence of Turkey-in-Asia as evidenced by the recommendations of an interdepartmental committee, headed by Sir Maurice de Bunsen of the Foreign Office, which regarded the preservation of a decentralized and largely intact Ottoman Empire as the most desirable option.[13] But just four months later the British high commissioner in Egypt, Sir Arthur Henry

McMahon, had been sufficiently impressed by Hussein's (false) pretence to represent 'the whole of the Arab Nation without any exception'[14] to tentatively accept his vision of an Arab successor empire (presumably headed by himself).

Hussein's achievement was nothing short of extraordinary given the near total lack of nationalist fervour among the Ottoman Empire's Arabic-speaking subjects. One historian has credibly estimated that a mere 350 activists belonged to all the secret Arab societies operating throughout the Middle East at the outbreak of World War I,[15] and even if one accepts that the leaders of these societies 'were mostly notables with substantial followings of their own',[16] they were but a drop in the ocean.

There was no 'Arab Nation' at the time, only an intricate web of local loyalties to one's clan, tribe, village, town, religious sect or localized ethnic minority; *ipso facto* there could be neither general craving for pan-Arab unification nor exasperation with the failure to achieve this objective. Most secret societies did not even seek Arab independence until after the outbreak of war but rather greater autonomy within the Ottoman Empire. No less important, they articulated not merely the refrain of pan-Arabism, as is universally believed, but even more so the cause of distinct local patriotism, the only message striking some responsive chord among their respective constituents. As T. E. Lawrence (better known as Lawrence of Arabia), probably the foremost Western champion of the pan-Arab ideal, put it in a 1915 memorandum on the conditions in Syria:

> Between town and town, village and village, family and family, creed and creed, exist intimate jealousies, sedulously fostered by the Turks to render a spontaneous union impossible. The largest indigenous political entity in settled Syria is only the village under its sheikh, and in patriarchal Syria the tribe under its chief ... All the constitution above them is the artificial bureaucracy of the Turk ... By accident and time the Arabic language has gradually permeated the country, until it is now almost the only one in use; but this does not mean that Syria – any more than Egypt – is an Arabian country.[17]

This means that Hussein represented little more than himself. The minimal backing he and his two prominent sons – Faisal and Abdullah – received from a few neighbouring tribes had far less to do with a yearning for independence than with the glitter of British gold and the promise of booty. The Hashemites could not even count on the support of their own local constituency. As late as December 1916, six months after the launch of their revolt, the residents of Mecca were 'almost pro-Turks',[18] and it would not be before the winter of 1917 that the pendulum would start swinging in the Hashemite direction.

Even then, the thought of the sharif of Mecca wresting the caliphate from the Ottoman sultan, with whom their loyalty had rested for centuries, was anathema to most Muslims. The vast majority of the eight to ten million Arabic-speaking Ottoman subjects remained loyal to their suzerain to the bitter end, and between 100,000 and 300,000 even fought in the Ottoman army during the war.

Unite and Rule

Just as there was no 'Arab Nation' that looked to Hussein as a would-be saviour, so the Hashemites were no champions of national liberation but imperialist aspirants anxious to exploit a unique window of opportunity to substitute their own empire for that of the Ottomans. Hussein and his sons had demonstrated no nationalist sentiments prior to the war when they had generally been considered loyal Ottoman apparatchiks, and neither of them changed in this respect during the revolt. They did not regard themselves as part of a wider Arab nation, bound together by a shared language, religion, history or culture. Rather, they held themselves superior to those ignorant creatures whom they were 'destined' to rule and educate. It was the 'white man's burden', Hijaz-style.

What the Hashemites demanded of Britain, then, was not self-determination for the Arabic-speaking Ottomans but the formation of a successor empire that would include Arabs, Turks, Armenians, Kurds, Assyrians and Jews, among others. As Hussein told Lawrence of Arabia in the summer of 1917: 'If advisable, we will pursue the Turks to Constantinople and Erzurum – so why talk about Beirut, Aleppo, and Hailo?' And Abdullah put it in similar terms when claiming that it was up to the British government 'to see that the Arab kingdom is such as will make it a substitute for the Ottoman Empire'.[19]

This expectation created a serious dilemma for British decision-makers. As imperialists themselves, they had no compunction about substituting a Hashemite empire for the Ottoman, especially if it were to fall under British tutelage. Yet given their keen awareness of the total lack of popular support for the revolt on the one hand, and the diversity and fragmentation of the Ottoman Arabic-speaking communities on the other, they had serious misgivings about the feasibility of the Hashemite project. Even Lawrence, who had done more than anyone else to impose Hashemite rule over much of the modern Middle East, would term Arab unity 'a madman's notion – for this century or next, probably ... I am sure I never dreamed of uniting even the Hijaz and Syria. My conception was of a number of small states'.[20]

This, however, was not how post-World War I British policymakers attempted to resolve the tension between their instinctive imperialist support for pan-Arab unity and their recognition that this goal was but a mirage. Contrary to the conventional wisdom, Britain's 'original sin', if such was indeed committed, lay not in the breaking up of Middle Eastern unity but in its attempted over-unification. As Winston Churchill, then the Colonial Secretary, told the House of Commons on 14 June 1921, shortly after presiding over the establishment of the states of Iraq and Transjordan (later Jordan), and the effective limitation of Palestine to the territory between River Jordan and the Mediterranean Sea:

> Broadly speaking, there are two policies which can be adopted towards the Arab race. One is the policy of keeping them divided, of discouraging their national aspirations, of setting up administrations of local notables in each particular province or city, and exerting an influence through the jealousies of one tribe against another. That was largely, in many cases, the Turkish policy before the War, and cynical as it was, it undoubtedly achieved a certain measure of success.
>
> The other policy, and the one which, I think, is alone compatible with the sincere fulfilment of the pledges we gave during the War to the Arab race and to the Arab leaders, is an attempt to build up around the ancient capital of Baghdad, in a form friendly to Britain and to her Allies, an Arab State which can revive and embody the old culture and glories of the Arab race, and which, at any rate, will have a full and fair opportunity of doing so if the Arab race shows itself capable of profiting by it. Of these two policies we have definitely chosen the latter.[21]

This process, nevertheless, was nothing like the caricature portrayed by the standard historiography, in which 'Europeans and Americans were the only ones seated around the table [where] Middle Eastern countries and frontiers were fabricated'.[22] Rather it was the aggregate outcome of intense pushing and shoving by a multitude of regional and international bidders for the Ottoman war spoils in which the local actors, despite their marked inferiority to the great powers, often had the upper hand.

Kingdoms for the Hashemites

Take the creation of the modern state of Iraq from the defunct Ottoman *vilayets* of Basra, Baghdad and Mosul, rather than the partitioning of this territory into three states in accordance with the existing realities of local patriotism and religious affinities: a Kurdish state in the north (as promised by the August 1920 Treaty of Sèvres), a Shiite state in the south and a Sunni state in the central and western parts.

On the face of it this was a purely British decision taken by the cabinet in March 1921 on the recommendations of a special conference held earlier that month in Cairo with the participation of Churchill and his advisers. But, in fact, it was the culmination of a sustained effort by Faisal to substitute Iraq for his Syrian kingdom, from which he had been expelled by the French the previous year. In July 1920 the emir was a spent force, desperately seeking his place in the sun, spurned both by his former British allies and by his father, who had by then become king of the Hijaz. Eight months later he and his British champions had talked the largest empire on Earth into enthroning him over the soon-to-be-established Iraqi state – created pretty much on his behalf against the wishes of London's wartime French ally – thus making him a preeminent figure in the post-war Middle Eastern architecture.

It was Faisal's erstwhile champions – Lawrence of Arabia, who at Churchill's request joined the colonial office as an adviser on Arab affairs, and Hubert Young, another veteran of the 'Great Arab Revolt' and head of the political and administrative branch of the newly established Middle Eastern department at the colonial office, charged with the administration of Mesopotamia, Palestine and Aden – who engineered the departmental consensus in this regard. Churchill had already been won over to the idea of Faisal's kingship before taking up his new post on 15 February 1921, while the colonial office itself was persuaded later that month. The issue was finally sealed at an interdepartmental conference on 26 February. In addition to Lawrence and Young, the meeting was attended by two other veterans of the revolt – colonels Kinahan Cornwallis and Pierce Joyce – as well as Sir Arnold Wilson, future British Commissioner in Iraq and a new convert to Faisal's cause. Not only was there no objection to Faisal's ascent to the Iraqi throne, but the Foreign Office representative reassured his colonial counterparts 'that the difficulty of getting the French to agree was not insuperable and that if they were faced with a fait accompli no trouble was likely to ensue'.

The Cairo Conference thus did little more than rubberstamp this collective recommendation. 'I think we shall reach unanimous conclusion among all authorities that Faisal offers hope of best and cheapest solutions', Churchill cabled Prime Minister David Lloyd George on 14 March, after two days of deliberations. 'I have no doubt personally Faisal offers far away best chance of saving our money. Please therefore endeavour to telegraph to me as soon as you possibly can that I am free to make plans on [the] basis of [this] formula.'[23]

No sooner had Churchill resolved the Iraqi problem than he was forced to accommodate another member of the Hashemite family: Faisal's elder brother Abdullah. Though the brightest and most politically astute of Hussein's sons and the main instigator of the Hashemite revolt, Abdullah had been marginalized by his younger brother, who, largely owing to Lawrence's exertions on his behalf, managed to win the most coveted imperial prize: Syria. Once Faisal had been driven from Damascus, Abdullah, who had earmarked Iraq for himself, knew that it was only a matter of time before his brother would elbow him out by substituting this country for his lost Syrian kingdom. In a bid to forestall this eventuality, at the end of September 1920 Abdullah left Mecca at the head of several hundred tribesmen for the small oasis town of Ma'an at the northern tip of the Hijaz, arriving there in mid-November. Ostensibly, the emir was responding to appeals by Syrian nationalists to help them drive the French out of Syria on behalf of his deposed brother; in reality, he was positioning himself as a key player in the scramble for the defunct Ottoman Empire.

The ploy had the desired effect. The British grudgingly began to view Abdullah as potential ruler of the vast, sparsely populated territory east of the Jordan River, or Transjordan as it would come to be known. Even Lawrence, who had developed an aversion to Abdullah during the revolt, joined Young in arguing, shortly before the Cairo Conference, that 'we are prepared to allow Abdullah to consolidate his position in this region, provided he is ready to act in general accordance with the advice of our political officers'. In Lawrence's and Young's view, it might even be possible at some future point to indicate to the French that if they wished to set Abdullah up in Damascus, 'such a solution will have our cordial approval and will be particularly agreeable to us as an unmistakable sign of Franco-British solidarity in Arabian policy'. 'We see no menace to French interests in this', they reasoned. 'On the contrary; Abdullah, like Faisal, will be much less dangerous as a settled ruler than as a freelancer'.[24]

This logic was fully endorsed by the Cairo Conference. At a Jerusalem meeting with Abdullah on 28 March 1921, Churchill proposed that Transjordan be constituted as an Arab province of Palestine, under an Arab governor acceptable to Abdullah and subordinate to the high commissioner for Palestine. This, however, was not good enough for the emir. He had gone to such great lengths in order to make himself an imperial ruler and a key player in regional affairs, not a subordinate provincial governor. If a certain territory had to be incorporated into another as a province, then it should be Palestine into Transjordan, under his headship, and not the other way round.

Churchill explained that since Britain was the mandatory power for Palestine, the Arab governor of Transjordan would have to recognize its authority and would be expected to refrain from any anti-French activities. At the same time he reassured Abdullah that 'Trans-Jordania would not be included in the present administrative system of Palestine, and therefore the Zionist clauses of the mandate would not apply'. As Abdullah indicated his readiness to accept the proposal, provided it was acceptable to his father and brother, Churchill offered the ultimate carrot. 'The French authorities in Syria were not at the moment pursuing a Sherifian policy and it was not for His Majesty's Government to press them to do so', he said. 'At the same time it appeared to him that if an example was set in the British sphere and at the same time His Majesty's Government could point to the admirable results achieved there by themselves, the French might possibly come round to the British way of thinking'.[25]

This was just what Abdullah wanted to hear. In contrast to his opposition to Transjordan's westward expansion, Churchill effectively signalled Britain's possible acquiescence in Hashemite domination of Syria, this time under Abdullah's, rather than Faisal's, rule. True, this was a long shot that might or might not pay off, but Abdullah felt that it was infinitely better to have a bird in the hand rather than two in the bush. Hence, in his second meeting with Churchill he went out of his way to reassure his interlocutor of his determination to prevent any anti-French activities in Transjordan; and when in their third meeting the colonial secretary suggested that 'the Emir himself should remain in Trans-Jordania for a period of six months to prepare the way for the appointment, with his consent, at the end of that time of an Arab Governor under the High Commissioner', Abdullah readily accepted, his only request being 'that he might be regarded as a British officer and trusted accordingly'. The relieved Churchill was only too happy to comply.[26]

'The Emir Abdullah has promised to work with us and for us to do his best to restrain the people from anti-French action and to form, with our assistance, a local administration which can later be handed over to a native Governor of less consequence than himself', Churchill reported on the meeting.

> His position will be informal, and no question either of governorship or sovereignty is raised. He must be given a very free hand, as he has a most difficult task to perform. Not only has he been checked in mid-career in his campaign against the French, but he has been asked to execute a complete *volte face* and to take active steps to nullify the effects of his previous policy.[27]

Churchill could not have been more mistaken. Far from being checked in mid-career, let alone forced to execute a complete about face, Abdullah had successfully recovered from a seemingly impossible situation. Having suffered a crushing defeat in May 1919 at the hands of rival Arabian potentates the emir was deprecated by the British, ridiculed in Arabia and disfavoured by his father. Now he had not only redeemed his lost honour but had talked London into putting him in charge of a new entity – created specifically on his behalf – thus making him a key contender against Faisal for pan-Arab leadership.

In the following years the two brothers would vie for championship of the unity ideal. Using his position as Iraq's founding monarch, Faisal toiled ceaselessly to bring about the unification of the Fertile Crescent under his rule, and this policy was sustained after his untimely death in September 1933 by successive Iraqi leaders, notably by Nuri Said, Faisal's comrade-in-arms and a long-time prime minister. For his part, Abdullah strove to transform the emirate of Transjordan into a springboard for the creation of a 'Greater Syrian' empire comprising Syria, Lebanon, Palestine and, possibly, Iraq and Saudi Arabia – an ambition that Abdullah was to nurture until the later 1940s, when it was dealt a mortal blow by the establishment of the state of Israel and its ability to withstand the pan-Arab attempt to destroy it at birth, thus forcing the king to content himself with the annexation of the territories occupied during the war (known since then as the West Bank of the Hashemite Kingdom Jordan).

Perfidious Albion or Perfidious Arabia?

Notwithstanding their vast territorial gains – several times the size of the British Isles – the Hashemites were never satisfied with their lot. And their complaint of being 'robbed' of the fruits of victory promised to them during the war has quickly become the standard anti-Western grievance that has dominated the Middle Eastern political discourse to date, with the Sykes–Picot Agreement on the partition of the Ottoman Empire gaining lasting notoriety as the epitome of the (alleged) Western duplicity. So much so that the Islamic State (IS) proclaimed its June 2014 conquest of Mosul, Iraq's second largest city, as the first step towards 'smashing the Sykes–Picot border'.[28]

'The Sykes–Picot Agreement is a shocking document', charged George Antonius in his celebrated book *The Arab Awakening*, a study that has had wide and lasting influence among intellectual and academic circles in both the Arab world and the West.

> The Agreement had been negotiated and concluded without the knowledge of the Sharif Hussein, and it contained provisions which were in direct conflict with the terms of Sir Henry McMahon's compact with him. Worse still, the fact of its conclusion was dishonestly concealed from him because it was realized that, were he to have been apprised of it, he would have unhesitatingly denounced his alliance with Great Britain. He only heard of the existence of the Agreement some eighteen months later.

In short, the Sykes–Picot Agreement is 'not only the product of greed at its worst, that is to say, of greed allied to suspicion and so leading to stupidity: it also stands out as a startling piece of double-dealing'.[29]

Who was duplicitous?

If Anglo-Hashemite negotiations involved 'a startling piece of double-dealing', as they most certainly did, it was on the part of Hussein and his sons rather than their British interlocutors. Not only did they initiate negotiations with London on the false pretence that they were representing the 'whole of the Arab Nation without any exception' and sustain this assertion throughout the talks; not only did they fantastically inflate their military strength and make a string of false promises (notably to detach the Arabic-speaking forces in the Ottoman army from their imperial master) that they knew they could never keep; but they secretly double-dealt with the Ottomans behind the backs of the British, both before the proclamation of the revolt and in the late stages of the war.

In a telegram to Minister of War Enver Pasha in mid-March 1916, Hussein styled himself as champion of the 'Arab nation', a habit that had by then become second nature, pledging 'to gather the Arab tribes for Jihad, under the command of my sons, in the territories of Iraq and Palestine' were the sharifate of Mecca to be vested in his family.[30] Since at the time Hussein had an understanding with London that he would launch a revolt, for which he had been promised far-reaching material and territorial gains, this overture was nothing but an unscrupulous act of betrayal. Had his demands been accepted, the revolt might have been averted altogether. As it was, Enver rejected Hussein's demands out of hand, ordering him to send his tribesmen to the front or face the dire consequences of insubordination.[31]

This, nevertheless, was not the Hashemites' last bid for a separate deal behind the back of their British ally; far more intricate negotiations were conducted between November 1917 and June 1918 by Faisal, who led the sharifian thrust into the Levant and who had been toying with the idea of winning his own separate Syrian empire. His interlocutors were Djemal Pasha, one of the triumvirs running the empire at the time (alongside Enver and Interior Minister Talaat Pasha) and the effective master of the Levant, and General Mustafa Kemal (later known as Atatürk), commander of the 7th Army and future founder of the Turkish republic. Neither the British nor Hussein were kept in the know.[32]

In his celebrated account of the 'Arab Revolt', *Seven Pillars of Wisdom*, T. E. Lawrence puts a romantic gloss on these contacts, portraying them as a clever ploy to widen the rift between the 'nationalist' and the 'Islamist' factions of the Ottoman leadership. In his claim the trick worked brilliantly: 'At first we were offered autonomy for Hijaz. Then Syria was admitted to the benefit: then Mesopotamia. Faisal seemed still not content; so Djemal's deputy (while his master was in Constantinople) boldly added a Crown to the offered share of Hussein of Mecca. Lastly, they told us they saw logic in the claim of the prophet's family to the spiritual leadership of Islam!'[33]

The truth was far less heroic. Faisal was engaged not in a brilliant feat of divisive diplomacy but in an unabashed exercise in duplicity, and none knew this better than Lawrence, who wholeheartedly endorsed this illicit adventure and kept most of its contours hidden from his own superiors. As he would tell one of his biographers years later, reluctantly admitting that the emir had hidden much of his double-dealing even from him, Faisal was 'definitely "selling us"'.[34]

There was no rift to widen between Djemal and Kemal: the two were at the time aligned in opposition to the military strategy of Enver and his German advisers. Nor were the wholesale Ottoman concessions recounted by Lawrence actually made; had they been, Faisal might well have seized them, as he had occasionally intimated to his British advisers. Indeed, on 10 June 1918, without informing Lawrence, Faisal passed Djemal his peace terms, which envisaged greater Arab autonomy under Ottoman suzerainty with Syria having dual Turkish-Arab rule on the Austro-Hungarian model.[35] In limiting his proposed arrangement to Syria, which he had earmarked for himself, Faisal was effectively accepting qualified Ottoman sovereignty in his own domain, and the continuation of absolute Ottoman rule in the rest of the Arabic-speaking territories. As Djemal remained unimpressed, Faisal scaled down his envisaged Ottoman-Arab political framework: now he was talking in terms of decentralization rather than full independence, something akin to Bavaria's existence as a separate kingdom within the German Empire. The Ottomans declined the proposal; the talks advanced no further.[36]

In contrast to this Hashemite perfidy, there was nothing deceitful about the Anglo-French talks. The two were war allies engaged in a mortal struggle over their destiny, and it was only natural for them to coordinate strategies, especially since this was officially required by the September 1914 Declaration of London obliging the Anglo-French-Russian Entente to coordinate its peace terms. If anything, it was France that should have harboured a grievance against Britain for breaching the terms of their wartime alliance by making unauthorized promises to a minor third party that had not even decided to ally itself with the Entente. It was precisely to staunch this grievance that the British initiated talks with the French: not to renege on their tentative understanding with Hussein but to give it the widest possible international recognition. In the words of British historian Albert Hourani: 'It seems clear now that the intention of the British government, when it made the Sykes–Picot Agreement, was to reconcile the interests of France with the pledges given to the Sharif Hussein.'[37]

In line with this goal, from the onset of the talks the British tried to convince their sceptical ally of the merits of both an Arab revolt and the establishment of an independent Arab state, or rather empire. They succeeded: the agreement contained a commitment 'to recognize and protect an independent Arab State or a Confederation of Arab States under the suzerainty of an Arab chief' occupying the territory from Aleppo to Rawandaz and from the Egyptian-Ottoman border to Kuwait.[38] This commitment represented a clear victory for British championing of Arab independence and unity over French opposition.

In other words, the Sykes–Picot Agreement constituted the first-ever great-power recognition of an Arab right to self-determination, well before US President Woodrow Wilson turned this principle into a driving force of international politics. As such, it was an agent of unification rather than the divisive instrument it is commonly thought to be.

Was the sharif aware of the agreement?

Nor was Hussein kept in the dark regarding the provisions of the Sykes–Picot Agreement, let alone its very existence. As early as October 1916 a Lebanese notable revealed the accord's details to Syrian circles in Cairo, and it is unlikely that the news evaded Hussein's dexterous secretary Fuad Khatib, himself a Lebanese.[39] In April 1917 Sykes and Picot themselves met a group of Syrian nationalists in Cairo to inform them of the agreement's main provisions and Sykes then set out to the Hijaz to brief Hussein in person.[40] On 2 May he met Faisal and explained to him the gist of the agreement, to which Faisal reportedly agreed 'after much argument and seemed satisfied'. Three days later Sykes explained to Sharif Hussein 'the principle of the agreement as regards an Arab Confederation or State'.

Sykes reported to Cairo that his interviews with the two men went well. Later that same month, on 19–20 May, he held two further meetings with Hussein, this time with Picot present. After much bargaining, Hussein agreed to declare that 'he would be content if the French Government pursued the same policy towards Arab aspirations on Moslem Syrian Littoral as [the] British did in Baghdad' and that he would be 'ready to cooperate with France in Syria to the fullest extent and England in Mesopotamia'.[41]

Sykes claimed that Hussein was given a thorough explanation of 'the outline and detail of the agreement'; an aide to Hussein said the sharif merely had 'a hasty perusal and explanation (with little opportunity given him to think it over or criticize)'.[42] But it makes no difference: either way, Hussein knew of the Sykes–Picot Agreement's existence and its main provisions, meaning that his later claim of having heard nothing about the agreement until its disclosure by the Bolsheviks in November 1917 was a falsehood.

Contradiction between Sykes–Picot and the Hussein–McMahon correspondence?

The charge of a fundamental contradiction between the provisions of the Sykes–Picot Agreement and those of the Hussein–McMahon correspondence overlooks the crucial fact that both agreements recognized the Arab right to self-determination and provided for the establishment of a large Arab state, or rather an empire. As such, their alleged incompatibility becomes a matter of degree rather than of substance, namely, the conformity between their territorial delineation of the prospective Arab empire. Moreover, it should be borne in mind that the McMahon–Hussein correspondence never culminated in an official and legally binding agreement – or, for that matter, in any agreement whatsoever. It was an intricate process of bargaining in which both parties pitched for the highest possible prize: Hussein for the largest empire he could secure for himself and his family; McMahon for harnessing the entire 'Arab Nation' to the Allied cause. Neither of them accepted the other's offers as final and both tried to improve on them until the territorial haggling was dropped without agreement. As far as the British were concerned, McMahon's tentative promises were nothing but a general statement of intent that had to be subjected to detailed scrutiny during the post-war negotiations. On 20 October 1915, Foreign Secretary Grey instructed McMahon to avoid concrete territorial pledges to Hussein unless these were absolutely necessary, only to be ignored by the latter, who believed that his promises were equivocal enough to leave 'as free hand as possible to His Majesty's Government in the future' and sufficiently definite to exclude those areas which involved British and French interests.[43] The problem was that it was precisely this equivocation which was to give rise to the longstanding charge of British perfidy.

In fact, there was no real contradiction between the Sykes–Picot Agreement and the Hussein–McMahon correspondence, which specifically excluded certain territories from the area of the prospective Arab state. Broadly speaking, these exclusions rested on four interconnected grounds, the first of which was Britain's existing treaties with other Arab chiefs, such as the sheikhs of Kuwait and Muhammarah, and Abdul Aziz ibn Saud. These in turn excluded much of the Arabian Peninsula from the prospective Arab empire, something that Hussein could never bring himself to accept. He repeatedly pleaded with Britain to goad these potentates into recognizing his supreme authority, to no avail; none of them was willing to come under his wing, and Ibn Saud eventually kicked the Hashemites out of the Hijaz.

Second, the British had to consider their Indian interests, which focused by and large on securing their position in Mesopotamia. This was presented by McMahon as follows: 'With regard to the *vilayets* of Baghdad and Basra, the Arabs will recognize that the established position and interests of Great Britain necessitates certain administrative arrangements in order to secure these territories from foreign aggression, to promote the welfare of the local populations and to safeguard our mutual economic interests'. When Hussein contested this provision, McMahon reiterated the importance of a 'friendly and stable administration in the vilayet of Baghdad' for British interests and suggested to leave the issue for the time being, since 'the adequate safeguarding of these interests calls for a much fuller and more detailed consideration than the present situation and the urgency of these negotiations permit'.[44]

In other words, not only was Hussein *not* promised the whole of Mesopotamia, the future of which remained open-ended, but he was informed of the extent of British interest in this area. In this respect the Sykes–Picot Agreement did little more than delineate those areas of British interests intimated by McMahon to Hussein.

Third, the British excluded areas that were not purely Arab, defined by McMahon as 'the two districts of Mersina and Alexandretta and portions of Syria lying to the west of the districts of Damascus, Homs, Hama and Aleppo [which] cannot be said to be purely Arab'.[45] This vague geographical expression was to become the central bone of Anglo-Arab contention, especially with regard to the exclusion of Palestine from the territory of the prospective Arab empire.

According to a standard British interpretation, first articulated in 1920, Palestine was indeed excluded from the envisaged empire due to its position west of the Ottoman district, or *vilayet*, of Damascus, which at the time included the area that was to become the emirate of Transjordan.[46]

The weakness of this contention, as Faisal pointed out in a London meeting (in March 1921), in what was to become the standard pan-Arab claim, was that

If His Majesty's Government relied upon the strict interpretation of the word 'vilayet', as applied to Damascus, they must also interpret the word to mean the same with regard to Homs and Hama. There was not, and never had been, a vilayet of Homs and Hama … [Hence] as the Arabic stood, it would clearly be interpreted by any Arab, and had been so interpreted by King Hussein, to refer to the four towns and their immediate surroundings. Palestine did not lie to the west of the four towns, and was therefore, in his opinion, included in the area for which His Majesty's Government had given pledges to his father.[47]

Declassified documents in the British archives confirm that contemporary officialdom in Cairo and London did indeed interpret McMahon's four 'districts' as meaning 'towns', but *not* in the expansive geographical sense claimed by Arab partisans. Quite the reverse, in fact. They viewed the four towns as synonymous with the entire territory of the prospective Arab empire in Syria, which in turn excluded Palestine from its territory. Indeed, even Faisal, in his above meeting, while contesting the British interpretation of McMahon's promises, said that 'he was quite prepared to accept … that it had been the original intention of His Majesty's Government to exclude Palestine'.[48]

The last, and probably the most important, reason McMahon was hesitant in his correspondence with the sharif was London's keen awareness of French interests in the Levant. In his letter of 24 October 1915, McMahon excluded from the area of the Arab empire all those regions in which Britain was not 'free to act without detriment to the interests of her ally, France'.[49] He did not go beyond this general formulation because he had no definite idea 'of the extent of French claims in Syria, nor of how far His Majesty's Government have agreed to recognize them', but he claimed to have 'endeavoured to provide for possible French pretensions to those places' by his general reservation.[50]

It was a matter of common knowledge at the time, however, that the French had a keen interest in, and a deep emotional attachment to, Syria, 'in which latter term they included Palestine and the Christian Holy Places'.[51] Indeed, in his reply to McMahon's promises, Hussein agreed to exclude the two *vilayets* of Mersina and Adana from the Arab kingdom, but insisted that 'the two *vilayets* of Aleppo and Beirut and their sea coasts are purely Arab *vilayets*'.[52]

Palestine at the time did not exist as a unified political or administrative entity but was rather divided into two separate units: the northern part, extending nearly to Jaffa, belonged to the *vilayet* of Beirut, and the southern part was defined as the independent *sanjak* of Jerusalem. In his letter of 24 October, McMahon avoided a specific definition of both the areas that 'cannot be said to be purely Arab' and those in which Britain was not 'free to act without detriment to the interests of her ally, France'. Had Hussein let this ambiguity stand, he could have later disowned any precise idea of its territorial delimitation. In choosing to interpret McMahon's vague reservation as including the *vilayet* of Beirut, however, he explicitly acknowledged its application to the northern half of Palestine – and, implicitly, to the entire country. Hence the exclusion of the northern part of Palestine from the area of the Arab empire by the Sykes–Picot Agreement could not have come as a surprise to Hussein; the southern part of Palestine, or much of the *sanjak* of Jerusalem, was in any event awarded by this agreement to the independent Arab empire.

All of this means that the depiction of the Sykes–Picot Agreement as the epitome of Western perfidy couldn't be further from the truth:

- It was the Hashemites who misled their British interlocutors rather than the other way round;
- The agreement served as a catalyst of Arab unification, not fragmentation;
- No fundamental contradiction existed between its territorial provisions and those of the Hussein–McMahon correspondence.

The Irrelevance of Sykes–Picot

But whatever the merits and flaws of the agreement, its standard castigation as the source of all evil is totally misconceived for the simple reason that the agreement *did not* shape the form of the contemporary Middle East, as even a casual glance at the map would reveal. The vast Arab empire it envisaged never materialized, its designated territory being divided between the present-day states of Iraq, Saudi Arabia, Syria, Transjordan (later Jordan) and Israel, as well as the Palestinian Authority (PA). Conversely, Turkey emerged from the war a significantly larger country than the truncated state it was intended to be. In brief, the new system devised by the Sykes–Picot Agreement in which the Arabs, or rather the Hashemites, would substitute for the Turks, that is, the Ottomans, as the Middle East's imperial masters gave way to a wholly different international order based on the newly articulated ideal of the nation state.

In fact, dissatisfaction with the provisions of the agreement was felt by its makers even before it was concluded. Both France and Britain were unhappy with its internalization of Palestine and planned to raise the issue in future negotiations, while London also resented the severance of Mosul from Mesopotamia and its inclusion in the French zone of influence. In their eagerness to gain international approval for their tentative understandings with Sharif Hussein, which is what the Sykes–Picot Agreement meant to them, British policymakers were prepared to pander to French (and Russian) imperial sensitivities; yet it was precisely these conjectural 'concessions' that made the agreement 'an egregious … foolish document', to use the words of Prime Minister David Lloyd-George (December 1916 – October 1922), and sowed the seeds of its undoing.[53]

This general disposition notwithstanding, it was the local actors who played the key role in the agreement's subversion. The state of Iraq (comprising Mosul) and the emirate of Transjordan, as we have seen, were created on behalf of the Hashemite brothers Faisal and Abdullah and at their instigation. Likewise, it was the ability of the Zionist movement to exploit a unique convergence of factors to harness British support to its national cause that produced the Balfour Declaration of November 1917, in which the British government endorsed 'the establishment in Palestine of a national home for the Jewish people' and pledged to 'use its best endeavours to facilitate the achievement of this object, it being clearly understood that nothing shall be done which may prejudice the civil and religious rights of existing non-Jewish communities in Palestine'.

These factors included Lloyd George's belief that 'the Jews might be able to render us more assistance than the Arabs' in easing the French out of Palestine;[54] the widespread conviction of British officialdom that Zionism held the key to the goodwill and support of 'World Jewry', whose mythical importance in British eyes did not subside following America's entry into the war (in April 1917) and even increased in tandem with Russia's slide into anarchy, as it was hoped that Jewish influence within revolutionary circles would counteract calls for Russia to leave the war; and the growing approval of Zionism as a worthy national movement, rather than as a merely handy tool, in the higher reaches of the British political and administrative establishment. Either way, the British desire to undo the Sykes–Picot Agreement created a unique opportunity that the Zionist leader, Dr Chaim Weizmann, was quick to exploit.

But the final nail in the coffin of the agreement was driven by none other than its intended victim: the collapsing Ottoman Empire, which was to be stripped not only of its vast Arabic-speaking provinces but also of most of the Turkish homeland itself. Istanbul and the straits were to go to Russia, together with most of Turkish Armenia, while the rest of Anatolia, apart from a tiny Turkish state in the eastern and north-central parts, was to be divided between France and Italy.

This stark prospect gave rise to a new and vibrant brand of Turkish nationalism, ready to disown the Ottoman imperial legacy but never to accept the partition and subjugation of the Turkish homeland. The person who, almost single-handedly, was to produce this historic turning point in Turkish and Middle Eastern history was the dashing war hero General Mustafa Kemal (Atatürk). In a sustained campaign between 1920 and 1922 that combined astounding battlefield victories with shrewd diplomatic manoeuvres, Kemal drove the foreign powers out of Anatolia, thus undoing the humiliating Treaty of Sèvres, imposed on Turkey by the great powers in August 1920, and laying the groundwork for the Treaty of Lausanne of July 1923. This recognized Turkish sovereignty over the whole of Anatolia, together with parts of eastern Thrace. Kurdistan and Armenia, envisaged as independent states by the Treaty of Sèvres, were effectively incorporated into Turkey and the Soviet Union, while Turkey renounced all rights and titles over Egypt and Sudan, a clear act of disengagement from its imperial past.

And thus it was that somewhere between the Hashemite dream of succeeding the Ottoman Empire, the French ambitions in the Levant, the Jewish quest for a homeland in Palestine, and Britain's regional desiderata; between the Italian and the Greek scramble for much of Anatolia and Rumelia, the Armenian and Kurdish yearning for self-determination, and the resurgent, non-imperialist brand of Turkish nationalism under Atatürk's capable stewardship, emerged the contemporary Middle East as it is known today. It was not like anything that had existed before, as the millenarian imperial unity characterizing the region from time immemorial had been irrevocably broken. Yet it was no less attuned to regional realities, sensibilities and yearnings than its precursor, as evidenced by its remarkable resilience to successive challenges to its existence, both by pan-Arabists seeking to eliminate the 'traces of Western imperialism' and unify the so-called Arab Nation, and by Islamists attempting to create a regional (indeed worldwide) religious community (*umma*) or caliphate.

2. BRITAIN'S PALESTINE MOMENT

The destruction of the Ottoman Empire left Britain the preeminent power in the Middle East. With over a million troops deployed in the region, Russia distracted by domestic turmoil, French presence hardly existent and the United States retreating to isolationism after its brief World War I intervention, Britain's regional supremacy seemed unassailable. This, nevertheless, implied no attempt to colonize the nascent Middle East, as is commonly claimed. Just as London had been amenable to the continued survival of the Ottoman Empire way after the latter's entry into the war, so it was happy to have its post-war interests secured under a mandate by the League of Nations, the newly established world organization and the United Nations' predecessor, rather than through direct imperial mastery.

Conceived by Lt Gen. Jan Christian Smuts, South Africa's Minister of Defence and a member of the British delegation to the post-war peace talks, the mandates system envisaged the placement of the territories of the defunct Austro-Hungarian, Russian, German and Ottoman empires under the control of a single power, accountable to the League of Nations. Annexation was forbidden, and the mandatory power was to oversee the mandated areas from tutelage to eventual independence. After much haggling, the territories of the Austro-Hungarian and Russian empires were excluded from the mandates system and given immediate independence; conversely, it was decided that 'the well-being and development' of those German and Ottoman territories 'inhabited by peoples not yet able to stand by themselves under the strenuous conditions of the modern world' formed 'a sacred trust of civilization and that securities for the performance of this trust should be embodied in the constitution of the League of Nations'. More specifically, it was agreed that 'Armenia, Syria, Mesopotamia, Palestine and Arabia must be completely severed from the Turkish Empire' and that certain communities in these territories 'have reached a stage of development where their existence as independent nations can be provisionally recognised subject to the rendering of administrative advice and assistance by a mandatory power until such time as they are able to stand alone'.[1] These principles were subsequently incorporated into Article 22 of the League of Nations' Covenant.

That British policymakers did not consider the mandates system a tool for imperial aggrandizement was evidenced by the fact that they were happy to let the United States administer these territories as was initially envisaged. As Washington shirked this responsibility, Britain was appointed the mandatory power for Mesopotamia (Iraq) and Palestine (with France assuming the mandate for Syria), and guided them to independence: in October 1932 Iraq was admitted to the League of Nations as a sovereign state; Transjordan (included in the Palestine Mandate) became independent in May 1946; and the state of Israel was proclaimed precisely two years later in accordance with UN General Assembly Resolution 181 of 29 November 1947, partitioning mandatory Palestine into two states – one Jewish, the other Arab. As for the prospective Palestinian Arab state, most of its designated territory was occupied by Transjordan and Egypt during their attempt to destroy Israel at birth, to be hitherto known, respectively, as the West Bank (of the enlarged Hashemite kingdom of Jordan) and the Gaza Strip.

This transit to statehood, to be sure, was hardly smooth and straightforward, as London's desire to secure its interests in the would-be independent states (e.g., the 1930 Anglo-Iraqi treaty giving Britain preferential political status and two military bases in independent Iraq) resulted in repeated tussles. Yet like the Anglo-Hashemite World War I interaction, the outcome of these clashes often corresponded to local wishes rather than to great-power interests. And nowhere was this reality more vividly illustrated than in Palestine, where British policy was largely dictated by Arab violence prior to World War II and by Jewish political and military pressure in its wake.

Violence Pays

On 25 April 1920, Britain was appointed by the San Remo peace conference as the mandatory power for Palestine, with the explicit purpose of 'putting into effect the declaration originally made on November 2, 1917, by the

Government of His Britannic Majesty [i.e., the Balfour Declaration], and adopted by the other Allied Powers, in favour of the establishment in Palestine of a national home for the Jewish people, it being clearly understood that nothing should be done which might prejudice the civil and religious rights of existing non-Jewish communities in Palestine, or the rights and political status enjoyed by Jews in any other country'. By way of achieving this general goal, Britain was required, among other things, to place Palestine 'under such political, administrative and economic conditions as will secure the establishment of the Jewish national home'; to ensure that 'no Palestine territory shall be ceded or leased to, or in any way placed under the control of the Government of any foreign Power'; to facilitate 'Jewish immigration under suitable conditions'; and to encourage 'close settlement by Jews on the land, including State lands and waste lands not required for public purposes'.[2]

These clear obligations notwithstanding, from the first days of the mandate the British government repeatedly gave in to Arab violence and to the demands that followed upon it. As early as March 1921, as we have seen, London sought to appease Emir Abdullah of Mecca by severing Transjordan from the prospective Jewish national home (though not from the Palestine Mandate) and making him its effective ruler. The following month the high commissioner for Palestine succumbed to pressure by the prominent Husseini clan and its British champions and appointed the militant Hajj Amin Husseini as the Jerusalem Mufti – Palestine's top religious post – despite his instigation a year earlier of an anti-Jewish pogrom in which five people were murdered and 211 wounded and for which he was sentenced to ten years' imprisonment (but evaded incarceration by fleeing the country).

This proved a catastrophic blunder that was to change Palestine's history for ever. In the immediate term it triggered a string of violent eruptions that claimed hundreds of Jewish lives. Over the long term it put the Palestinian Arabs on a collision course with their Jewish compatriots against the wishes of ordinary Palestinians who would rather have coexisted with their neighbours yet paid the ultimate price for their leaders' folly: homelessness and statelessness.

Within a month of the Mufti's appointment, 90 Jews were murdered by Arab rioters; in the summer of 1929, another wave of violence resulted in the death of 133 Jews and the wounding of hundreds more. In response, the British issued two White Papers, in 1922 and 1930 respectively, which severely compromised the Jewish national home by limiting immigration to the 'economic capacity of the country at the time to absorb new arrivals' and imposing harsh restrictions on land sales to Jews.

In July 1937, Arab violence reaped its greatest reward when a commission of inquiry headed by Lord Peel, appointed 11 months earlier to ascertain the causes of the mufti-instigated 'revolt' that had been raging since April 1936 and suggest ways and means for pacifying the country, recommended the repudiation of the terms of the mandate altogether and, instead of 'placing the country under such political, administrative and economic conditions as will secure the establishment of the Jewish national home', the partition of Palestine into two states: an Arab state, united with Transjordan, that would occupy some 85 per cent of the mandate territory; and a Jewish state in the remainder. Jerusalem, Bethlehem and a corridor connecting them to the Mediterranean Sea were to remain a British mandatory zone. To reduce future friction between the two communities, the commission proposed a land and population exchange between the Jewish and the Arab states, similar to that effected between Turkey and Greece in the wake of World War I.[3]

After a heated debate, the Zionist leadership gave the plan its qualified support. The Palestinian Arab leadership and the Arab governments dismissed it out of hand, with the sole exception of Abdullah, who viewed the unification between the prospective Arab state and Transjordan as a stepping stone to the vast pan-Arab empire he had been striving to create throughout his career. The uprising was thus renewed with increased ferocity, only now it was primarily directed against the Mufti's Arab rivals and ordinary Palestinian Arabs, many of whom had become deeply disillusioned with the ongoing violence. The number of Arabs murdered by the gangs thus surpassed that of Jewish and British victims, driving many of them to flee the country in a foretaste of the 1947–8 exodus. While in 1936, according to official British statistics, 195 Arabs were murdered by their Arab brothers, compared with 37 British and 80 Jews, two years later these figures rose to 503 Arab fatalities, compared with 255 and 77 Jewish and British deaths respectively. Fatalities in 1939 remained on a similar level: 414 Palestinian Arabs murdered by Arab gangs, as opposed to 94 Jews and 37 Britons. Some Palestinian Arab sources put the number of murdered Arabs at a staggering 3,000–4,500.[4]

It didn't take long for the British government, headed since late May 1937 by the timid Neville Chamberlain, to cave in to Arab violence yet again. In October 1938, another commission of inquiry, headed by Sir John Woodhead, recommended dropping the partition plan, and three months later the colonial secretary, Malcolm MacDonald, concluded that 'active measures must be taken' to improve Anglo-Arab relations. On 17 May

1939, the government issued the Palestine White Paper which provided for 'the admission, as from the beginning of April [1939], of some 75,000 immigrants over the next five years … After the period of five years no further Jewish immigration will be permitted unless the Arabs of Palestine are prepared to acquiesce in it'. Also imposing severe restrictions on Jewish purchase of land, the White Paper envisaged an independent state in which the Jews would comprise no more than one-third of the total population. And as if to add insult to injury, in July MacDonald announced that all Jewish immigration to Palestine would be suspended from October 1939 until March 1940.[5]

Given the rapidly deteriorating position of Europe's Jews and the fact that Jewish immigration (which Britain was obliged to facilitate) had been both the leading symbolic and practical indicator of the permanency and success of the Zionist project, it was hardly surprising that world Jewry responded with vehement indignation to what it saw as the subversion of the Jewish national revival in Palestine and the abandonment of European Jewry to their Nazi persecutor. Chief Rabbi Isaac Herzog of Palestine wrote to the London *Times* that the White Paper was 'a sin against the spirit of God and the soul of Man'; Chaim Weizmann, who had played a key role in the issuance of the Balfour Declaration, called it a 'liquidation of the Jewish national home'; while the American Zionist leader Rabbi Stephen Wise denounced it as a policy that 'repudiates the letter and the spirit of the Mandate'. So did a number of British politicians, including the surviving members of the Peel Commission, while the League of Nations' Permanent Mandate Commission asserted (in an August 1939 report) that 'the policy set out in the White Paper was not in accordance with the interpretation which, in agreement with the Mandatory Power and the [League's] Council, the Commission had always placed upon the Palestine Mandate'.[6]

Courting Hitler

If the Chamberlain government hoped that this latest act of appeasement would rally the Arabs behind its cause in the looming confrontation with Nazi Germany, it was to be bitterly disappointed. Just as its shameful betrayal of Czechoslovakia (in the September 1938 Munich Agreement) served to whet Hitler's appetite rather than curb his expansionism, so the 1939 White Paper, augmented in February 1940 by draconian Land Transfer Regulations that left a paltry 5 per cent of Palestine fully accessible to Jews,[7] reinforced Arab perceptions of Britain as a spent force at pains to hold its own in the face of the rising Nazi power. In the words of Reader Bullard, the veteran British ambassador to Saudi Arabia: 'I suppose that, seeing us in a hole, they propose to take full advantage of the opportunity in order to extract, if possible, their full demands'.[8]

In line with this thinking, not only did the Arab leaders (apart from Abdullah) dismiss the White Paper as insufficient, demanding the immediate creation of an Arab state in Palestine, the complete cessation of Jewish immigration and a review of the status of every Jew who had entered the country after 1918, but they refused to declare war on Germany (again, with Abdullah's sole exception: Iraq did so in January 1943 after the Nazi threat to the Middle East had been irrevocably defeated at Alamein, while Egypt, Syria, Lebanon and Saudi Arabia followed suit as late as February 1945, three months before the end of the war). Indeed, many Arabs had been looking to the Third Reich for help and inspiration even before the war began. This included, aside from Hajj Amin and other Palestinian leaders who made their pro-Nazi sympathies known within weeks of Hitler's rise to power, such prominent figures as King Ibn Saud, who sought German weapons and ammunition; Iraqi Prime Minister Hikmat Suleiman (October 1936 – August 1937), who plotted a pro-German coup in Baghdad; and Hassan Bana, founding leader of the militant Muslim Brothers Society and an unabashed admirer of Hitler and Mussolini, as well as numerous pan-Arab activists throughout the region.

As the Nazis went from strength to strength, their prestige in the Middle East shot to new heights. In a secret message to Hitler, passed by his father-in-law and ambassador to Tehran, Egypt's King Faruq expressed 'strong admiration for the Führer and respect for the German people, whose victory over England he desired very sincerely'. He also emphasized his determination to withhold support from Britain as demonstrated by his refusal to declare war on the Axis despite relentless British pressure. In a meeting with Lt Col James Roosevelt, eldest son of the US president and then attached to the British army headquarters in Cairo, the king had nothing but praise for Nazism, which in his view had proved its mettle, unlike the sluggish and inefficient Western democracies.[9]

Even Nuri Said, one of Britain's foremost Arab champions, began hedging his bets. As prime minister of Iraq he had succumbed to British pressure and severed diplomatic relations with Germany upon the outbreak of hostilities (while refusing to go a step further and issue a declaration of war). A year later, as foreign minister in a cabinet headed by his political rival, the staunchly pro-Nazi Rashid Ali Kailani, he sought Hajj Amin Husseini's good offices in making contacts with the Axis powers.[10]

Hajj Amin, however, felt no gratitude to the person who had welcomed him to Iraq after his flight from Palestine (in October 1937). Just as he had won the post of the Jerusalem Mufti by pledging to promote Arab-Jewish coexistence only to do precisely the opposite, he had no compunction in reneging on his promise to be on his best behaviour in Baghdad. Within a fortnight of his arrival, British intelligence sources reported his efforts to revive the dying Palestine 'revolt' while later briefs had him forbidding ordinary Palestinians to volunteer for military service, ordering them to keep their weapons and ammunition hidden until needed. In the 1940 celebrations of the birthday of the 'Prophet Moses' (Nabi Musa) at a shrine bearing his name near Jerusalem, the same event that had sparked the first anti-Jewish pogrom in April 1920, the Mufti's loyalists urged villagers and tribesmen to renew the revolt at the earliest opportunity. Capitalizing on the German successes in France, they also spread the rumour throughout Palestine that Hajj Amin had been promised the headship of a new Palestinian Arab government independent of, but friendly toward, Nazi Germany.[11]

Nor were the Mufti's machinations confined to Palestine. He rapidly immersed himself in Iraq's domestic affairs, fomenting sedition among the Shiite clergy with a view to sparking mass violence in the mid-Euphrates as a stepping stone to a wider anti-British rebellion throughout the Middle East, and seeking to undermine the pro-British elements in government and parliament so as to steer the country in the direction of the Axis.[12] This, however, didn't represent the farthest limits of the Mufti's ambitions. Styling himself to Hitler and Mussolini as a spokesman of the entire 'Arab Nation', he argued that the Palestine problem necessitated an immediate solution not because of the national aspirations of the Palestinian Arabs but because it constituted 'an obstacle to the unity and independence of the Arab countries by pitting them directly against the Jews of the entire world, dangerous enemies, whose secret arms are money, corruption, and intrigue'. His proposed solution, therefore, was not Palestinian statehood but 'the independence of [unified] Palestine, Syria, and Iraq' under his leadership. As he put it in one of his letters to Hitler, '[T]he Arab people, slandered, maltreated, and deceived by our common enemies, confidently expects that the result of your final victory will be their independence and complete liberation, as well as the creation of their unity, when they will be linked to your country by a treaty of friendship and cooperation'.[13]

'Getting Too Much at the Head of the Queue'

Even as Hajj Amin became 'the most important Arab Quisling in German hands' (to use the words of a contemporary British report)[14] – broadcasting Nazi propaganda to Arabs and Muslims worldwide, recruiting Arab prisoners of war and Balkan Muslims for the Nazi fighting and killing machine, and urging the extermination of Jews wherever they could be found – the British government still hoped for appeasement to work.

At a meeting with David Ben-Gurion (in August 1941) the British colonial secretary, Lord Moyne, questioned the prudence of Jewish insistence on Palestine, suggesting that the Jewish state be established in East Prussia, whose German inhabitants would be expelled after the war by the victorious allies. 'You may be able to expel the Germans', the astounded Zionist leader retorted. 'But the Jews will not go there; it will take machine guns to force them to go; the Jews will not settle in a country whose inhabitants have been expelled by you'. As Moyne dismissed the view as moralistic naivety, Ben-Gurion ended the discussion: 'We have a country and will settle there'.[15]

As a life-long admirer of Zionism, Prime Minister Winston Churchill drastically diverged from his close friend Moyne regarding the Jewish historical attachment to Palestine. Yet he rarely used his wartime dominance of British politics to help the Zionists (or indeed European Jewry). However appalled by the White Paper, he failed to abolish this 'low grade gasp of a defeatist hour' (to use his own words),[16] refrained from confronting his generals and bureaucrats over the creation of a Jewish fighting force, which he wholeheartedly supported, and gave British officialdom a free rein in the running of Middle Eastern affairs, which they readily exploited to further erode Britain's international obligations to the Jewish national cause and to get the Arab case across to the American public. In November 1943, for example, Freya Stark, the acclaimed author, orientalist and Arabian adventurer, was sent to the US on a seven-month propaganda campaign aimed at undercutting the Zionist cause and defending Britain's White Paper policy.[17]

That this could happen at the height of the Nazi extermination of European Jewry, of which Whitehall was keenly aware, offered a stark demonstration of the mindset of British officialdom, which was less interested in stopping genocide than in preventing any potential survivors from reaching Palestine after the war. Such was the depth of the indifference to Jewish suffering and the preoccupation, even obsession, with fighting Zionism during the war that senior Foreign Office members portrayed Britain, not Europe's Jews, as the main victim of the Nazi atrocities. So much so that a prominent Syrian politician told a Zionist acquaintance that whenever he discussed Palestine with British officials he was left with the distinct impression that it was them, rather than the Arabs, who were Zionism's main enemies.[18]

This anti-Zionism was promptly adopted after the war by the Labour Party, which in July 1945 swept to power in a landslide electoral victory. Only 13 months earlier the party, which had vehemently opposed the White Paper and had maintained a close relationship with its Labour Zionist counterpart, proposed to allow the largest possible number of Jews into Palestine so as to enable them to become the majority, for otherwise 'there is surely neither hope nor meaning in a "Jewish National Home".' It moreover suggested encouraging the Palestinian Arabs to emigrate to the neighbouring states and extending Palestine's existing boundaries, by agreement with Egypt, Syria or Transjordan, to accommodate the nascent Jewish state. 'There was a strong case for this before the War. There is an irresistible case now, after the unspeakable atrocities of the cold and calculated German Nazi plan to kill all Jews in Europe', read the party's proposed programme. 'Let the Arabs be encouraged to move out as the Jews move in. Let them be compensated handsomely for their land and let their settlement elsewhere be carefully organized and generously financed. The Arabs have many wide territories of their own; they must not claim to exclude the Jews from this small area of Palestine, less than the size of Wales'.[19]

No sooner had Labour come to power, however, than these recommendations – some of which, notably encouraging Arabs to leave Palestine, were opposed by the Zionists[20] – were all but forgotten as Prime Minister Clement Attlee and Foreign Secretary Ernest Bevin began to take their cue from their bureaucrats. The empathy for the Jewish tragedy in Europe was forgotten, replaced by the belief that the Jews were receiving a disproportionate amount of sympathy at the expense of other victims of Nazi persecution. This was most publicly aired by Bevin, who in November 1945 criticized the Jewish tendency 'to get too much at the head of the queue' in demanding help. 'Is it "getting too much to the head of the queue" if, after the slaughter of six million Jews, the remnant of a million-and-a-half appeal for shelter in their homeland?' the mild-mannered Weizmann responded. 'What sorry epitaph the new declaration of policy seeks to write over the graves of the six million of our dead!'[21]

Four months earlier, US President Harry Truman, who had considered the White Paper a shameful product of the 'Munich mentality', demanded the immediate admission of 100,000 Holocaust survivors into Palestine. To abort the idea, perfectly congruent with Labour's pre-election position but now viewed as 'calculated to embarrass the Labour Government', Bevin suggested the establishment of an Anglo-American committee of inquiry 'to examine what could be done immediately to ameliorate the position of the Jews now in Europe' and 'the possibility of relieving the position in Europe by immigration into other countries, including the United States and the Dominions'. The committee was also 'to consider how much immigration into Palestine could reasonably be allowed in the immediate future', but the phrasing of this question, let alone the keeping of the White Paper's restrictions (loathed by Labour while in opposition) in place, left little doubt as to what Bevin had in mind. 'Should we accept the view that all the Jews or the bulk of them must leave Germany?' he cabled the British ambassador to Washington, Lord Halifax. 'I do not accept that view. They have gone through, it is true, the most terrible massacre and persecution, but on the other hand they have got through it and a number have survived. Now what succour and help should be brought to assist them to resettle in Germany and to help them to get over the obvious fears and nerves that arise from such treatment?'

In public Bevin was considerably subtler, if hardly more accommodating. 'The Jewish problem is a great human one', he told the House of Commons on 13 November 1945, in an official policy statement on Palestine. 'We cannot accept the view that the Jews should be driven out of Europe and should not be permitted to live again in these countries without discrimination, and contribute their ability and talent towards rebuilding the prosperity of Europe.'[22]

Had the foreign secretary genuinely been interested in harnessing Jewish ability and talent to the rebuilding of Europe, let alone in relieving the plight of these survivors, largely congregated in congested camps in the country that had just butchered six million of their co-religionists, he could easily have shown the way by seeking their admittance into Britain; after all, a few minutes before being asked to approve the Anglo-American committee, the cabinet was told of representations from the chief rabbi to admit displaced Jews who had no wish to be settled in Germany. The burden on British society would not have been that onerous: even Truman's proposed 100,000 refugees amounted to a mere 0.2 per cent of the existing British population. But Bevin didn't give the idea – and for that matter the wishes of these Holocaust survivors, the vast majority of whom wanted to go to Palestine – a fleeting thought: under no circumstances were they to be allowed to complicate Britain's relations with the Arabs by emigrating to the Promised Land. As he put it in his letter to Halifax: 'I think that to fly in the face of the Arabs after all the undertakings that have been given would cause a breakdown at the beginning'.[23]

By way of avoiding this breakdown, Bevin unflinchingly flaunted Britain's obligations to the Zionist movement. 'The mandate for Palestine requires the mandatory to facilitate Jewish immigration and to encourage close settlement by Jews on the land, while ensuring that the rights and positions of other sections of the population are not prejudiced thereby', he asserted in the parliamentary address noted above, conveniently overlooking the fact that immigration and settlement (draconically curtailed by the 1939 White Paper) were but means to the ultimate goal of 'putting into effect the declaration originally made on 2 November 1917 by the Government of His Britannic Majesty ... in favour of the establishment in Palestine of a national home for the Jewish people'.[24]

Bevin's omission of the mandate's raison d'être was anything but accidental. In a closed meeting with prominent Labourites a few weeks before making his policy statement, he categorically rejected the idea of a Jewish state; shortly after his parliamentary address he told members of the press that 'the British Government had never undertaken to establish a Jewish State in Palestine'. (Attlee was similarly opposed to the idea of Jewish statehood, so much so that years after Israel's establishment he would still refer to it in private as Palestine).[25]

This blatant misrepresentation of the letter and spirit of the mandate (and effective repudiation of the electoral platform on which Labour had risen to power) echoed the imperialist creed of British officialdom, which had no empathy for the yearning of subject peoples and communities for national liberation but rather viewed them as thankless natives who failed to appreciate the White Man's 'civilizing message'. In the case of Jewish nationalism, this outlook was aggravated by the pervasive anti-Semitism within British officialdom (the last high commissioner for Palestine, General Sir Alan Cunningham, for example, described Zionism as a movement where 'the forces of nationalism are accompanied by the psychology of the Jew, which it is important to recognize as something quite abnormal and unresponsive to rational treatment'),[26] and by frustration with their inability to patronize the Jews in the way they condescended to the Arabs. 'These officials aren't really anti-Semitic', the prominent British politician Richard Crossman noted after his meetings with British officials in Palestine during his tour of duty on the 1946 Anglo-American committee, 'but they certainly are anti-Jewish and they are either pro-Arab or strictly impartial in detesting both sides ... Off the record, most of the officials here will tell you that the Jews are above themselves and want taking down a peg'.[27]

But even if the Jews had been on their best behaviour, the government would still have ridden roughshod over their national aspirations, owing to the simple fact that as occupiers of vast territories endowed with natural resources (first and foremost oil) and sitting astride strategic waterways (e.g., the Suez Canal), the Arabs had always been far more meaningful for British imperial (and post-imperial) interests than the Jews. 'No solution of the Palestine problem should be proposed which would alienate the Arab states', the chiefs-of-staff advised the cabinet in July 1946, and seven months later the chief of the air staff told the cabinet that if 'one of the two communities had to be antagonized, it was preferable, from the purely military angle, that a solution should be found which did not involve the continuing hostility of the Arabs; for in that event our difficulties would not be confined to Palestine but would extend throughout the whole of the Middle East'. Cunningham put the matter in far blunter terms: 'Zionism has exhausted its usefulness to Great Britain and has become more of a liability than an asset'.[28]

Final Retreat

Heeding its military advisors, at the end of July 1946 the government unveiled its plan for the partition of Palestine into four autonomous (but not independent) entities – a Jewish province (comprising some 17 per cent of Palestine's territory), an Arab province (40 per cent of the country), and the British-controlled districts of Jerusalem and the Negev (53 per cent of Palestine) – and invited the two adversaries for talks in London in September. When neither the Zionists nor the Palestinian Arabs would come and subsequent attempts at persuasion came to naught, Bevin decided to up the ante and on 18 February 1947 told parliament of the government's decision to refer the Palestine question to the United Nations. He apparently hoped that the newly established world organization would refer this explosive political issue back to Britain with a clear mandate to enforce its trusteeship over Palestine, or better still, to establish a unitary Arab state (in which the Jews would remain a small minority) that would be either absorbed or dominated by Transjordan.

This is not what happened. Although at Britain's request the UN General Assembly convened for a special session (from 28 April to 15 May) that appointed the United Nations Special Committee on Palestine (UNSCOP) to study the question and suggest ways for its resolution, the committee's report, published at the end of August 1947, was a far cry from British hopes and expectations. Urging the earliest possible termination of the mandate and the granting of independence to Palestine, it diverged over the nature of the envisaged independence. Seven of the committee's eleven members (the representatives of Canada, Czechoslovakia, Guatemala, Holland, Peru, Sweden and Uruguay) proposed the partition of Palestine into two independent states – one Jewish, the other Arab – linked in an economic union, with Jerusalem internationalized by means of a trusteeship agreement that would designate the UN as the administering authority. Three members (the representatives of India, Iran and Yugoslavia) proposed the creation of an independent federal state of Palestine (with Jerusalem as its capital) comprising Jewish and Arab districts that would enjoy full powers of local government but not supreme authority over such issues as national defence, foreign relations, immigration, currency, taxation, and transport and communication, which would be vested in the federal government. The eleventh member, Australia, abstained from voting on either scheme.

The British, however, did not lose hope of subverting this 'clear victory for the principle of partition' (in the words of UN Secretary-General Trygve Lie). As an Ad Hoc Committee on the Palestinian Question comprising representatives of the world organization's 57 member states began deliberating (on 25 September) the two UNSCOP reports with a view to submitting final recommendations to the General Assembly's annual session, Britain cajoled and intimidated the smaller members in an attempt to raise wide-ranging concerns over the adverse implications of the creation of a Jewish state. It warned of an Arab oil embargo that would subvert Europe's fledgling economic recovery after the destruction wrought by the war, as well as a violent pan-Islamic backlash against the West. It claimed that the Jewish state was certain to become a Communist bridgehead in the Middle East and that the only way to contain Soviet expansionism was to establish a bulwark of Arab states – Transjordan, Iraq, Egypt and an Arab Palestine – backed by British forces in the region.

In an ironic twist of history the first great power to have publicly endorsed the right of the Jewish people to national self-determination in its ancestral homeland, and to have been given an international mandate to implement this right, had not only discarded this international trust but become its foremost enemy. In the words of Sir John Troutbeck, head of the British Middle East office in Cairo: 'A Jewish state is no more in our interest than it is in the Arabs'.[29]

Partners in Adversity

With its efforts to prevent the passing of the partition resolution aborted, London used its position as Palestine's occupying power to launch a sustained campaign to subvert the will of the international community. It announced that its forces in Palestine would not help enforce the UN resolution or maintain law and order in the country until the end of the mandate, yet obstructed a Jewish initiative for the deployment of an international force that would do precisely this; prevented a special UN commission tasked with ensuring Palestine's smooth transition to independence from entering the country as stipulated by the partition resolution and rejected its request for a month 'overlap' with the mandatory administration; refused to provide the Jewish community with a free port as required by the partition resolution, knowing full well that this 'seriously prejudiced the Jews by depriving them of freedom to import arms … in view of the ease with which the Palestinian Arabs could obtain arms from neighbouring countries';[30] and sustained a naval blockade around Palestine to prevent Jewish immigration in flagrant violation of the UN resolution, or indeed its mandated duty 'to facilitate Jewish immigration', herding dozens of thousands of Holocaust survivors in overcrowded camps in Cyprus. (Of the 70,000 'illegal immigrants' trying to brave the blockade in the three-year period between the end of World War II and the establishment of Israel, only 2,500 managed to enter the Promised Land.)[31]

Once the state of Israel was nevertheless proclaimed on 14 May 1948, the government welcomed the immediate pan-Arab invasion as a golden opportunity to undo the partition resolution and cut the nascent Jewish state 'down to size', with Bevin expressing the hope that 'it might well be that if the two sides ever accept a compromise it would be on the basis of boundaries differing from those recommended in the Partition Plan of the General Assembly'.[32]

That these border revisions were not conceived in terms favourable to Israel was evidenced by the tireless British efforts to convince the UN mediator, Swedish Count Folke Bernadotte, who arrived in the Middle East at the end of May 1948, to devise a solution that would reduce Israel to approximately the extent envisaged by the 1937 Peel plan – about half the size allotted to the Jewish state by the UN resolution. This included inter alia the surrender of Palestine's southern part, or the Negev, to Transjordan and Egypt, with the attendant detrimental consequences for Israel's strategic and economic interests;[33] the prevention of a Jewish land corridor between the coastal plain and Jerusalem; the surrender of some territory in the eastern Galilee to Syria;[34] and the creation of a substantial ex-territorial enclave in the Haifa Bay, under UN auspices, that would serve as a 'free port' for the 'movement of sealed trains and of transfer on specified roads between the free port and the neighbouring Arab countries including Iraq'. In other words, Israel was to avail its primary naval outlet, vital economic installations and national transport infrastructure to the strategic and economic needs of its enemies.[35] And while British officials were keenly aware that 'life for the Jews in such a small State would sooner or later become intolerable and it could be eliminated altogether',[36] they accompanied their attempts to bring about this eventuality with a spirited effort to stunt Israel's population growth, claiming that the Arabs would never accept the existence of an independent Jewish state unless 'there should be international agreement to accept numbers of Jewish displaced persons elsewhere than in Israel, and conceivably also to limit immigration to Israel'.[37] These dual goals of reducing Israel's size and limiting its population growth was duly incorporated into Bernadotte's report (published on 16 September 1948),[38] only to be dismissed out of hand by the Israeli government.

This, to be sure, was by no means the farthest limit of Britain's support for the pan-Arab assault. It also sought to dictate the scope and pace of the war by providing weapons and technical/advisory services to the invading Arab armies and starving Israel of arms and war materiel through a tight naval blockade on the one hand, and timing the cessation of hostilities to Arab political and military needs on the other.

At the initial stage of the war, when the invading Arab armies went from strength to strength, the British strove to prevent an immediate Security Council ceasefire resolution, both because it invoked the threat of sanctions under the UN charter and because the Arab invaders seemed well poised to make further territorial gains. Once the Arabs had conquered substantial chunks of mandatory Palestine, thus reducing Israel's territory to a fraction of that awarded by the partition resolution, London changed tack and sought a swift termination of hostilities so as to secure these gains. 'I am convinced that the continuance of the truce will benefit the Arabs and that its breakdown would be disastrous from their point of view', Bevin opined a few days before the expiry of the four-week ceasefire that had come into effect on 11 June.

> If they were responsible or could plausibly be represented as responsible for the renewal of fighting, it would probably be impossible for H.M. Govt. as a member of the United Nations to supply them with ammunition or indeed to give them any material assistance whatsoever. At the same time the Jews would be able to raise large sums of money in the United States and to purchase armaments either there or from other sources of supply. On the other hand the conditions now prevailing under the truce must be a source of grave embarrassment to the Jewish leaders. With much of their restricted manpower under arms and with serious interruption of their foreign trade their economic situation must be increasingly precarious.[39]

Underlying this prognosis were also the mounting anti-British sentiments in the United States and the distinct possibility that Washington would rescind its arms embargo (imposed in December 1947), which had severely harmed the Israeli war effort but had no impact on its British-armed Arab adversaries. On 20 May Secretary of State George Marshall told a press conference that 'the lifting of the embargo by the United States was under consideration'. Four days later Weizmann asserted after a meeting with Truman that 'the President gave him hope that the United States would lift the embargo on export of arms to Middle East in the not too distant future', and on 26 May congressman Jacob Javits introduced legislation authorizing a $100 million loan to Israel for the acquisition of military supplies and technical assistance.[40] And to make matters worse for London, the Senate Appropriations Committee demanded an official investigation to determine whether US funds to Britain had been used to assist the Arab invasion of Israel, driving the Chancellor of the Exchequer to warn the cabinet that 'this enquiry might cause us some embarrassment, for, when we excluded Palestine and Transjordan from the sterling area, we had provided them with United States dollars with which to finance their current transactions'.[41]

Told by a senior Egyptian official that the Arab states 'would be better advised to continue fighting now while their armies were advancing, rather than await such results from a conference under the mediator', Bevin exploded. 'What would happen if the Arab States did not accept the ceasefire, in which case the efforts he had made to prevent the raising of the arms embargo would prove in vain', he blustered. 'Would the Arabs prefer military defeat to a settlement now?'[42] Yet, apparently anticipating their advice on the truce to be ignored, the British urged their Arab allies to exploit this valuable respite to 'establish some real authority in the areas behind the lines occupied by their forces' so as to ensure their lasting control of these territories in the undesirable event of the resumption of hostilities. 'This is particularly important in the area to the south of the Egyptian front line', they reasoned. 'The greater part of this area was awarded to the Jews last November and the Jewish settlements there are still holding out and presumably maintaining contact with Tel-Aviv. We shall have great difficulty in supporting the Arab claim to retain this part of Palestine unless it can be shown that it is in fact and not in name only under Arab administration during the truce'.[43]

When the Arabs failed to heed this advice and resumed hostilities the British did their utmost to stop the fighting, going so far as to send a military force to Aqaba and to state their readiness to fend off an Israeli incursion on Transjordanian territory. When Israel expelled the Egyptian forces from the Negev and invaded the Sinai Peninsula in early January 1949, the British threatened to invoke their 1936 bilateral treaty with Egypt if the Israeli forces were not immediately withdrawn; and by way of underscoring this threat they sent several aircraft to the combat zone, only to have five of them shot down by the Israeli air force.

By the time fighting was over in early 1949, Israel had defeated the pan-Arab attempt to destroy it at birth and had asserted its control over wider territories than those assigned to it by the partition resolution, albeit at the exorbitant human cost of 1 per cent of its population. The Palestinian Arab community was profoundly shattered, with nearly half of its members becoming refugees in other parts of Palestine and the neighbouring Arab states. Already before the end of hostilities the president of Syria was overthrown by a military coup, and the king of Egypt followed suit in the summer of 1952. Within two years of the war Jordan's King Abdullah, the foremost Arab combatant in the conflict, was assassinated, as were the prime ministers of Egypt and Lebanon. For decades the 'Palestine problem' would dominate inter-Arab relations as the Arab states and the Palestinians sought to undo the consequences of the *Nakba* – 'the catastrophe', as the 1948 defeat came to be known in Arab discourse – and bring about Israel's demise by military, political and economic means.

As for Britain, the humiliation attending its ignominious departure from Palestine was to scar Anglo-Israeli relations for many years to come. As a veteran British diplomat candidly admitted, 'Many of us, including myself, who spent the last years of the British Mandate in Palestine, will never recover fully from the shame and humiliation of the dismal retreat in the spring of 1948'.[44]

3. INNOCENTS ABROAD

Wherever we went, in Europe, Asia, or Africa, we made a sensation
… We always took care to make it understood that we were
Americans – Americans! When we found that a good many foreigners
had hardly ever heard of America, and that a good many more
knew it only as a barbarous province away off somewhere, that had
lately been at war with somebody, we pitied the ignorance of the Old
World, but abated no jot of our importance … The people stared at
us everywhere, and we stared at them. We generally made them feel
rather small, too, before we got done with them, because we bore
down on them with America's greatness until we crushed them.

MARK TWAIN,
THE INNOCENTS ABROAD (1869)

Twain's humorous depiction of his fellow travellers' blissful innocence is as pertinent today as it was 150 years ago. To be sure, apart from a brief expansionist spell in the late nineteenth century, and unlike its European counterparts, the United States has never been an overseas imperial power in the traditional sense of the word.[1] On the contrary, as the first modern day post-colonial republic, its national ethos and international outlook have been driven from the outset by an instinctive anti-imperialist and anti-colonial impulse linked to an abiding belief in a unique moral mission 'to give to mankind the magnanimous and too novel example of a people always guided by an exalted justice and benevolence' (to use George Washington's farewell words).[2] And with the exception of America's fin de siècle imperial moment, this precept has been expressed not in the glorification of territorial aggrandizement and foreign domination but in an outspoken commitment to the championship of such lofty ideals as freedom, national self-determination and liberal democracy. It is indeed the inherent tension between this benevolent naivety and the realities on the ground that has generated a rather schizophrenic foreign policy swinging from excessive interventionism to no less disproportionate isolationism and vice versa; from extending social, economic and cultural aid to supporting brutal regimes violating every principle held dear by the American public and its elected leaders.

A False Start

No one personified this cognitive dissonance more clearly than President Woodrow Wilson, the moving spirit behind the ideals of national self-determination and collective security. From the moment he placed the United States at the centre stage of world affairs in April 1917 by entering World War I, the president took the moral high ground, disavowing any ulterior motives for his decision and presenting it as a selfless move to make the world 'safe for democracy'. Keeping his distance from his European partners and their imperial schemes, he chose to be designated an 'associate' rather than a fully fledged ally, and he never declared war on the Ottoman Empire. On 8 January 1918, in an address to a joint session of Congress, Wilson proclaimed his famous Fourteen Points that were to form the basis for the post-war settlement and the conduct of international politics generally. Of these, three were of direct relevance to the Middle East: Point One, renouncing secret diplomacy and secret agreements; Point Fourteen, calling for the formation of a general association of nations to guarantee the independence and territorial integrity of all states; and Point Twelve, specifically addressing the future of the Ottoman Empire: 'The Turkish portions of the present Ottoman Empire should be assured a secure sovereignty, but the other nationalities which are now under Turkish rule should be assured an undoubted security of life and an absolutely unmolested opportunity of autonomous development'.

Yet for all his high rhetoric and self-righteous pretences Wilson was as much a power broker as his European allies. He was ostensibly opposed to the Sykes–Picot Agreement, yet having joined the war did his utmost to keep it secret, going so far as to try – unsuccessfully – to prevent its publication in the United States after the Bolsheviks had revealed the accord's contents.[3] More important, as a prominent member of the Anglo-French-Italian-American Council of Four, whose deliberations were held in the strictest secrecy, Wilson became a party to precisely the same secret diplomacy he had so loudly derided.

Even the president's celebrated Point Twelve was regressive in comparison with the much-maligned Sykes–Picot Agreement. The latter provided for 'an independent Arab State or a Confederation of Arab States' and was followed in November 1918 by an Anglo-French declaration that promised 'complete and definite emancipation of the peoples so long oppressed by the Turks, and the establishment of National Governments and administrations deriving their authority from the initiative and free choice of the indigenous populations'. In contrast, not only did Point Twelve not envisage the full independence of the former Ottoman nationalities (only their 'autonomous development'), it did not even preclude possible great-power annexation of these territories so long as their inhabitants were assured 'an undoubted security of life and an absolutely unmolested opportunity of autonomous development'.

All this, nevertheless, did not prevent Wilson from seeking to overturn Sykes–Picot, and his primary tool for achieving this goal was the mandatory system associated with the nascent League of Nations. But then, given the chance to implement his lofty ideals as London and Paris welcomed an American mandate over the defunct Ottoman territories, Wilson would not deliver the goods, failing not only to have the move approved by the US Senate but also opposing the British proposal for an immediate assignment of mandates. Lloyd George was particularly contemptuous of the president and his attempt to determine the future of the Middle East without having sent a single soldier to fight there, indeed, without even declaring war on the Ottoman Empire. 'Our people are fed up with Wilson', he declared. 'They are tired of playing second fiddle, considering what we have done in the war'. Even when the mortally ailing Wilson was confined to his bed, the British prime minister remained vindictive: 'The only faculty which remained unimpaired to the end – which was delayed for four years – was his abnormal stubbornness'.[4]

Nothing underscored the gap between these two positions more starkly than Wilson's suggestion to send an inter-Allied commission to Syria to gauge opinion there and to tell the conference 'the facts as they found them'. While the president promptly appointed the commission's two American members – Henry Churchill King, president of Oberlin College and a firm believer in Anglo-Saxon superiority over the French, and Charles Crane, an influential contributor to the Democratic Party and a rabid anti-Semite – the British and the French were in no hurry to nominate their delegates. In late May 1919 the frustrated Wilson decided to go it alone, only to have King and Crane – chosen to go to Syria 'because they knew nothing about it'[5] – played by Faisal ibn Hussein. A few months earlier the emir had signed an agreement with Chaim Weizmann, the upcoming head of the Zionist movement, which endorsed the Balfour Declaration.[6] Now that the commission presented him with a golden opportunity 'to try to appropriate' the 'ownerless merchandise' that was Syria (to use his own words), Faisal left nothing to chance. Extensive propaganda, orchestrated demonstrations and intimidation of opponents were all employed to sway the hostile Syrian population behind his cause. No less important, a General Syrian Congress was swiftly assembled to tell the commission of the (alleged) Syrian desire for an independent constitutional monarchy under Faisal.[7] But the congress, which convened for the first time on 3 June 1919, just after the commission had set off to the region, was anything but representative. No real elections were ever held, and its delegates came by and large from the ranks of the small circle of nationalists who fought alongside Faisal during the war and who controlled his administration in its wake.[8]

Some of the commission's staffers did not fall for these machinations, as illustrated by a confidential appendix to its report underscoring 'evidences of considerable pressure exerted by the Government to secure the union of all elements upon one program … government agents tried hard to persuade, cajole, or threaten all, Christians and Moslems alike, into subscribing'.[9] Yet so mesmerized were King and Crane by Faisal's charade that they preferred his self-serving solution to their staffers' recommendation that Syria be placed under a joint Anglo-French mandate, Lebanon under a French mandate, and Palestine under a British mandate.

By this time, however, the Treaty of Versailles had been signed and Wilson had left for America. Hence the commission's report had no impact whatsoever on the future of the modern Middle East; indeed, Wilson did not even bother to send it to the deliberations over the Turkish Peace Treaty that continued after the conclusion of the Paris Peace Conference, leaving it to Britain and France (with a little help from Italy) to complete the destruction of the Ottoman Empire in the August 1920 Treaty of Sèvres (which was in turn subverted by Kemal Atatürk).

The Question of Palestine

With its grand entry into Middle Eastern high politics ending in a whimper, Washington redirected its attention to the issues that had dominated its past policy, notably protection of American missionary, philanthropic and educational interests in the Levant and cultivation of economic relations with the region, which since the 1930s gained considerable importance for US strategic interest with the growing significance of its oil deposits for the world economy.

It was only after World War II, having eclipsed Britain and France as the foremost Western power, that the United States found itself immersed in Middle Eastern affairs: not as a traditional imperial power bent on the acquisition and safeguarding of 'tangible and territorial interests',[10] but as an extension of its instinctive anti-imperialist impulse and the attendant idealistic worldview. This was primarily manifested in the sustained effort to contain what was seen as an expansionist drive by the Soviet Union, which emerged from the war as the world's second superpower alongside the US, to dominate the region; but it was also directed against America's Western allies, first and foremost Britain. This ranged from Wilson's failed attempts to influence the post Ottoman architecture, to Roosevelt's belief in the inevitable collapse of the European empires and the decolonization of their subject populations,[11] to Eisenhower's staunch opposition to the 1956 Anglo-French Suez war, which played a key role in the campaign's failure and drove the final nail in the coffin of Britain's imperial moment in the Middle East. But the first Anglo-American confrontation revolved around the creation of a Jewish state in a partitioned Palestine.

As we have seen, in deference to Arab violence Britain consistently reneged on its internationally mandated duty to facilitate the establishment of a Jewish national home in Palestine, to the extent of becoming the foremost opponent of the idea in the immediate post-war years in a desperate bid to salvage whatever regional assets it could from the looming collapse of its world empire. In the words of Foreign Secretary Bevin, 'The whole strategic position of the Western Powers is dependent on how and in what way we handle this Middle East situation.'[12]

This prognosis struck a responsive chord among State Department bureaucrats. As early as December 1917 Secretary of State Robert Lansing had informed Wilson of the department's opposition to 'turning the Holy Land over to the absolute control of the race credited with the death of Christ', totally unaware of the president's acceptance of the Balfour Declaration nearly two months earlier. Five years later the department opposed Congress's endorsement of the Palestine Mandate and in the coming decades did its utmost to bring about its demise. This ranged from support for the 1939 White Paper (in defiance of Roosevelt's specific instructions to the contrary), to opposition to Jewish immigration to Palestine even as the Nazis were systematically slaughtering European Jewry, to efforts to devise a joint Anglo-American statement disavowing the Balfour Declaration.[13]

Once Britain had surrendered the mandate to the nascent United Nations, the department collaborated with the British Foreign Office, as well as with the Pentagon and the American oil companies, to prevent the creation of a Jewish state. In March 1947 the US president proclaimed what came to be known as the Truman Doctrine, pledging American support to all nations facing Soviet or Communist threats, and shortly afterwards Washington planners began working on the enormous aid package for European recovery and reconstruction that would be remembered as the Marshall Plan. The establishment of a Jewish state, it was argued, would jeopardize both ambitious efforts and weaken the West in the evolving Cold War with the Soviet bloc.

Time and again Secretary of Defense James Forrestal underscored the critical need for Arab oil in the event of future war, while the State Department stressed the importance of close relations with the Arabs so as to prevent them from turning to the Soviets in their fight against Jewish statehood – a move that would give Moscow a firm foothold in the Middle East and necessitate American military intervention to save the nascent Jewish state from being 'extinguished in blood'.[14] When Moscow defied this prediction and chose to endorse partition, which it deemed the most effective means to ease Britain out of Palestine, the State Department quickly changed tack and claimed that, if established, a Jewish state would become a Soviet forward detachment in the Middle East.[15]

As the UN vote on partition neared with Truman throwing his weight behind this solution, US diplomats joined their British peers in an attempt to deprive the prospective Jewish state of vast territories, notably the Negev desert in the south of the country – nearly half of Palestine's total size.[16] Supported by senior officials, including Undersecretary of State Robert Lovett, Assistant Secretary for Near Eastern and African Affairs Loy Henderson, and Assistant Secretary of State for UN affairs Dean Rusk, this scheme would have reduced the Jewish state to a large ghetto and rendered it totally indefensible. It was only Truman's last-minute intervention on 19 November, after a dramatic secret meeting with Weizmann, which nipped this plan in the bud hours before it was publicly announced. When Forrestal reminded him of the importance of Arab oil for US strategic interests, Truman retorted that 'he would handle the situation in the light of justice, not oil.'[17]

To the president's critics, this was self-righteous rhetoric aimed at winning Jewish votes and campaign contributions (though Truman would go on to win the elections despite losing the three key states of Pennsylvania, New York and Illinois where most American Jews lived). In fact, his pronounced sentiments harped not only to George Washington's vision of 'exalted justice and benevolence' but also to the pervasive religiously based support for the restoration of the Jews in their ancestral homeland dating back to the Republic's early days (President John Adams, 1797–1801, famously hoped to see 'the Jews again in Judea an independent nation'), or indeed to pre-independence times. Hence Wilson's endorsement of the Balfour Declaration stemmed not only from its compatibility with the ideal of national self-determination, or the influence of close Jewish associates such as Chief Justice Louis Brandeis or Rabbi Stephen Wise, but also from a prophetic-like conviction of being destined 'to help restore the Holy Land to its people' (as he told Wise). So did Roosevelt's sympathy for the ingathering of the Jews in their ancestral homeland, which led him so far as to entertain the transfer of Palestine's Arab population to the neighbouring states, while the more devout Truman proudly styled himself as 'Cyrus the Great' – the sixth-century BCE Persian monarch who subdued proud Babylon and allowed the return of Jewish exiles to their homeland.[18]

Small wonder therefore that *all* American presidents without any exception endorsed the Balfour Declaration. So did Congress in a joint resolution on 30 July 1922, amplifying this move during World War II with several resolutions and declarations supporting unrestricted Jewish immigration and the creation of a Jewish state in Palestine. In July 1945 the newly inaugurated Truman was handed a letter, signed by a majority of both Houses of Congress and urging 'all interested governments to join with the United States toward the end of establishing Palestine as a free and democratic Jewish commonwealth at the earliest possible time'. A similar letter signed by 40 governors of the 48 states of the United States was submitted on the same day, while a December 1945 congressional resolution urged the US to use its good offices towards the establishment of a democratic commonwealth in Palestine.[19] When King Ibn Saud protested at his demand for the immediate admission of 100,000 Holocaust survivors to Palestine, Truman replied that, 'The Government and people of the United States have given support to the concept of a Jewish National Home in Palestine ever since the termination of the First World War. It is only natural, therefore, that my Government should favor at this time the entry into Palestine of considerable numbers of displaced Jews in Europe, not only that they may find shelter there, but also that they may contribute their talents and energies to the upbuilding of the Jewish National Home'. As the Saudi monarch remained unmoved, Truman insisted that, 'There was a strong feeling in this country that the Jewish people who had made so many notable contributions to the world were entitled to a national home of their own, and it seemed appropriate that this national home should be established in a land which for thousands of years had been regarded by Jews as their spiritual home'.[20]

Now that the General Assembly was about to vote on partition, there was overwhelming support for the idea in all walks of American life – from Congress to the media, to the public at large – as evidenced inter alia by a Gallup poll taken a day before the passing of the partition resolution that found 65 per cent of Americans supportive of the idea, with opposition running as low as 10 per cent.[21] This gave Truman a unique opportunity, in the words of his young confidant Clark Clifford, to do well by doing good.

To this must be added America's anti-imperialist impulse. For it was not only the perennial restorationist sentiments and post-Holocaust sympathies that underlay the sweeping American support for the creation of a Jewish state but also the Zionist movement's position as the most effective anti-imperialist Middle Eastern force in the immediate wake of World War II. In the grudging words of the British ambassador to Washington: 'As far as the general public is concerned there is a natural predisposition to sympathize with any group seeking to establish a new nation (May 15th has been described as the Jewish equivalent of July 4th); to support an anti-Colonial cause; and, other things being equal, to cheer the efforts of the underdog ... This feeling will be all the stronger because [Israel] is popularly regarded as a progressive and democratic republic striving to make its way against backward greedy and reactionary opponents'.[22] Hence Truman's deep conviction that the United States, having played the leading role in the UN's formation, must not repeat its World War I mistake of walking away from the world organization it had helped create; all the more so since the specific issue at hand involved the realization of the anti-colonial principle of national self-determination for both Jews and Arabs in Palestine.

To the State Department bureaucrats, however, these general sentiments mattered little. Hailing by and large from the White Anglo-Saxon Protestant upper and upper middle classes, educated in prestigious private boarding schools and universities, and imbued with an inflated sense of self-importance and elitist condescension of their less privileged fellow Americans,[23] they were determined not to allow ignorant public opinion or ill-conceived UN resolutions to stand in the way of their deeply held convictions and prejudices, even if this meant effectively subverting the president's will.

These efforts seemed to bear fruit as the situation in Palestine deteriorated. Within hours of the passing of the partition resolution the Palestinian Arab leadership waged a violent struggle aimed at its subversion, bolstered since January 1948 by the infiltration of a substantial pan-Arab irregular force into the country. By April, nearly 900 Jews had been killed and another 1,900 wounded (twice the relative casualty rate of the Palestinian Arabs),[24] leading to manifestations of disorientation and declining morale. 'It is becoming increasingly apparent that the Yishuv [Palestine's Jewish community] and its leaders are deeply worried about the future', read a British report. 'The 100,000 Jews of Jerusalem have been held to ransom and it is doubtful whether the Arab economic blockade of the city can be broken by Jewish forces alone. If the Jewish leaders are not prepared to sacrifice the 100,000 Jews of Jerusalem, then they must concede, however unwillingly, that the Arabs have won the second round in the struggle which began with a Jewish victory in the first round on the 29th November'.[25]

With their scepticism of the viability of Jewish statehood ostensibly vindicated by the Arab successes, the State Department's bureaucrats sought to seize the moment. Amplifying past admonitions of the 'manifestly unworkable' partition resolution and its adverse implications, they proposed 'to investigate the possibilities of any other suggested solution such as a federal state or trusteeship, which would not require outside armed force for implementation'.[26] When in mid-February 1948 the United Nations Palestine Commission (UNPC) urged the formation of an international security force to help enforce the resolution, the department warned that such a move would endanger US security and that 'In the event of reconsideration of the Palestine problem by the General Assembly, the United States should propose the creation of a trusteeship in Palestine with the UN Trusteeship Council as the administering authority'.[27]

This is indeed what happened. On 19 March the US representative to the United Nations, Senator Warren Austin, announced that since the ongoing conflict in Palestine proved partition to be no longer feasible, and since London's determination to vacate its forces by 15 May was certain to plunge the country into chaos, 'my government believes that a temporary trusteeship for Palestine should be established under the Trusteeship Council of the United Nations to maintain the peace and to afford the Jews and Arabs of Palestine, who must live together, further opportunity to reach an agreement regarding the future government of that country'.[28]

The statement took Truman by complete surprise. The previous day he had secretly assured Weizmann of his unwavering support for partition, only to wake up two days later to a barrage of public criticism. 'This morning I find that the State Dept. has reversed my Palestine policy', he angrily recorded in his diary. 'The first I know about it is what I see in the papers! Isn't that hell? I'm now in a position of a liar and a double-crosser. I never felt so in my life. There are people on the 3rd and 4th level of the State Dept. who have always wanted to cut my throat. They are succeeding in doing it'.[29]

In fact, Truman had broadly approved the departmental line a few weeks earlier, though he did so in the course of routine signing of working papers without realizing its true agenda, and on condition that 'nothing should be presented to the Security Council that could be interpreted as a recession on our part from the position we took in the General Assembly' and that Austin's speech be cleared with him in advance – which clearly had not been done.[30] Yet notwithstanding his exasperation with the 'striped-pants boys' (as he dismissively called state bureaucrats), the drop in his approval rating to a mere 36 per cent following the abrupt policy reversal, UN Secretary-General Lie's threatened resignation in protest of the move, and the Jerusalem consulate's warning that 'both Arabs and Jews regard the trusteeship scheme undesirable and most observers feel bloodshed will now increase tremendously with Jews desperate and Arabs feeling new strength',[31] Truman refrained from disavowing the statement so as not to antagonize Secretary of State Marshall, his most illustrious cabinet member, who positioned himself squarely behind the move. At a press conference a week after Austin's speech, the president sought to square the uneasy circle by presenting trusteeship not as a substitute for partition but as a temporary measure 'to fill [the] vacuum soon to be created by termination of [the] mandate on May 15' that did not 'prejudice [the] character of [the] final political settlement'. Asked whether this meant continued support for partition, Truman said that he remained in favour of the solution 'at some future date'.[32]

The Zionists, however, would not sit idly and wait for this 'future date'. With the US reversal coming on the heels of a string of military setbacks, they decided to move on to the offensive, both politically and militarily. On 1 April Moshe Shertok, the Jewish Agency's 'foreign minister', told the Security Council that the Jews would not accept the postponement of independence; the same message was relayed to Truman a week later in a personal letter from Weizmann, and on 12 April the Zionist General Council in Tel Aviv announced its intention to proclaim statehood upon the termination of the mandate and appealed to the Palestinian Arabs and the neighbouring Arab states 'for brotherhood, cooperation, and peace'.[33]

Meanwhile, a series of successful military operations were turning the tables on the Arabs. By mid-April the siege of Jerusalem had been breached with the conquest of several Arab villages on the Tel Aviv–Jerusalem road, and a few days later Jewish forces captured the mixed-population city of Tiberias, overlooking the Sea of Galilee, where some 6,000 Jews and about as many Arabs were living. Ignoring pleas by the local Jewish leadership to stay put, the Arabs chose to leave Tiberias en masse and were evacuated by the British army.[34] The same scenario was to recur on 21–22 April in the city of Haifa, home to 75,000 Jews and 62,500 Arabs, where tens of thousands of Arabs were ordered or bullied into leaving by their national leadership despite strenuous Jewish efforts to persuade them to stay.[35] In Jaffa, Palestine's largest Arab city, the municipality organized the transfer of thousands of residents by land and sea before the city's surrender to the Jews on 13 May, despite strenuous British military efforts to save the day. By the time the British high commissioner left Palestine on 14 May, Palestinian Arab society had all but disintegrated, with 300,000–400,000 of its members fleeing their homes to other parts of the country and to the neighbouring Arab states.[36]

Stung by these developments, the State Department was enticed into action. 'We should abandon our present defensive attitude and take the offensive in a confident and courageous manner', Assistant Secretary Henderson wrote to Under Secretary Lovett on 22 April. 'We must persuade the more moderate Jews in this country to break the hold which a minority of extreme American Zionists now has on American Jewry so that Jewish leaders in this country, instead of continuing to push Palestine Jews into an extremely nationalistic position, will endeavor to impress upon them the importance of assuming a reasonable and moderate attitude with the Arabs'.[37]

One such 'reasonable and moderate' person was Judah Magnes, the American-born president of the Hebrew University in Jerusalem, and Henderson lost no time in bringing him over to Washington. There he met Marshall on 4 May, telling him that the administration had been 'too apologetic' in pushing forward its trusteeship proposals and urging American sanctions that would stop 'the Jewish war machine in Palestine' dead in its tracks and disabuse the country's 'artificial' Jewish community of its state-hood dreams. Impressed by 'the most straightforward account on Palestine' he had heard, Marshall arranged for his guest to be seen by Truman.[38] Yet while Magnes's words were music to departmental ears, his proposed bi-national Arab-Jewish state was anathema to most Jews (or, indeed, Palestinian Arabs, who had insisted on a unitary Arab state where Jews would be reduced to a small minority) and had no chance of being considered now that statehood seemed only ten days away. As a Zionist official told Henderson: 'The Jewish State already exists and the Jews have no use for trusteeship.'[39]

This upbeat prognosis was reaffirmed by the American consul in Jerusalem, who reported on 3 May that, 'In Jewish areas Jews have taken effective control and are maintaining public services within those areas. Preparations for [the] establishment [of a] Jewish state after termination [of] mandate are well advanced. Confidence in [the] future [is] at high peak and Jewish public support for leaders overwhelming.'[40] Yet despite this state of affairs and indications of Truman's intention to recognize the prospective Jewish state, the State Department remained hopeful. Austin proposed a General Assembly resolution deriding the imminent proclamation of a Jewish state as a violation of a recently passed Security Council truce resolution, while Rusk supported an old-new British proposal handing most of Palestine to neighbouring Arab states and 'leaving the Jews a coastal state running from Tel Aviv to Haifa'[41] – a fraction of the territory assigned to them by the partition resolution. More important, having identified Shertok as dithering, the department strove to exacerbate his seeming doubts. This culminated in a personal meeting with Marshall on 8 May, where the Jewish 'foreign minister' was unceremoniously warned of the insurmountable military risks attending the proclamation of statehood. 'There was no doubt but that the Jewish army had gained such temporary success but there was no assurance whatever that in the long-range the tide might not turn against them', the decorated World War II general cautioned. 'If the tide did turn adversely and [you] came running to us for help [you] should be placed clearly on notice now that there was no warrant to expect help from the United States, which had warned [you] of the grave risk [you] were running.'[42]

This message failed to have the desired effect, as vividly illustrated by an 11 May *New York Times* article titled 'Jews to proclaim state despite U.S.' .

Citing a Jewish Agency spokesman at the UN headquarters, the paper reported that 'despite continued efforts by the United States to persuade it not to do so, the Jewish Agency for Palestine intends to proclaim a Jewish state in Palestine as soon as the British mandate is terminated'.

By now, some of the department's stalwarts seemed to have given up the fight. Briefing members of his UN team, Rusk argued that since the administration had never 'fundamentally abandoned' the partition plan, and since 'the President never did decide we had to impose a trusteeship against the wishes of either community', Truman would never oppose the proclamation of Jewish statehood if his opposition was 'the only thing that would prevent it from succeeding'. This assessment was reinforced by a departmental legal opinion that 'The Arab and Jewish communities will be legally entitled on May 15, 1948 to proclaim states and organize governments in the areas of Palestine occupied by the respective communities', and that the question whether to recognize these states was 'a matter of executive discretion which may be decided upon the basis of the political interests of the United States'.[43]

Matters came to a head during a White House meeting on 12 May. Having been treated to an impassioned plea by presidential special counsel Clifford for a prompt recognition of the Jewish state upon the termination of the mandate, Lovett decried the move as a transparent ploy for Jewish votes that would backfire on the president. To recognize a Jewish state prematurely, he argued, would not only be injurious to the United Nations but would also be 'buying a pig in a poke'. 'How did we know what kind of Jewish State would be set up?' he reasoned before producing a pile of intelligence reports alleging that many Jewish immigrants were effectively Soviet agents.

An enraged Marshall then took over from his deputy. 'The counsel offered by Mr. Clifford was based on domestic considerations, while the problem which confronted us was international', he said, warning that 'the great dignity of the office of the President would be seriously diminished' if Truman were to follow his counsel's advice. So much so that 'if in the elections I were to vote, I would vote against the President'.[44]

While Truman refrained from responding to his secretary of state, two days later Clifford met Lovett for lunch and told him that the president was under 'unbearable pressure' to recognize the Jewish state, which had been proclaimed that morning in Tel Aviv and which proposed to live within the partition resolution boundaries. After six o'clock in the evening (US eastern time) there would be no government or authority of any kind in Palestine, he said, and the president was inclined to recognize the new state should it make a formal appeal for recognition. Could the State Department 'recommend language to put into effect recognition in the event the President decided upon it'?

Conceding that there was no legal bar to recognition, Lovett nevertheless urged that it be withheld for another day or so to allow the department to study the proclamation's text and to inform the UN delegation, Senator Austin, and the British, French and Belgian governments, with which it collaborated in arranging a new truce resolution. Clifford refused on the grounds that the president could not afford to have any leaks at that time, and the two returned to their offices where Lovett continued to work on a statement in connection with the US truce efforts, while Clifford called the Jewish Agency's Washington representative Eliahu Epstein to tell him that recognition would be forthcoming that day and to ask that the official request be submitted to the White House without delay, which it was.

In a last-ditch bid to postpone recognition, Lovett called Clifford at 5:30 p.m., half an hour before the expiry of the mandate. He said that the General Assembly was in session and would probably finish its deliberations around ten o'clock, and asked if it were possible to delay the announcement until then. After a quick consultation with Truman, Clifford declined the request yet authorized informing Austin of the imminent action. This was done by Rusk at 5:45 p.m., only to have the enraged ambassador leave the UN headquarters and go home without telling any of his colleagues of the imminent action.

When at 6:11 p.m. White House spokesman Charlie Ross announced the president's de facto recognition of the state of Israel, the American delegation to the United Nations was caught by complete surprise. 'When I use the word pandemonium, I think I am not exaggerating', Rusk recalled. 'I was later told that one of our U.S. Mission staff men literally sat on the lap of the Cuban Delegate to keep him from going to the podium to withdraw Cuba from the United Nations. In any event, about 6:15 I got a call from Secretary Marshall who said: "Rusk, get up to New York and prevent the U.S. delegation from resigning *en masse*". Whether it was necessary or not, I scurried to New York and found that tempers had cooled sufficiently so that my mission was unnecessary'.

'My protests against the precipitate action and warnings as to consequences with the Arab world appear to have been outweighed by considerations unknown to me', an embittered Lovett summed up the episode, 'but I can only conclude that the President's political advisors, having failed last Wednesday [May 12] to make the president a father of the new state, have determined at least to make him the midwife'.[45]

4. ADRIFT IN IRAN

If support for the establishment of the state of Israel represented by and large the triumph of the intrinsic American values of anti-imperialism, national self-determination and the spread of democracy (not to mention deeply ingrained religious affinity) over self-serving material interests, Washington's relations with the rest of the region have been predicated on precisely such interests, notably the supply of cheap Middle Eastern oil and the containment of (the perceived) Soviet expansionism. It is true that both interests can be viewed as essential for the wellbeing and security of the Western nations and as such commensurate with American values. Yet it is no less true that their pursuit through alignment with brutal local dictatorships (a rather common feature of US Third World policy in the post-World War II era) has not only been at odds with the greater good it has purported to promote but has often proved counterproductive, making Washington more dependent on its local allies than the other way around and immersing it in foreign machinations and misadventures it would have rather avoided.

The Rise of the Shah

Take the case of US-Iranian relations. From the first days of its direct involvement in this vast, strategically located, oil-rich, non-Arab Muslim country in the midst of World War II, the US hinged its local fortunes on the autocratic Shah Mohammed Reza Pahlavi rather than attempt to encourage the advent of a more pluralistic society. Installed in September 1941 by the Anglo-Soviet forces that had invaded Iran the previous month and deposed his pro-Nazi father Reza Shah Pahlavi (1925–41), the

21-year-old sovereign lost no time in trying to recoup his father's absolute powers and to reverse the shift towards constitutional monarchy initiated by the occupying forces. He quickly set about consolidating his grip on the army with American support and in contravention of the constitutional subordination of this force to the minister of war, and in December 1942 exploited serious food shortages to instigate widespread riots in an attempt to force the government to resign and to establish martial law under his control. When the following year the government pushed for the early departure of the occupying forces and the restoration of full Iranian sovereignty, the shah secretly told the US ambassador of his opposition to the move so long as he hadn't prevailed over his domestic opponents.[1] And while President Roosevelt felt 'rather thrilled with the idea of using Iran as an example of what we could do by unselfish American policy' (as he asserted after the December 1943 Anglo-American-Soviet Tehran summit), his bureaucrats had a far less idealistic worldview of what could and should be done.

Echoing the shah's prognosis that his country was not yet ripe for constitutional government, the Office of Strategic Services (OSS), the CIA's predecessor, stated that 'Iran, like a small child, needs a strong governing hand until education had done its work', while ambassador Leyland Morris suggested (in September 1944) that 'the strengthening of [the shah's] hand would be one of the roads out of the internal political dilemma in which this country finds itself'. This judgement was endorsed by Morris's successor, Wallace Murray, who deemed Mohammed Reza a compassionate and caring ruler 'of a mental maturity that belies his 25 years', and by George Allen, the highly regarded youngest American ambassador then on duty, who in May 1946 replaced Murray at the Tehran embassy.[2]

For his part the shah toiled tirelessly to convince Washington of his indispensability for its interests, especially after Moscow sought to extend its post-war control of northern Iran by creating two puppet 'republics' there. When in April 1946 Prime Minister Ahmad Qavam agreed to give the Soviets a fifty-year concession for the development of Iran's northern oil deposits (through the creation of a joint oil company with majority Soviet control) and four months later appointed three ministers from the Tudeh communist party to his cabinet, the shah urged 'forceful measures to prevent [the] country from becoming [a] puppet of [the] USSR', while former court-minister-turned-Washington-ambassador Hussein Ala gauged American amenability to Qavam's removal. Not only was the prime minister operating without consulting his lawful sovereign, he told

Secretary of State Byrnes, but he often acted against his wishes, as with the dismissal and arrest of the Iranian chief-of-staff 'who was serving his country'. This persistent insubordination would have already driven the shah to 'make a decision' had he not feared that Qavam 'would rally a large following and bring on civil war, which would cause the Russians to come back with their troops'.[3]

While Byrnes would not pick up the gauntlet, Ambassador Allen was warming to the idea and in mid-October told the shah that he 'should force Qavam out and should make him leave the country or put him in jail if he caused trouble'. 'It has become clear to our Ambassador and to us that Qavam is now virtually a prisoner of his own policy of retreating before Soviet pressure and that Iran is daily losing what remains of its independence', Director of the Office of Near Eastern and African Affairs Loy Henderson reported to Under Secretary of State Dean Acheson. 'It is quite possible that within the next few days the Shah will remove Qavam and appoint a new prime minister. If such an event should take place, in our opinion we should at once give to the new government all appreciative moral support and at the same time make it clear that we are now prepared to extend to Iran the economic assistance we have been promising for the last three years'.[4]

The shah, however, failed to seize the moment, preferring to give Qavam another chance, provided he purge the Tudeh ministers from his cabinet (which he swiftly did), only to find himself embroiled in a bitter tussle with the prime minister over the ratification of the Soviet oil concession. By the summer of 1947 the shah was lamenting to Allen that while he had retained Qavam because of the latter's pledge to reject any Soviet deal, the prime minister was now exploiting the election of a new parliament (or *Majlis*), which made his dismissal constitutionally more difficult, 'to carry out a policy he may have favored all along, of giving the Russians some kind of oil concession'. This prognosis struck a responsive chord in Washington. '[It] is difficult for us to believe that Qavam who cannot be entirely ignorant of [the] manner in which international relations are conducted acted in good faith in requesting that we inform [the] Soviet Union that [the] US would declare hostilities in case of Soviet aggression against Iran', Secretary of State Marshall wrote to Allen. 'We are wondering whether Qavam by making requests of a character which clearly be met by us is not trying to produce a situation which would justify his accession to various Soviet demands on grounds of lack of assurance of US support against Soviet aggression'.[5]

By 22 October 1947, when the Majlis voted 102 to 2 to abolish the Soviet concession, despite an impassioned plea by Qavam not to close the door to further negotiations with Moscow, the State Department informed the Tehran embassy that, 'If Shah displays cooperative attitude and despite this Qavam so conducts himself that distrust cannot be dispelled, and if Shah should therefore consider new PriMin desirable, it is hoped that change of govt. could be brought about in manner not to create wide rift in Iranian body-politic'.[6]

The ambassador needed no further prodding. Convinced that Qavam had been deliberately prolonging the crisis, both as a means of projecting himself as 'the indispensable Persian who alone can maintain friendly enough relations with [the] USSR to avoid an actual attack' and out of fear that his job might be terminated once the problem was resolved, he gave the shah a green light to dismiss his troublesome prime minister. Having secured the blessing of the British ambassador as well, on 4 December the monarch forced the government's collective resignation and shortly afterwards parliament approved the move. 'One is frequently made aware here that Iran is not ready for full democracy and that, as the result of insisting on democratic processes in a country not ready for them, we often get more fraud, corruption, and self-seeking than we do good government', Allen reflected on the episode.

> One is tempted by the thought that, although a dictatorship of the Reza Shah variety would be undesirable, perhaps a middle ground of a somewhat stronger government would be preferable to the chaotic and corrupt condition we now have. However, I have steadfastly resisted the temptation, and my own policy continues to be based firmly on support of democratic principles, no matter how badly they may be carried out in practice. The Shah sometimes uses cogent arguments with me on the subject, but I continue to argue for the ways of democracy.[7]

America's Foremost Middle Eastern Ally

As the ambassador argued the ways of democracy, the Iranian monarch was steadily steering his country towards enlightened despotism, Pahlavi-style. Considering himself the scion of a great millenarian imperial tradition (in his November 1949 meeting with Truman he spoke at some length on the

Persian Empire under Darius the Great, 550–486 BCE),[8] Mohammed Reza embarked on a sustained effort to reform the constitutional bequest left by the Anglo-Soviet occupation; and while the US administration was far from happy with 'any diminution of Majlis power in favor [of] apparent one-man rule [that] would almost certainly evoke unsympathetic reaction on [the] part [of the] American public', it refrained from public criticism of the shah lest this 'be construed by Iranians as interference in [an] internal matter, just as expression of views by foreign diplomat in Washington on US constitutional amendment would be properly resented'.[9]

When in April 1949 the shah rode a tidal wave of public sympathy attending a failed attempt on his life to ban the Tudeh party, declare martial law and appoint a constituent assembly to approve his constitutional reform, first and foremost the dissolution of parliament and the creation of a new upper house with half of its members elected and half appointed by the shah, Washington remained conspicuously silent. 'We have never advanced, nor are we inclined now to advance, any argument against Iranian constitutional reform per se', Secretary of State Acheson commented on the impending move. 'On the contrary, [it] must be clear to any observer [of] Iranian politics that [the] present constitution is faulty in certain respects and [that] legislative process might be improved by amendment'.[10]

By the end of the year the administration had come to equate the shah with the Iranian national interest.[11] This perception was to remain virtually intact until his downfall three decades later despite several major 'bumps on the road', notably the August 1953 Anglo-American overthrow of Prime Minister Mohammed Musaddeq, who endangered the viability of the shah's regime.[12] Moreover, from the 1960s onwards the shah gradually transformed Tehran into Washington's foremost regional collaborator, so much so that by the end of the decade Iran was calling most of the shots in the bilateral relationship to its senior ally's benevolent consent.

As early as January 1964 the shah alerted President Lyndon Johnson to the massive Soviet buildup of Egypt's military capabilities, which, he claimed, posed a clear and present danger not only to Iranian security but to that of the wider Middle East, or indeed the Western world as a whole. '[U]pon the stability of Iran depends the security of the entire Middle East', he enunciated what was to become his strategic rationale for Iran's military buildup over the next fifteen years. 'If the United States is not in a position to meet our clear and urgent military needs … we might advisedly arrange for the purchase of our additional needs, under favorable conditions, from the United States of America or from elsewhere'. And in a thinly veiled hint as to what other suppliers he had in mind, the shah lauded Leonid Brezhnev's recent visit to Tehran as an indicator of the warming relations between the two countries.[13]

While Johnson seemed unimpressed by this reasoning, some of his senior cabinet members took it far more seriously. In a memo on the eve of the shah's US visit (in June 1964), Secretary of State Rusk argued that 'a secure, long-range, close military relationship with the U.S. is necessary if [the shah's] concerns are to be satisfied and our influence in Iran is to be maintained in the future'.[14] This message seemed to have the desired effect. Notwithstanding the Pentagon's recommendation to restrict arms sales to Iran lest their cost endanger the ambitious socioeconomic reforms pursued by the shah since the early 1960s (dubbed the White Revolution), the visit culminated in a $250 million five-year arms deal that corresponded more to the shah's ambitions than to those of his Washington sceptics.[15]

This, to be sure, didn't prevent the Iranian monarch from manipulating superpower rivalry to his advantage. Having pledged in 1962 not to deploy Western missiles on Iranian soil, in June 1965 he paid a state visit to Moscow that culminated in a large commercial agreement and, no less important, a $140 million arms deal. In the next few years Tehran's relations with the Soviet Union and Communist bloc countries perked up further, lending greater credence to the shah's pronounced intention to broaden Iran's sources of military equipment, credits and trade. And while US officials doubted the shah's 'Soviet option', given his perennial fear of Communist penetration, they were nevertheless forced to concede that Moscow had become 'an active contender for influence in Iran' to the extent that 'in the event of the Shah's demise, the USSR would be in a better position to influence the course of events'.[16] With its warnings that Tehran's courting of Moscow 'would call into question the fundamental basis for the U.S.-Iranian military supply relationship' answered in yet another Iranian-Soviet arms deal, Washington saw no choice but to agree (in 1968) another five-year plan for the annual supply of $100 million-plus worth of arms (instead of its proposed $75 million) – after the shah threatened to shop elsewhere for the missing sum. In the words of a State Department memorandum, 'Unless we remain Iran's principal military supplier our interests in Iran, including our ability to maintain our own strategic interests there and to influence the Shah in the direction of constructive foreign and domestic policies, will be seriously weakened'.[17]

This prognosis proved prescient. With Iran's oil revenues shooting from some $300 million in 1961 to around $900 million in 1968; the White

Revolution making impressive advances; the economy expanding at an annual rate of 10 per cent; the domestic opposition in complete disarray (with its foremost spokesman, Ayatollah Ruhollah Khomeini, forced into exile); and Tehran courted by East and West alike, the shah's self-confidence was growing by the day. Viewing Iran's domestic and foreign successes – many of which were achieved against US advice – as vindication of his strategic vision and political infallibility, he was now bent on substituting Iran for Britain as 'Guardian of the Persian Gulf' after the latter's scheduled withdrawal from the region in 1971.[18]

To justify this policy, the shah claimed that the responsibility for maintaining Gulf security lay solely with the local states and that no external powers had the right to interfere in the affairs of the region. As the largest and most powerful Gulf country, he believed Iran had a moral, historical and geopolitical responsibility to ensure peace and stability in the region not only for local benefit but for the good of the world. As his self-confidence grew still further, the shah cast his sights way beyond the Persian Gulf. 'World events were such that we were compelled to accept the fact that the sea adjoining the Oman Sea – I mean the Indian Ocean – does not recognize borders', he stated. 'As for Iran's security limits – I will not state how many kilometers we have in mind, but anyone who is acquainted with geography and the strategic situation, and especially with the potential air and sea forces, knows what distances from Chah Bahar this limit can reach.'[19]

These growing ambitions meshed with the Nixon administration's determination to extricate the US from its Vietnam quagmire and to avoid similar entanglements in the future. In July 1969, during a visit to the Asian island of Guam, the president announced what came to be known as the Nixon Doctrine. He reaffirmed Washington's unwavering commitment to its treaty obligations, but made clear that 'as far as the problems of internal security are concerned, as far as the problems of military defense, except for the threat of a major power involving nuclear weapons, the United States is going to encourage and has a right to expect that this problem will be increasingly handled by, and the responsibility for it taken by, the Asian nations themselves.'[20] While Iran was not specifically mentioned, its unique geopolitical location in direct contiguity to the Soviet Union in the north and to the world's largest oil deposits in the south made it invaluable for US strategic interests and in November 1970 Nixon decided to predicate American interests in the Gulf after the British withdrawal on the 'twin pillars' of Iranian-Saudi collaboration 'while recognizing the preponderance of Iranian power'.[21]

This policy seemed to pay handsome dividends the following year when Iran agreed to act as a conduit for the supply of US weapons to Pakistan in its armed confrontation with India,[22] and in May 1972, during an official visit to Tehran, Nixon gave the shah a blank cheque to buy whatever conventional weaponry he wished.[23] As the monarch took the administration at its word, Iran evolved into the most lucrative market for US military and civilian goods. Between 1972 and the shah's downfall in January 1979, the value of US arms sales to Iran amounted to some $20 billion, including the highly advanced F-14 aircraft, attack helicopters, M-60A main battle tanks, and various types of sophisticated missiles and laser-guided bombs. By 1975 Washington had overtaken Bonn as the largest supplier of civilian goods and services to Tehran, and the two parties signed a five-year trade agreement for the supply of $20 billion worth of non-military American goods, which would have resulted in a trade surplus for the United States despite the sharp increase in its oil purchases from Iran. On the eve of the Iranian revolution, the number of Americans working in Iran exceeded 35,000, while over 30,000 Iranian students – the largest contingent from any foreign country – studied in the United States and over fifty American universities maintained collaborative ties with Iranian institutions.[24]

This state of affairs gave the shah an ever-growing leverage over his much larger ally. He was no longer the young malleable ruler of 1953, reinstated through a Western cloak-and-dagger operation, but rather a confident autocrat keeping his subjects in permanent awe and playing a key role on the world stage. And while there is little doubt that the shah's grand ambitions would have been far less tenable without American aid and support, this dependence was more than matched by Washington's need for Tehran: a cornerstone in the containment of Soviet ambitions in the Middle East; an important oil supplier; the foremost protector of Western interests in the Gulf; the only regional power maintaining close relations with both Israel and its Arab foes; and a key provider of sensitive international services (e.g., restoration of Indian-Pakistani relations after the 1971 war, aiding South Vietnam at the time of the 1973 Paris Peace Accords, suppression of the Oman insurrection in 1973–6, loans to India, Pakistan, Afghanistan, Egypt and Jordan, etc.).[25] 'Iran under the shah', Henry Kissinger wrote in his memoirs, 'was one of America's best, most important, and most loyal friends in the world ... Under the Shah's leadership, the land bridge between Asia and Europe, so often the hinge of world history, was pro-American and pro-West beyond any challenge'.[26]

In these circumstances policymakers in Washington were happy to let Tehran dictate the general direction of the bilateral relationship.[27] They ignored the virulent anti-American attacks by the Iranian media on account of the shah's vocal international support for US policies; they disregarded the shah's persistent striving for higher oil prices (and repeated rebuffs of US representations on this matter), instead lauding his refusal to participate in the 1973–4 Arab oil embargo and his attempts to preserve stability in the world oil market; they conveniently overlooked their longstanding opposition to nuclear proliferation and agreed to sell Iran nuclear power plants for civilian purposes;[28] and they supported the shah's subversive activities in Iraq in the early 1970s, through the Kurdish uprising in the north of the country, then looked the other way when he betrayed the Kurds to the Iraqi regime once they had outlived their usefulness to his purposes.[29]

Even President Jimmy Carter, who in the spring of 1977 cancelled the pending sale of 160 F-16 fighter aircraft to Iran, went out of his way to placate the shah by presenting the move as part of 'a broader program to reduce arms buildups around the world' and boasting that 'since becoming president, I have approved the sale of military equipment to Iran which, in total dollar volume, is greater by half than that approved for any other nation in the world'.[30] Indeed, not only did the Carter administration fight tooth and nail to gain congressional approval for the sale of AWACS intelligence aircraft to Tehran (despite the president's lack of appetite for the deal), but in 1977 it tabled plans to increase Iranian military purchases to $3.98 billion for the year, with orders pending through 1981 to the tune of $9 billion approved by the president.[31]

So pervasive had the US-Iranian symbiosis become that successive administrations came to view Iranian interests as indistinguishable from their own. The shah was seen as a permanent feature of the Middle Eastern political landscape, something that had always been there – and always would be. No writing on the wall, however ominous, was allowed to shake this illusion. Even the rare warnings of the risks attending the shah's ambitious programmes, or the odd questioning of the prudence of predicating US national interests on the fortunes of one person, however powerful, would normally end on a positive chord emphasizing the remoteness of the identified threats and the stability of the shah's position. In the words of Stansfield Turner, CIA director at the time of the shah's fall: 'U.S. policy in that area of the world was so dependent on the Shah that it was all too easy for us to assume that he would do what was necessary to play the role we had in mind for him'.[32]

Losing Iran

Upon entering the White House in January 1977 Carter was presented with a rosy picture of the domestic situation in Iran and the stability of the regime. 'The Shah is the unquestioned leader of the modern Iranian state', ran a report by the Tehran embassy:

> His almost unchallenged domination of the political scene rests on 2,500 years of monarchical tradition, and his own extraordinary skill in exercising his powers for the benefit of the nation … He has presided over almost unprecedented economic development over the past decade – which has brought its own problems – and achieved for Iran an impressive international stature which has created popular pride in the country's achievements.[33]

A memorandum by the State Department's Bureau of Intelligence and Research (INR) was no less effusive. 'Iran is likely to remain stable under the Shah's leadership over the next several years, and committed to its relationship with the US as long as the Shah rules', it argued. 'The prospects are good that Iran will have relatively clear sailing until at least the mid-1980s, when oil production will probably slow and when the Shah says he will step aside in favor of the Crown Prince'. But even if the shah were to change his mind and remain in power after that date, this was no cause for concern: 'At age 57, in fine health, and protected by an absolute security apparatus, the Shah has an excellent chance to rule for a dozen or more years'.[34]

In fact, the shah's health was anything but fine. He was suffering from terminal cancer, diagnosed a few years earlier by French physicians. But what had been probably known to the French secret service for quite some time remained unknown to the American intelligence and foreign affairs community, despite the shah's centrality for US national interests.[35] As late as July 1978, when Iranian cities were awash with rumours of the shah's ill health, including terminal malignancy, the Tehran embassy blamed the Russians for 'spreading the stories'. 'At this time I tend to discount well over 90 per cent of the nonsense,' US Ambassador William Sullivan wrote to Secretary of State Cyrus Vance, 'but we shall continue to try to keep ourselves informed. We are taking the line, when comment is unavoidable, that "to the best of our knowledge the shah is fine"'.[36]

Small wonder, therefore, that the administration remained largely oblivious to the gathering storm in Iran until it blew down the house built by the shah. In a memorandum to Vance in July 1977, his assistant for Near Eastern and South Asian Affairs, Roy Atherton, opined that 'Iran has been remarkably stable for many years' and that 'there is less chance of a dramatic shift in direction in Iran than in most other countries'.[37] CIA reports throughout the summer and autumn of 1977 were similarly upbeat. Predicting that, 'The Shah will be an active participant in Iranian life well into the 1980s', they anticipated 'no radical change in Iranian political behavior in the near future' and estimated that, if anything, 'we are looking at evolution not revolution'. In line with the standard misattribution of Middle Eastern developments to external influences rather than to indigenous dynamics, these assessments struck an exceedingly upbeat bottom line:

> The Shah seems to have no health or political problems at present that will prevent him from being the dominant figure in Iran into and possibly throughout the 1980s. His style of rule and his general policies will probably remain the same unless dramatic developments in the international environment force him to make a change.[38]

Washington decision-makers remained sanguine even when Iran began sliding to catastrophe in January 1978, after the killing of scores of demonstrators in the holy city of Qom fuelled violent eruptions throughout the country that gained momentum in forty-day intervals, with the ending of the mourning period for the 'martyrs' of the previous round of violence. While the Tehran embassy was quick to identify the exceptional severity of the violence and the role played by the clergy in its initiation and expansion, inundating Washington with a steady stream of stark reports as the situation deteriorated,[39] it failed to draw the self-evident conclusions emanating from its own reports. In early June, Sullivan reported that the 'shah and his establishment stay firmly in control'[40] and at the end of the month left Iran on a two-month 'home leave' that sent the unmistakable message that the crisis need not cause undue alarm. This notion was reinforced during his absence by the embassy reporting that the situation was not 'as bad as tableau being painted by pessimists' and that Iran was not 'going to hell in a hand basket', as well as by a CIA assessment that the country 'is not in a revolutionary or even a prerevolutionary situation'.[41]

Shortly after returning to Tehran in late August, Sullivan reported that the shah had decided 'to transform his authoritarian regime into a genuine democracy'.[42] When this thesis collapsed a week later with the imposition of martial law and the killing of hundreds of demonstrators by the security forces, the ambassador preferred to view the move as a necessary facilitator of the shah's liberalizing agenda. 'I found him tired and unhappy, but considerably more spirited than he was a week ago', he reported on his meeting with the beleaguered monarch on 10 September, two days after the mass killings. 'He is convincing when he says that he has sided with those who want reform and [that] we can expect him to attempt to carry out those changes ... He has a more coherent plan of action than he earlier displayed. He categorically eschews any suggestion that he will abdicate or flee the current situation'.[43] Two weeks later the embassy estimated that, given the glaring disunity within the opposition, 'it seems inevitable that despite lack of enthusiasm for his leadership, the Shah will continue as Iran's ultimate political arbitrator'.[44] This view was echoed both by a Defense Intelligence Agency assessment that 'the Shah will probably be able to maintain his position through the early 1980s', and by a CIA National Intelligence Estimate ruling out the possibility of the shah's abdication before the mid-1980s:

> Because he has for so long identified his fate with that of Iran, the current political instability is likely to reinforce the Shah's determination to restore order and work toward an orderly succession to his son, the 18-year old Crown Prince Reza ... Should still more serious disorders recur, the monopoly of force held by the Iranian armed and security forces theoretically provides them with the capability to prevent the disturbances from growing out of control, either in the immediate future or in 1979 if an extension of martial law becomes necessary.[45]

As late as 22 October, while highlighting the usual sources of instability and violence, Sullivan maintained that 'there are encouraging indications that the Iranian crisis may have passed a fever point and opened some prospects for its constructive resolution'. This was mainly reflected in the fact that 'political figures among the opposition, who attempted to ride the popular discontent led by Ayatollah Khomeini and the mullahs, have begun to lower their apparent ambitions. While two or three weeks ago, many of these politicians were openly calling for the dismissal of the shah, most of them now quietly state that they accept the need for the shah's continued leadership, albeit within the framework of a democratic, constitutional society'. In another cable on the same day the embassy reported the departure of moderate opposition leaders to Paris for talks with Khomeini that 'if sufficiently favorable to some form of cooperation between in-country religious leaders and GOI [Government of Iran], could help start tension-reduction process'.[46]

By the end of the month, however, the ambassador was rapidly changing his tune. Though reporting that many oppositionists were still willing to live with the shah for lack of a viable alternative, he emphasized that this predilection was coming under increasing strain.[47] On 2 November, just as Vance voiced confidence in the shah's ability to 'restore order', Sullivan reported that the monarch was contemplating abdication, and this prognosis was echoed by the INR, which opined that if the shah 'does nothing to channel the course of events, he is likely to be ousted'.[48] A week later the ambassador took this theme a major step forward, urging his superiors to start 'thinking the unthinkable' and make plans for a post-shah Iran. Yet even as he made this bold proposition Sullivan could not reconcile himself to the real consequences of this momentous change, anticipating the successor Islamist regime to sustain 'Iran's general international orientation except that it would cease its ties with Israel and associate itself with the Arabs, probably closer to the rejectionist front than to Saudi Arabia'. 'It would probably be a Kuwait writ large in its general orientation', he argued, and 'although U.S. involvement would be less intimate than with the shah, it should be an essentially satisfactory one, particularly if the military preserves both its integrity and its status as one of the "pillars" of the nation'.[49]

If the ambassador hoped that his upbeat portrayal of the post-shah regime (he went as far as to describe Khomeini as a 'Gandhi-like' figure) would make the administration amenable to the looming change, he was to be bitterly disappointed. Ignoring his assessment altogether, the State Department asserted that the shah 'remains in firm control and has stated categorically that he will not step down',[50] while the CIA maintained that 'if the Shah holds firm – and is perceived to be holding firm – he probably will retain the backing of the military and will slow the growing popular momentum against this'. But even if the shah were to lose his nerve, and his throne, this need not necessarily mean a total disaster, since 'it is more likely that a military regime would succeed him than that he would be replaced by a civilian government of either the religious right or the secular left'.[51]

To make matters worse, Sullivan's new thesis made him the implacable enemy of the White House. Shortly after the fall of the shah Carter blamed this debacle on an 'intelligence failure', a charge that was ostensibly reaffirmed by a 1979 congressional report.[52] Yet, as candidly admitted by National Security Advisor Zbigniew Brzezinski, what transpired in Iran was a 'failure of political intelligence in the widest meaning of the term "intelligence"' rather than a matter of deficient intelligence-gathering and reporting.[53] What he failed to note, however, is that culpability for strategic blunders of this magnitude usually rests with the top political echelon as subordinate agencies strive to adjust their assessments to their superiors' perceived worldview.

So it was in the case of Iran. As long as Sullivan subscribed to the received wisdom that the shah was perfectly capable of riding the storm, against all evidence to the contrary provided by the Tehran embassy, his judgement was not questioned. Once he dared challenge this orthodoxy he was instantaneously transformed into an outcast, and his ostracism intensified by the day as he stood his ground against what he considered the White House's 'gross and perhaps irretrievable mistake' of refusing to negotiate with Ayatollah Khomeini, who had emerged as the indisputable leader of the anti-shah coalition. So much so that on 10 January 1979, a week before the shah's flight from Iran, Carter ordered Sullivan's dismissal, only to be talked out of the idea by Vance. This, however, did not prevent the president from publicly (mis)claiming a day after the shah's departure that 'the rapid change of affairs in Iran has not been predicted by anyone so far as I know'.[54]

At no stage of the crisis, not even when all was over, did the administration realize that what was transpiring in front of its eyes was a revolution in the grand style of the French or the Russian, not merely turbulence on a large scale. Tehran had long been America's 'only building block ... between Japan, and NATO, and Europe ... that is strong, that is sound, that is aggressive, and that above all regards us as just about as its firmest friend',[55] and no Cassandra 'motivated by doctrinal dislike of the Shah' should be allowed to question this fundamental truth – be it Sullivan or his Washington alter ego Henry Precht, the State Department's head of the Iran Desk.[56]

Wedded to the standard misconception of Middle Eastern affairs as an offshoot of global politics, Carter and Brzezinski (and Washington bureaucracy for that matter) viewed the Iranian crisis through a Cold War prism that was largely oblivious to regional intricacies and considered any American loss a Soviet gain. Suspecting an invisible Soviet hand behind the anti-shah opposition, Brzezinski became increasingly alarmed by the crisis in the spring of 1978 following a successful pro-Soviet coup in neighbouring Afghanistan.[57] When on 18 November Soviet leader Brezhnev responded to Carter's public support for the shah by warning against US intervention in Iran, Brzezinski overrode Vance's conciliatory reply in favour of a sharp rebuke to Moscow. A couple of weeks later he went so far as to request that the Defense Department initiate contingency plans for the deployment of US forces in southern Iran to secure the oilfields from a possible Soviet grab.[58]

It never occurred to the president and his top advisor that Moscow might be no less alarmed by the prospect of having a militant Islamist regime on its southern border, and that a modicum of US-Soviet collaboration could consequently be arranged to preempt such an eventuality by either propping up the shah or seeking a more acceptable successor regime. As far as they were concerned, the Soviets posed no less a threat to US regional interests than the domestic Iranian opposition, hence had to be deterred while the shah was being bolstered to crush the opposition come what may.

In an ironic twist of history, the president who had made the promotion of human rights a defining issue of his administration, and whose pressure on the shah in this regard played a role in the eruption of the Iranian cauldron,[59] was being transformed into a champion of repression. Contemptuously dismissing Sullivan's pleas to give up on the shah and his Western-educated Prime Minister Shahpour Bakhtiar (appointed on 4 January 1979) and to establish direct contact with Khomeini, Carter and Brzezinski, who marginalized Vance and his State Department bureaucrats in managing the crisis, urged the monarch to suppress the protest without delay. As the shah would not play this role and plunge his country into a bloodbath, they concluded that a military government could save the day; and while the president was loath to accept his advisor's persistent advocacy of a military coup, both because of his distaste for covert operations and because he saw no military figure capable of executing this feat (CIA Director Turner, too, viewed Brzezinski as prone to 'unrealistic expectations of what could be achieved by covert action'), in early January he nevertheless dispatched General Robert Huyser, Deputy Commander of the Supreme Allied Command in Europe, to Iran to do precisely that in the event of the collapse of the Bakhtiar government.[60]

This mission, to be sure, was totally useless. Apart from serving as an echo chamber for his superiors' fatal misconceptions, Huyser stood no chance of galvanizing the Iranian generals into action for the simple reason that, for all their large size and material prowess, the Iranian armed forces were a clear case of 'lions led by donkeys', as British World War I high command is infamously known. Not only were Iranian officers appointed and promoted on the basis of loyalty and sycophancy rather than professional competence, but as supreme commander the shah sterilized the armed forces of independent thinking and esprit de corps: he prevented the creation of a unified command structure – a basic component of any military establishment – thus emptying the post of chief-of-staff (and minister of defence) of any concrete substance; he treated his senior officers with high-handed disrespect that generated perennial self-abnegation and submissiveness; he used a string of divide and rule tactics – from appointing ethnic minority members to senior posts (thus alienating them from their subordinates) to eschewing group discussions in favour of individual meetings with officers; and he maintained tight surveillance of the officer corps to prevent 'misconduct' and 'deviations'. As a result, the Iranian high command was not the cohesive supreme decision-making body it was supposed to be but a disparate agglomeration of individuals, beset by jealousies, rivalries and distrust, unversed in operational or organizational collaboration, and lacking a collective (and personal) backbone. Small wonder that it failed to induce the shah to revert to iron-fisted tactics, deemed necessary by most senior officers, and once abandoned by its towering monarch collapsed like a house of cards (on 9–10 February 1979) at the first major test.[61]

As a tearful Shah left Iran on 16 January 1979 and a buoyant Khomeini made a triumphant return home after 16 years of exile, the supremacy of indigenous dynamics in Middle Eastern affairs and the limits of superpower influence had been reaffirmed yet again. While there is little doubt that the Carter administration mismanaged the crisis on a grand scale, the fact of the matter is that Washington was reacting to events that were not of its own making and over which it had but limited control. The Iranian Revolution was a volcanic eruption of long-suppressed popular passions and desires rooted in millenarian traditions and legacies – the first popular revolution in the history of the modern Middle East (though most regional coups misnamed themselves as revolutions). Putting this genie back into the bottle was well beyond America's power. All the administration could realistically do was to try to limit the damage to US interests to the barest minimum. As things were, the perennial constraints on superpower regional policy came to the fore in a particularly devastating fashion: excessive Cold War mentality to the exclusion of local realities; competing international priorities (e.g. the Egyptian-Israeli peace talks,

SALT negotiations with Moscow); bureaucratic infighting and inability to transcend cultural barriers – all coalesced to produce a setback that even a decade of bitter regional conflict (the Iran-Iraq War, that is) and momentous global changes would fail to redress.

5. THE CAUTIOUS BEAR

Geopolitical considerations have played the key role in Moscow's policy towards the Middle East. To Russia and its short-lived Soviet incarnation the vast territory on its southern border has never been yet another Third World area: it is *the area*, for no other reason than it is the only part of the Third World immediately adjoining Russian territory, and as such is an integral component of its security perimeter.[1] Russia's interest in the Middle East has therefore been essentially identical (albeit less intense) to that held by its immediate European neighbours – Poland, Finland, the Baltic states, and the Balkans prior to the Second World War and Eastern Europe during the Cold War – namely, securing an effective buffer zone through the prevention of foreign intervention and the preservation of benevolent local regimes. In the case of the Middle East, this interest was further reinforced by Russia's long-standing desire to control the Bosphorus and the Dardanelles straits so as to provide an outlet for its naval activities in the Mediterranean and to block the passage of Western warships into the Black Sea.

This in turn makes Moscow's preoccupation with the Middle East qualitatively different from that of any other great power. While Western interest in the region, however important, is circumstantial and ephemeral, the Russian interest is structural and perennial: for the West, Middle Eastern affairs are an offshoot of global politics; for Moscow they are a predominantly regional issue.[2] This is not to deny the relevance of global considerations in the making of Russia's Middle Eastern policy, given that the main threats to its southern border over the past two centuries emanated from external rather than indigenous powers, be it Britain's interference in Iran and Afghanistan, the Anglo-French invasion of the Crimea or Turkey's membership in NATO. Nevertheless, due to its predominantly regional perspective, Moscow's policy revealed far greater constancy and far less susceptibility to global vicissitudes than Western policy. It was only during Mikhail Gorbachev's tenure (1985–91) that the Russians came to subordinate their Middle Eastern interests to global considerations, and even this brief detour seems to have reverted to its old self under Boris Yeltsin and Vladimir Putin.

Moscow's geopolitical outlook is vividly illustrated by the fact that it has never viewed the region adjacent to its southern border as a unified whole but has rather made a clear distinction between its immediate neighbours – Turkey, Iran and Afghanistan (defined as the *Srednii Vostok*, the Middle East) – and the rest of the region, which it calls the Near East (*Blizhni Vostok*); and it is this distinction that largely accounted for its lack of interest in the Arabic-speaking world before the 1950s.

Since the existence of independent Arab states was a relatively new phenomenon and since most of them remained under Western tutelage till the late 1940s or early 1950s, the Soviets were slow to discover their 'revolutionary potential' (in the 1948 Arab-Israeli war, for example, they extended indirect military support to 'revolutionary' Israel as a means of easing the British out of Palestine); instead they focused on their direct neighbours in an attempt to incorporate them into an effective buffer zone that would resist external domination and prevent the projection of religious and nationalist incitement into Russian territory. By way of achieving this goal the Soviets encouraged strong national leaders such as Turkey's Mustafa Kemal (Atatürk) and Iran's Shah Reza Pahlavi and proved ready to settle for 'good neighbourly relations' with their southern neighbours, often based on bilateral treaties stipulating non-intervention in internal affairs and neutrality in case of war (e.g., the Soviet-Iranian treaty of 1921).[3]

This approach gave way to an assertive, indeed aggressive, policy in the immediate wake of World War II as Stalin capitalized on Moscow's growing preeminence to tighten its control over its southern neighbours. Hence his refusal to withdraw from Iran, occupied in 1941 together with Britain, in flagrant violation of his wartime undertaking, and hence his demands for Turkish concessions including the return of the Kars and Ardahan districts (ceded to Ankara in 1921), the establishment of Soviet bases on the straits, and the revision of the Montreux Convention regulating the navigation law there. Yet even as Moscow embarked on this assertive course it took care to present it as designed to preempt capitalist encirclement, a claim that was not without some merit, especially with regard to Iran, where London seemed eager to retain its physical presence and economic and political influence.[4]

It was not long, however, before this strategy backfired, as Ankara and Tehran drew closer to the West (while exploiting their growing geostrategic importance to extract handsome military and economic returns for this shift). In March 1947, President Truman announced his famous doctrine aimed at shielding Turkey and Greece from the threat of 'international communism' and five years later Ankara became a formal member in NATO. In 1955 Turkey joined Iraq, Iran, Pakistan and Britain in forming the Baghdad Pact, which transformed what had been an effective buffer zone in the prewar era into an important link in the worldwide chain of Western containment and extended NATO's military power to Moscow's backyard, turning it into a potential theatre of great-power confrontation;[5] and it was the desire to breach this encirclement that kindled the Soviet interest in the Arab states.

With Egyptian President Gamal Abdel Nasser considering the Baghdad Pact a major obstacle to his burning ambition for pan-Arab leadership, the Syrian regime fearful of its hostile Turkish and Iraqi neighbours, and the Saudis resentful of any strengthening of their Iraqi nemesis, in March 1955 the three states formed an alliance to counterweight the pact. Capitalizing on this unique convergence of interests, Moscow quickly signed large arms deals with Cairo and Damascus in what heralded a prolonged and multifaceted procurement relationship with the Arabic-speaking world. Three years later, following a bloody coup that overthrew the Hashemite monarchy and took Iraq out of the pact (which had come to be known as the Central Treaty Organization, or CENTO), Baghdad, too, drifted towards the Soviet orbit. By the end of the 1970s Moscow had supplied its Arab allies nearly $26 billion worth of weapons and military equipment (and some $4.7 billion in economic aid), with thousands of Soviet advisers and technicians (but not independent units) deployed in the local armies in training and maintenance roles.[6] Yet if the Soviets had any hopes that these burgeoning ties would give them leverage over their Arab clients, especially in relation to the cardinal issues of war and peace, they were to be bitterly disappointed.

Failing to Prevent Arab-Israeli Wars

It has of course been widely claimed that the Soviets sought to foment local tensions, if not to keep the Middle East in a permanent state of low intensity conflict, as a means of enhancing their influence and deepening Arab dependence.[7] Yet not only did this supposed conduct contravene Moscow's perception of regional instability as a magnet of external intervention that had to be deflected but it also ran counter to Soviet strategic doctrine, which until the late 1960s considered military intervention in Third World conflicts a certain catalyst to world war.[8] Indeed, unlike the United States, which by the 1960s had been drawn into two prolonged local wars (Korea and Vietnam) aside from a string of small scale military interventions (e.g., the 1958 dispatch of marines to Lebanon, the Bay of Pigs fiasco), Moscow refrained from any intervention in Third World conflicts until the June 1967 Arab-Israeli war, when it made some modest demonstrative moves on behalf of its Arab allies yet declined an official request for direct intervention. Even the false Soviet warnings of an imminent Israeli attack on Syria that set in train the rapid deterioration to the 1967 war were apparently the result of faulty intelligence estimates rather than a deliberate grand design to trigger an all-out war.[9] Indeed, during the 25-year period from the war to the disintegration of the Soviet Union in December 1991, Moscow did its utmost to prevent further conflagrations and to convince its Arab allies of the merits of a peaceful resolution of the conflict.

Take the Egyptian war of attrition against Israel along the Suez Canal (March 1969–August 1970). The Soviets pleaded with Nasser to forgo the use of force and, once hostilities nevertheless broke out, to stop fighting and reach a negotiated settlement; they even threatened him with military sanctions – to no avail.[10] Not only did these pressures fail to impress the Egyptian president, but during a secret visit to Moscow at the end of January 1970 he managed to implicate Egypt's bigger ally in his war by threatening to resign in favour of a pro-American leader unless Soviet-manned aircraft and air defence units were immediately sent to the war zone to neutralize Israel's overwhelming air supremacy. 'As far as I can see, you are not prepared to help us in the same way that America helps Israel', Nasser reportedly told his hosts: 'This means that there is only one course open to me: I shall go back to Egypt and I shall tell the people the truth. I shall tell them that the time has come for me to step down and hand over to a pro-American president. If I cannot save them, somebody else will have to do it. This is my final word'.

Taken aback by their client's uncompromising stance, the Soviet leaders broke for immediate consultations and, after a prolonged deliberation, grudgingly acquiesced in his demand, but not before emphasizing the seriousness of this military intervention – the kind of which had never been taken before outside the Communist bloc. '"Comrade Nasser",

Secretary-General of the Communist Party Leonid Brezhnev said, 'the Soviet Union has today taken a decision fraught with grave consequences. It is a decision unlike any we have taken before. It will need your help in carrying out, and it will call for restraint on your part'.[11]

An even starker demonstration of the limits of Soviet influence was afforded by the outbreak of the October 1973 war. When Anwar Sadat, who in the autumn of 1970 assumed the presidency following Nasser's premature death, began threatening Israel with war unless it accepted his demands for a negotiated settlement, the Soviets were greatly alarmed lest a new conflagration jeopardize the cause of global détente and force them to expand their military support for the Arabs who, they believed, were certain to be thoroughly defeated yet again. For over a year they tried to prevent the outbreak of hostilities by withholding arms supplies. Yet after an initial success in forcing Sadat to postpone his deadlines for launching war this strategy backfired in grand style: determined to enter Sinai 'even if we only have rifles', in July 1972 the Egyptian president ordered the expulsion of the 15,000 Soviet military personnel brought to Egypt in 1970 at Nasser's demand.[12]

This move took the Soviets by complete surprise. Notwithstanding their reluctance to deploy these troops in the first place and their attendant unease about retaining them, this was certainly not the way they envisaged their departure. They therefore sought to cut their losses by resuming arms deliveries to Egypt, albeit not at the pace and scope desired by Sadat, while trying to convince the Arabs of the perils of war and the benefits of a negotiated settlement. These efforts were accompanied by warnings to the US administration in the hope of driving it to pressure Israel to accommodate the Arab demands.

As early as February 1973 Brezhnev warned Nixon that in the absence of immediate progress towards a settlement 'the Arabs can turn to the use of other possible means of its solution'. Three months later he made an even starker prognosis during a meeting with National Security Advisor Henry Kissinger in the Soviet leadership's retreat in Zavidovo. 'It is impossible not to take some steps or President Nixon and I might find ourselves in an impossible situation', he warned. 'After all, nothing in the world is eternal – similarly, the present military advantage enjoyed by Israel is not eternal either'.[13]

Brezhnev knew what he was talking about. In May 1973 he and his colleagues managed to persuade Syria's President Hafez Assad, who had joined Sadat's war preparations some time earlier, to talk his partner into postponing their planned attack that month so as to give Moscow a final chance to plead their case in the forthcoming US-Soviet summit in June;[14] and knowing full well that the Egyptian-Syrian acquiescence hung by a thread the Secretary-General went out of his way to convince his American counterparts of the situation's volatility. So much so that on the last night of the summit (23 June), in the western White House in the Californian resort of San Clemente, he demanded an immediate meeting with Nixon, who was already asleep. When this unusual session was arranged at 10:30 p.m., the Secretary-General proposed that the two superpowers agree then and there on a Middle East settlement that would provide for an Israeli withdrawal to the 1967 lines in return for an end to the state of belligerency – but not peace, which would have to be subsequently negotiated with the Palestinians. 'If there is no clarity about the principles we will have difficulty keeping the military situation from flaring up', he warned. 'I am categorically opposed to the resumption of the war. But without agreed principles … we cannot do this'.

The Americans remained unmoved. Viewing Brezhnev's warnings as a blatant attempt 'to bulldoze us into solving his dilemmas without paying any price' by 'shifting the onus of a deadlock unto us and to prevent a further erosion of the Soviet position in the Arab world', Nixon declined his demand for an immediate agreement yet promised to move energetically towards a settlement. 'It would be very easy for me to say that Israel should withdraw from all the occupied territories and call it an agreed principle', he said. 'But that's what the argument is about: I will agree to principles which will bring a settlement. That will be our project this year. The Middle East is [a] most urgent place'.[15]

As the Arabs responded to the summit's inconclusive outcome by accelerating their covert war preparations, the Soviets sustained their stream of public and private warnings of the non-tenability of the situation. This culminated in Andrei Gromyko's address to the UN General Assembly (on 25 September) urging the necessity of a political settlement,[16] and three days later the foreign minister warned Nixon in a White House meeting that 'we could all wake up one day and find there is a real conflagration in that area'.[17]

When their warnings failed to dispel American complacency (as late as 6 October, a few hours before war broke out, the CIA and DIA estimated that the Egyptians and the Syrians 'do not appear to be preparing for a military offensive against Israel' and that 'for the normally cautious Syrian president, a military adventure now would be suicidal'),[18] the

Soviets made a last-ditch attempt to alert the Israelis to the impending war by withdrawing their civilian dependants from Egypt and Syria in a massive air- and sealift on 4 October, immediately upon learning that war would ensue in two days.[19] This move was drastic enough to enrage Sadat, who feared that his meticulously prepared surprise attack would be jeopardized at the last moment, and to raise a few eyebrows within the Israeli intelligence community. Yet since the Israelis believed that the Soviets would alert the Americans to an impending war (which they did) and that the Americans would in turn warn them (which they did not), they concluded, with considerable misgivings, that the evacuation signified another rupture in Arab-Soviet relations of the sort that had taken place in Egypt in July 1972.[20]

The outbreak of the October 1973 war was thus a glaring failure of Moscow's political and diplomatic power. Not only did it expose its lack of influence over the US and Israel (both of which turned a deaf ear to its warnings) but it also underscored its inability to dissuade its closest Arab allies from undertaking a course of action deemed harmful to its interests. Indeed, within hours of the outbreak of hostilities Sadat angrily rejected a ceasefire proposal passed to him by the Soviet ambassador to Cairo, Sergei Vinogradov. Undaunted, Vinogradov approached the Egyptian president the next day with the same proposal, only to be turned down for the second time.[21]

Failing to Facilitate Peace

The Soviets were no more successful in bringing their Arab allies to the negotiating table than they had been in preventing them from waging war. As co-architects of the November 1967 Security Council Resolution 242, which established the principle of 'land for peace' as the cornerstone of future Arab-Israeli peace negotiations and accepted Israel's right to a peaceful and secure existence, the Soviets considered the document 'the only way to peace in the Middle East'.[22]

By adopting this position, despite the fact that the resolution left the door open to Israel's retention of some land by requiring its withdrawal 'from territories occupied in the recent conflict' (the absence of the definite article 'the' before 'territories' – which, had it been included, would have required a complete Israeli withdrawal – was no accident and reflected the contemporary awareness of the existential threat posed by Israel's pre-1967 lines), Moscow indicated its reluctance to side with the extremist Arab demands. Indeed, in a 1968 meeting with the Israeli ambassador to the UN, the Soviet deputy foreign minister implied his government's readiness to support minor border adjustments between Israel and its Arab neighbours.[23] It was only in December 1968, upon announcing its own comprehensive peace plan, that Moscow endorsed the Arab interpretation of the resolution as necessitating complete Israeli withdrawal. After the October 1973 war the Soviets took this position a major step further by claiming that the resolution required the establishment of an independent Palestinian state – though it actually made no mention of the Palestinians whatsoever (only noting the need 'for achieving a just settlement of the refugee problem', which could well be applied to the hundreds of thousands of Jewish refugees expelled from the Arab states during and after the 1948 war).[24]

This policy shift failed to impress the Arabs. Convinced that the key to a political settlement lay in Washington rather than in Moscow, Sadat began extricating Egypt from the Soviet orbit already in the early 1970s. The breach between the two countries was rapidly widened in the wake of the October war as Cairo tied its political, economic and military fortunes to Washington and was made absolute in March 1976 with the unilateral abrogation of its 1971 Friendship and Cooperation Treaty with Moscow and the termination of the extensive Soviet naval services in Egyptian ports.

Nor were Moscow's other allies more receptive to its wishes. Violently opposed to Israel's right to exist, Syria and the Palestine Liberation Organization (PLO) dismissed the idea of a political settlement altogether and voiced their commitment to Israel's destruction via the 'armed struggle'. Ignoring repeated Soviet pleas, Damascus refused to attend the Arab-Israeli peace conference convened in Geneva in December 1973 – the first such gathering since the aftermath of the 1948 war. Shortly afterwards, much to Moscow's chagrin, it opted for a US-sponsored disengagement agreement with Israel and, moreover, accompanied the negotiation process with a war of attrition on the Golan Heights; and while the Syrians would eventually come to adopt the preferred Soviet way to a negotiated settlement, namely, an international peace conference, they would nevertheless remain adamantly opposed to Moscow's perception of the essence of such a settlement, predicated as it was on the right of all regional states, Israel included, to secure existence.

As a result, a delicate 'balance of tolerance' evolved from the mid-1970s onwards whereby the two allies agreed to disagree. The Syrians supported the future convocation of an international conference on the Middle East but continued to reject Israel's right to exist, and indeed viewed the conference as a means of preventing a bilaterally negotiated Egyptian-Israeli peace agreement and the possible drift of other Arab states in this direction. For their part the Soviets made no bones about their acceptance of Israel yet refrained from overtly pressuring Damascus to accept this position; they reluctantly signed a bilateral friendship and cooperation treaty in October 1980 yet told the Syrians not to interpret it, and for that matter their military and political support, as endorsement of their political stance.[25]

Even Gorbachev, the first Soviet leader to attempt an even-handed approach that put the Arab and Israeli causes on a par and called for a solution based on a 'balance of interests among all sides',[26] was forced to recognize the limits of Soviet influence. Going much further than his predecessors to eradicate Assad's intransigence he repeatedly declined his requests for state-of-the-art weaponry; sought to isolate Damascus by supporting the conservative Arab regimes; restored diplomatic relations with Israel (severed since the 1967 war); and allowed a mass exodus of Soviet Jews to Israel. When Assad questioned the prudence of these actions he was bluntly told to seek a peaceful solution with Israel since 'reliance on military force in settling the Arab–Israeli conflict has completely lost its credibility'. The quest for 'strategic parity' with Israel, the cornerstone of Syria's regional policy since the mid-1970s, drew a particularly scathing criticism for 'diverting attention from the question of achieving security and peace in the Middle East'.[27]

While there is little doubt that this approach heightened Assad's sense of vulnerability, it also intensified his hostility towards Gorbachev and left him totally impervious to his wishes. 'Anyone remote from the region and taken in by the brilliance of the détente process can be dragged into the position of equating the aggressor and the victim of aggression', argued the Syrian media. However, 'What is called the balance of interests cannot be achieved in the Middle East, where the nature of the problem and the conflict differs from other regional problems and conflicts'.[28]

When in November 1988 the PLO feigned recognition of Israel's existence and declared Palestinian independence (in Arafat's meeting with Gorbachev in April 1988, the first of its kind in five years, he was told that Israel, too, had legitimate security concerns and was urged to recognize the Jewish state),[29] the Syrians denounced this move as a sell-out and refused to recognize the self-declared Palestinian state. 'We do not ignore or belittle the importance of world public opinion', Assad sardonically commented on the move. 'But we will not allow ourselves to concede our rights for the sake of winning its support'. 'What is the use of asking others to support our legitimate rights', he reasoned, 'if we ourselves concede these rights'.[30] When the PLO took this pretence a step further by signing the September 1993 Declaration of Principles (DOP) with Israel, which provided for Palestinian self-rule in the entire West Bank and the Gaza Strip for a transitional period of up to five years as a prelude to a negotiated peace settlement, it was strongly condemned by the Syrian regime with the Damascus-based Palestinian terrorist Ahmad Jibril threatening Arafat with death.

Crisis over Lebanon

While the question of Arab-Israeli peace constituted a protracted bone of contention between Moscow and Damascus with occasional outbursts of sharp differences, since the mid-1970s Soviet-Syrian relations became increasingly captive to the vicissitudes of the Lebanese civil war. As the country formed the stage for a string of Israeli-Syrian crises, and eventually war, as well as a vicious power struggle between Damascus and the PLO, it constituted the backdrop against which Soviet-Syrian relations played out some of their most trying moments.

To be sure, when Assad decided to send his troops into Lebanon on 1 June 1976, he had no reason to anticipate a Soviet-Syrian rift. By that time Damascus had become Moscow's foremost Middle Eastern ally following Cairo's defection from the Soviet fold, and its pacification efforts since the outbreak of the Lebanese civil war the previous year had been favourably received by the Soviets. Moscow viewed the conflict as an 'imperialist-Zionist plot' to divide the Arabs and had no objection to its ally's growing influence in a pro-Western state, especially since this strengthened the 'progressive' PLO-leftist coalition.[31] Yet as the indirect and cautious Syrian intervention failed to stabilize the situation, the Soviets grew increasingly alarmed lest matters get out of hand given Israel's vocal concern about the growing instability along its northern border. Ignoring these warnings entailed the risk of a renewed Israeli-Syrian conflagration; alleviating Israel's apprehensions, on the other hand, required a measure of coordination that only Washington could offer. Indeed, as early as October 1975 the US administration acted as a back channel between Jerusalem and Damascus to prevent an undesirable escalation and several months later sent a veteran diplomat to Beirut to mediate a compromise between the rival factions.

Soviet unease about the Lebanese situation intensified in March 1976, when Damascus turned against its former 'progressive' allies in an attempt to prevent them from gaining the upper hand in the war. With two of its allies locked in a vicious fight, Moscow threw its weight behind Damascus, both because its strategic value far exceeded that of the Lebanese left and the PLO put together and because the latter's growing extremism posed a clear and present danger to Lebanon's delicate sectarian edifice (e.g., the PLO's January 1976 massacre of hundreds of civilians in the Christian town of Damour, south of Beirut). As late as 28 May, three days before Syrian tanks began rolling into Lebanon, Moscow strongly decried 'the attempt to besmirch the Syrian mediation mission in Lebanon' as 'another aspect of imperialist and reaction pressure on Damascus ... with the aim of driving Damascus out of the anti-imperialist line and destroying the [Palestinian] resistance and the nationalist movement in Lebanon'.[32] In his visit to Damascus amid the Syrian intervention (1–4 June), Prime Minister Alexei Kosygin reportedly told Assad that while the Soviets approved of this action he 'should not expect any public declarations of support because of the Soviet commitment to the Palestinians'. Still the final communiqué contained a veiled endorsement of the Syrian intervention with more pronounced expressions of support following in the next few days, coupled with the establishment of a Soviet naval presence opposite Lebanon.[33]

Before long, however, Moscow was to change tack as its expectations of a swift and decisive pacification of the situation were dashed. 'The Syrian Arab Republic has repeatedly stated that the mission of the troops sent by it to Lebanon was to help stop the bloodshed', ran a statement by the TASS official news agency on 9 June. 'Attention must, however, be drawn to the fact that an ever swelling river of blood continues to flow in Lebanon today ... The first thing to be done in Lebanon, therefore, is to stop the bloodshed. All those parties involved in the Lebanese events, in one way or another, must cease fire forthwith'.

A week later, while avoiding a direct demand for withdrawal, TASS cited the Syrian minister of information as saying that Damascus had sent its troops to Lebanon to create conditions 'for a dialogue among the Lebanese' and would withdraw them as soon as this goal had been attained. This thinly veiled hint was accompanied by a reported rejection of a Syrian request for financial aid to offset the cost of its fresh Lebanese intervention, and on 11 July Brezhnev sent a personal message to Assad that harshly criticized the Syrian intervention, called for an immediate truce, and raised the spectre of Soviet sanctions should Damascus fail to withdraw its troops from Lebanon. The seriousness of these threats was evidenced within days by the significant slowdown of arms supplies and technical assistance to Syria as well as the launch of an anti-Syria propaganda campaign by the official Soviet media. A July visit to Moscow by the Syrian foreign minister, Abdel Khalim Khaddam, only served to underscore the widening rift between the two allies; a return visit to Damascus later that month by the Soviet deputy foreign minister proved equally futile.[34]

These measures won Moscow precious little. As early as 10 June Damascus responded to TASS's criticism of the previous day by pledging to maintain its Lebanese policy. Ten days later, during Assad's first visit to France – in itself a clear signal of his determination to keep his options open – the Syrian president had nothing but praise for his hosts' mediation attempts in Lebanon. More galling to Moscow, Assad harnessed French tacit support for 'the Syrian efforts to help the warring parties in Lebanon to achieve a political solution to the Lebanese crisis'. These efforts, Assad promised, would continue until Lebanon was 'rescued from its painful ordeal'.[35] Yet notwithstanding this open act of defiance, the Syrian president was careful to avoid an open rift with Moscow, refraining from overt criticism of its actions and making the odd gesture – from voicing support for the reconvening of the Geneva conference to deriding Washington's Lebanon policy. In a policy statement published on 12 October, the Syrian government openly pronounced its interest in 'strengthening relations of cooperation with the friendly socialist states'.[36]

This combination of relentlessness and pragmatism had a moderating impact on the Soviets. Assad's steadfastness underscored the extraordinary lengths required for twisting his arm; his avoidance of direct confrontation, on the other hand, illustrated the benefits of the special relationship. Hence, during the autumn of 1976, Moscow's Lebanon policy shifted from exclusive pressure on Syria to a more balanced approach of mediating a settlement between the warring factions. Within this framework, in mid-September Farouq Qaddumi, the PLO's 'foreign minister', was invited to Moscow where he was apparently pressured to reach an understanding with Damascus. Reinforced by several meetings between Arafat and the Soviet chargé d'affaires in Beirut, this pressure seemed to bear the desired fruit: on 24 September, the day after the Syrian-sponsored president, Elias

Sarkis, had entered office, Arafat sent a letter to the newly inaugurated head of state informing him of the PLO's decision to adopt a unilateral ceasefire and conform to the agreements regulating Palestinian-Lebanese relations. When in mid-October 1976 a mini-conference in Riyadh, with the participation of Syria, Lebanon, Egypt, Kuwait and the PLO, agreed measures to stabilize the Lebanese civil war, Moscow stopped its criticism of Damascus altogether and gradually came to view the Syrian military presence in Lebanon as 'peacekeeping forces'. By early 1977 Soviet-Syrian relations had fully recovered with the restoration of arms deliveries and technical assistance to Damascus.

Subsequently, in each of the Syrian-Israeli crises and clashes over Lebanon in the late 1970s and early 1980s, notably the 1982 Lebanon war, the Soviets zealously defended the legitimacy of Damascus's presence in Lebanon. This reached its peak in the staunch support offered during Yuri Andropov's brief term in office (November 1982–February 1984) to the relentless Syrian campaign against the Israeli (and American) presence in Lebanon, despite its escalatory potential. Yet even Andropov took great care to reduce the risk of a general conflagration by clarifying to Assad that he could not expect Soviet intervention in Lebanon should events there get out of control.

This symbiosis of uneasy approval of Syria's presence in Lebanon and fears of its escalatory potential persisted during the Gorbachev era, as starkly illustrated in the missile crisis of December 1985–January 1986 when Jerusalem and Damascus came close to war following the deployment of Syrian surface-to-air missiles in Lebanon. While justifying the move as an act of 'self-defense and the protection of Syria's ally, sovereign Lebanon' and rejecting the Israeli (and American) demand for their withdrawal as an 'impudent interference in Syria's internal affairs', Moscow was careful not to indicate any readiness to support Damascus militarily should the crisis escalate to open confrontation. So much so that the Soviet media portrayed the deployment as taking place within Syria, rather than on Lebanese territory, thus signalling a measure of disapproval of the Syrian action and delineating the geographical limits of support for Damascus.[37]

The Afghan Misadventure

But the foremost example of the limits of Soviet power was afforded by the December 1979 invasion and subsequent occupation of Afghanistan.

Contrary to its widespread interpretation as an expansionist bid to 'give the Soviets a deep penetration between Iran and Pakistan and pose a threat to the rich oil fields of the Persian Gulf area and to the crucial waterways through which so much of the world's energy supplies had to pass',[38] the invasion was a last-ditch attempt to prevent the descent of a strategic neighbouring country into anarchy after the exhaustion of all other means to achieve this goal. Had the newly established communist regime in Kabul heeded Moscow's advice and acted with due prudence and restraint, the invasion might have been averted altogether. As it was, the Soviets were reluctantly driven to their largest Third World military undertaking ever, knowing full well that there might be no light at the end of the tunnel yet unable to arrest their steady slide towards the abyss. There was no fantasizing about new imperial vistas or control of the world oil market, only grim realization that given the existing balance of risks and opportunities direct military intervention was the least of all evils.

The countdown to invasion began in the spring of 1978 when the ambitious reforms initiated by the small communist People's Democratic Party of Afghanistan (PDPA), which seized power in a military coup in April, sparked widespread disturbances that escalated by the end of the year to a fully fledged uprising. With the PDPA's popular base further narrowed by vicious infighting between its radical Khalq ('Masses') faction, headed by Muhammad Nur Taraki and Hafizullah Amin, and the more moderate Parcham ('Flag'), led by Babrak Karmal, the nascent regime was soon looking to Moscow for aid and support.

Having long considered Afghan stability an integral part of its southern buffer zone, first against the threat posed by British India and then vis-à-vis Pakistan (a close US ally and a member of the Baghdad Pact and its CENTO offspring), Moscow followed the brewing crisis in Kabul with deep concern. A communist seizure of power in the deeply devout Middle East, where the 'godless' communists were persecuted and oppressed as a matter of course, was an extraordinary achievement that the Soviets were anxious to secure come what may, not least since it constituted an important barrier to the projection of Islamist influences into their Muslim republics, especially in the wake of the Iranian revolution. They therefore threw their weight behind the nascent regime despite their overt displeasure with its aggressive pursuit of reform (which they feared might alienate the highly conservative Afghan society) and the repressive measures enacted by the Khalq, which quickly marginalized its more moderate rival, cautiously supporting its counterinsurgency campaign with arms supplies and the deployment of advisors throughout the Afghan army (about 600 by the end of 1978) yet resisting repeated pleas for direct intervention.[39]

On 17 March 1979, amid heavy fighting in the country's third largest city of Herat and the defection of entire units to the insurgents with their weaponry, the Soviet highest decision-making body, the Politburo, held an extraordinary session to decide whether to up the ante and dispatch regular units to prop the fledgling regime. After some deliberation it was agreed that while Moscow could under no circumstances 'surrender Afghanistan to the enemy', and while emergency intervention plans had been drawn, it was imperative 'to use all political means in order to help the Afghan leadership to strengthen itself, to provide the support which we've already planned, and to leave as a last resort the use of force'. Not merely because of the international ramifications of such a move but also because it was unclear 'whom will our troops be fighting against if we send them there[?] Against the insurgents? Or have they been joined by a large number of religious fundamentalists, that is, Muslims, and among them large numbers of ordinary people? Thus, we will be required to wage war in significant part against the people'.

In these circumstances, it was decided to expedite arms deliveries to the Afghan army ('but only if we are convinced that they will not fall into the hands of the insurgents'), to increase the amount of economic aid (e.g., higher prices for Afghan natural gas, larger food supplies), and to vigorously back the beleaguered Afghan regime in the face of Iranian, Pakistani, Chinese and American pressure. At the same time, the Khalq leadership was to be told in no uncertain terms to stop its repressive tactics, which weakened the regime's long-term survivability, and instead strive to expand its popular base by pandering, among other things, to the population's religious sentiments.[40]

These decisions were relayed the same day to Taraki in a phone conversation with Prime Minister Kosygin, only to encounter an adamant demand for direct intervention. The situation in Herat was bad and getting worse, the Afghan leader argued. There was no active support on the part of the population, which was almost wholly under the influence of Shiite propaganda, and the army was in no position to rout the rebels who were busy preparing a major offensive with Iranian and Pakistani assistance. The only way 'to save the revolution' was for the Soviet army to 'launch a decisive attack on Herat'. Otherwise, 'the enemy will go in the direction of Kandahar and on in the direction of Kabul. They will bring half of Iran into Afghanistan under the flag of the Herat division'.

'We have decided to quickly deliver military equipment and property to you and to repair helicopters and aircraft,' Kosygin sought to allay his interlocutor's fears. 'All this is for free. We have also decided to deliver to you 100,000 tons of grain and to raise [Afghan] gas prices from $21 per cubic meter to $37.82'.

'That is very good, but let us talk of Herat. Why can't the Soviet Union send Uzbeks, Tajiks, and Turkmens in civilian clothing? No one will recognize them. We want you to send them. They could drive tanks, because we have all these nationalities in Afghanistan. Let them don Afghan costume and wear Afghan badges and no one will recognize them. It is very easy work, in our view'.

'I do not want to disappoint you, but it will not be possible to conceal this. Two hours later the whole world will know about this. Everyone will begin to shout that the Soviet Union's intervention in Afghanistan has begun'.[41]

Reporting the conversation to the Politburo the next day, Kosygin found his colleagues equally lukewarm to Taraki's intervention pleas. 'What is the problem? Why is this happening?' Defence Minister Dmitri Ustinov squarely blamed the Afghan government for the rapid deterioration. 'The problem is that the leadership of Afghanistan did not sufficiently appreciate the role of Islamic fundamentalists. It is under the banner of Islam that the soldiers are turning against the government, and an absolute majority, perhaps only with rare exceptions, are believers'.

KGB director and future national leader Yuri Andropov took this prognosis a step further. '[W]e must consider very, very seriously the question of whose cause we will be supporting if we deploy our forces into Afghanistan', he said.

It's completely clear to us that Afghanistan is not ready at this time to resolve all of the issues it faces through socialism. The economy is backward, the Islamic religion predominates, and nearly all of the rural population is illiterate. We know Lenin's teaching about a revolutionary situation. Whatever situation we are talking about in Afghanistan, it is not that type of situation. Therefore, I believe that we can suppress a revolution in Afghanistan only with the aid of our bayonets, and that is for us entirely inadmissible. We cannot take such a risk ... we should say to Taraki bluntly that we support all their actions and will render the kind of support that we agreed upon yesterday and today, but that in no case will we go forward with a deployment of troops into Afghanistan.

This view was echoed by Foreign Minister Gromyko. 'I completely support Comrade Andropov's proposal to rule out such a measure as the deployment of our troops into Afghanistan', he said.

> The army there is unreliable. Thus our army, when it arrives in Afghanistan, will be the aggressor. Against whom will it fight? Against the Afghan people first of all, and it will have to shoot at them. Comrade Andropov correctly noted that indeed the situation in Afghanistan is not ripe for a revolution. And all that we have done in recent years with such effort in terms of détente, arms reduction, and much more – all that would be thrown back. China, of course, would be given a nice present. All the nonaligned countries will be against us. In a word, serious consequences are to be expected from such an action … One must ask, and what would we gain? Afghanistan with its present government, with a backward economy, with inconsequential weight in international affairs. On the other side, we must keep in mind that from a legal point of view too we would not be justified in sending troops.

The next day Leonid Brezhnev joined his colleagues to wrap up the discussion. 'The question was raised as to the immediate participation of our troops in the conflict that has arisen in Afghanistan', he said. 'In my view the Politburo has correctly determined that the time is not right for us to become entangled in that war. We must explain to Comrade Taraki and our other Afghan comrades that we can help them with everything that is necessary for the conduct of all activities in the country. But the involvement of our forces in Afghanistan would harm not only us, but first of all them'.[42]

Taraki was thus flown to Moscow on 20 March, where he received a solemn pledge for political, economic and military support – short of direct intervention. 'We examined this question from every angle, weighed it carefully, and, I will tell you frankly: this should not be done', Brezhnev told his guest. 'This would only play into the hands of the enemies – yours and ours'. Moscow had warned Tehran and Islamabad in the strongest terms to stop interfering in Afghanistan's internal affairs, the Soviet leader added, yet found it inexplicable that Kabul did practically nothing to stem the influx of Iranian and Pakistani terrorists into its territory. This was an abnormal situation that had to be rectified without delay if the regime wished to survive, just as it was absolutely imperative for it to desist from its repressive measures, expand its popular base and split the ranks of the religious opposition: 'This could well be achieved by getting at least a part of the clergy, if not to actually support the government openly, then to at least not speak out against it'.[43] The importance of this last point was hammered shortly afterwards in a Politburo memo that defined the clergy and tribal leaders as the most influential forces in Afghanistan and identified 'the situation in Iran and the spark of religious fanaticism all around the Muslim East [as] the underlying cause of the activization of the struggle against the government of Afghanistan'.[44]

In the coming months the Soviets were to reject repeated Afghan pleas for direct intervention while at the same time pressuring the regime to appease the opposition and reach an agreement with Pakistan (and if possible Iran) on the cessation of their meddling in the conflict. During a visit to Kabul at the end of July, for example, Politburo member Boris Ponomarev fended off repeated pleas for the dispatch of Soviet forces 'at the request of the legal government of Afghanistan'. Undeterred, Prime Minister Amin reiterated the demand to the Soviet ambassador, to the chief Soviet military advisor in Afghanistan, and to the deputy minister of defence, General Ivan Pavlovsky, who arrived in Kabul in mid-August at the head of a delegation to monitor the situation – only to be turned down time and again.[45] Meanwhile the East German ambassador to Kabul was busy assuring his American counterpart of Moscow's lasting distaste for direct military intervention. The Soviets were keenly aware, he argued, that while such a move 'could eliminate the present govt. thereby solving one problem' it would create a much bigger problem by turning the 'entire Afghan nation' against them 'just as the Afghans turned against the "British invaders" in the nineteenth century'. Hence 'it made no sense for the Soviets to intervene militarily' and they would continue their efforts to solve the crisis through political means, notably a change in leadership in Kabul.[46] This, however, was not to be. In a clear snub to Moscow, which in August had reportedly hatched a plot against him and which had no qualms indicating its preference of President Taraki, on 16 September Amin overthrew (and subsequently executed) his longtime mentor in a bloody coup and seized the country's top spot.[47]

Shocked and dismayed, the Soviets decided to cut their losses and go along with the new ruler, while closely monitoring his conduct. Four days after the coup Brezhnev told the Politburo that 'events developed so swiftly that essentially there was little opportunity for us, here in Moscow, to somehow interfere in them' and that handling Amin would likely be 'difficult and delicate'. Yet he surmised that 'Soviet-Afghan relations will not sustain some sort of major changes, and, it seems, will continue in their previous course. Amin will be pushed toward this by the current situation and by the difficulties which the Afghan government will face for a long time to come. Afghanistan will continue to be interested in receiving from the USSR military, economic and other aid, and possibly even in increased amounts'.[48]

Two weeks later Brezhnev was even more upbeat. 'We now see that Amin is implementing what I told Taraki', he told his East German counterpart Erich Honecker.

> Frankly, we are not pleased by all of Amin's methods and actions. He is very power-driven. In the past he repeatedly revealed disproportionate harshness. But with regard to his basic political platform, he has decidedly conformed to the course of further development of the Revolution, of furthering cooperation with the Soviet Union and other countries of the Socialist community. It is a fact that many of Amin's followers and partisans are honourable people who are faithful to the ideas of Marxism-Leninism and take a good attitude towards us. By taking into consideration the actual situation, we will continue to support Afghanistan and give it a variety of support and help it in its fight against foreign aggression and the domestic counterrevolution.[49]

By December, however, these hopes had all but vanished. Not only had Amin lost control of much of the country but he seemed to be doing his utmost to eradicate the regime's power base through systematic purges of the party, army, state bureaucracy and civic organizations, thus driving the Soviets to entertain new options. On 1 December, Andropov informed Brezhnev of a fresh overture by Babrak Karmal, Parcham's exiled leader, gauging the possibility of Soviet military assistance for an anti-Amin coup. 'The implementation of the given operation would allow us to decide the question of defending the gains of the April revolution, establishing Leninist principals in the party and state leadership of Afghanistan, and securing our positions in this country', the KGB director favourably commented.[50]

That Brezhnev was warming to the idea was evidenced by the dispatch of a deputy minister of internal affairs to Kabul with a reported mandate to 'pressure Amin to step aside in support of Babrak'[51] and, more importantly, by a Politburo recommendation (on 6 December) to capitalize on Amin's latest request for Soviet forces and dispatch 500 KGB commandos 'in a uniform which does not reveal its belonging to the Armed Forces of the

USSR' – precisely the kind of forces earmarked for cloak and dagger operations.[52]

Two days later, in a meeting with Andropov, Ustinov, Gromyko and Mikhail Suslov, the party's leading ideologue, Brezhnev was given a grim survey of the risks attending the Afghan situation. Washington had long been at work to create a 'new Great Ottoman Empire' comprising the Islamic Soviet republics, Andropov argued, and would readily exploit the fall of the Kabul regime to realize this goal. Then there was the viable possibility of the stationing of ballistic Pershing missiles in Afghanistan which, given the absence of a reliable air defence system in Moscow's southern republics, would pose a clear and present danger to many vital Soviet objects. To this must be added, among other risks, the likely formation of militant regimes in northern Afghanistan, the possible annexation of that region by Pakistan, and the use of Afghan uranium deposits for the benefit of the Pakistani and Iraqi nuclear weapons programmes.

By way of preempting these perceived threats it was decided to substitute Karmal for Amin in a KGB-orchestrated coup. Yet when ordered to prepare the necessary forces to secure the putsch, the chief of the general staff, Marshal Nikolai Ogarkov, demurred. This was a reckless move that would fail to stabilize the situation while turning the Muslim world against Moscow, he argued, 'and we will lose politically in the entire world'. Promptly summoned to Brezhnev's office, where the 'small Politburo' (Andropov, Gromyko and Ustinov) was in session, Ogarkov made an impassioned plea for resolving the crisis by political means, warning that Afghanistan's long history of armed resistance to foreign invaders was certain to generate the most inhospitable reception.[53]

His arguments proved unavailing. The die was cast. On 10 December secret military preparations began in earnest, notably the formation of a new army in the Turkestan military district, and two days later the Politburo unanimously approved the dispatch of Soviet troops to Afghanistan with a view to toppling Amin (Kosygin, who opposed the move, did not attend) and authorized Andropov, Ustinov and Gromyko to implement the decision.[54] Two weeks later, in the morning hours of 25 December, KGB commandos supported by an armoured column attacked the presidential palace and after heavy fighting killed Amin.

As large Soviet units were being flown into Afghanistan to secure the nascent putsch, Moscow announced Karmal's appointment as head of state. In a special communiqué circulated two days later to the Soviet wider leadership, the invasion was presented as a limited and temporary pre-emptive move to prevent 'armed attacks of hostile foreign forces (mainly from Pakistan) and the attacks of domestic counterrevolutionary forces'. 'The Soviet military contingent', it was promised, 'will be withdrawn from Afghanistan as soon as the situation there stabilizes and the reasons which occasioned this action disappear'.[55]

It would take nearly ten years, dozens of thousands of Soviet casualties, over a million Afghan fatalities, and untold mayhem and dislocation before this pledge would be fulfilled.

6. THE ONLY REMAINING SUPERPOWER?

While refusing to give Moscow the benefit of the doubt and acknowledge the Afghan invasion for what it was – a defensive bid to isolate its southern republics from the Islamist genie unleashed by the Iranian revolution – US policymakers were stunned by the fall of their foremost regional ally and his replacement with a ferociously anti-American Islamist government headed by the zealous Ayatollah Ruhollah Khomeini. The hostage crisis, in which more than 50 Americans were held by Islamist militants with the connivance of the Tehran mullahs for 444 days until the end of the Carter presidency, underscored America's growing impotence and finished the president's dwindling chances of re-election.[1]

Ronald Reagan exploited this sense of malaise during the 1980 election campaign and his administration presided over a hawkish foreign policy supporting anti-communist groups throughout the world, from the Mujahedin in Afghanistan to the Angolan UNITA to the Nicaraguan Contras. Yet while this tough image temporarily shored up America's tarnished image (as vividly illustrated by the prompt release of the hostages upon Reagan's inauguration, giving birth to a conspiracy theory of collusion with the Iranians to delay the move until after the election),[2] its influence over Middle Eastern developments remained as limited as it had been during the Carter years. For a full eight years Washington watched helplessly the horrendous bloodletting between Iran and Iraq in the vicinity of the world's largest oil deposits, with its sporadic and often contradictory interventions (e.g., providing intelligence information to Iraq, secretly selling arms to Iran in return for the release of US hostages in Lebanon, reflagging of Kuwaiti tankers) having little impact on the course of the conflict.[3]

The deployment of a US peacekeeping force in Lebanon in the wake of Israel's June 1982 invasion proved similarly futile. With 241 marines (and

58 French troops) killed in a suicide bombing of their Beirut barracks on 23 October 1983 – the first such attack in a Middle Eastern conflict – the administration swiftly withdrew the force in early 1984 despite Reagan's solemn pledge to keep it in place. This led to an intense debate within the administration over the prerequisites for a successful military intervention, with Secretary of Defense Caspar Weinberger making a strong case for non-intervention in conflicts where success was not assured and certainly not without the backing of the American people – a rather unlikely eventuality given the lingering Vietnam legacy on the one hand, and the growing woes of the Western economies on the other.

If there was one seeming ray of light in the Reagan administration's Middle Eastern policy it was the covert military support for the Islamist resistance in Afghanistan that helped make Moscow's presence in the country untenable (though this would prove a Pyrrhic victory that would come to bite America at home and throughout the world a decade later). This process came to fruition under Mikhail Gorbachev, who considered disengagement from the Afghan misadventure a small price to pay for improving Soviet-Western relations, deemed essential for his ambitious domestic reforms, and who keenly recognized the growing unpopularity of the costly and seemingly unwinnable conflict with the Soviet public. In 1988 a withdrawal agreement was reached, and by mid-February 1989 the last Soviet troop had left Afghanistan.

By now Reagan had been succeeded by his deputy, George H. W. Bush, and Western attention had been fixated on Eastern Europe, where Gorbachev's reformed foreign policy had set in train a string of peaceful popular revolutions that overthrew the ruling Communist regimes (the only exception to this peaceful pattern being Romania, whose long-reigning dictator Nicolae Ceausescu was summarily tried and executed together with his wife Elena). As the Berlin Wall was literally torn down by hundreds of thousands of ecstatic demonstrators on 9 November 1989, Gorbachev consented to the unification of Germany within NATO in return for promises to cut the German armed forces and substantial economic assistance. In March 1990 the Soviet-controlled East Germany held the first free elections in its history and seven months later, on 3 October, the two Germanys were united.

The significance of this change cannot be overstated. In one fell swoop Gorbachev dispensed with Russia's geopolitical concept of keeping its enemies at arm's length through the preservation of a buffer zone along its entire defence perimeter; and not just another enemy, but the most powerful and dangerous of them all, which less than half a century earlier had almost knocked the Soviet Union out of existence. Small wonder therefore that these developments were widely seen in the West not only as a victory in the Cold War but as a triumph of Western ideals and way of life. A brave new world led by the 'only remaining superpower' (as the United States came to be known) and its fellow Western democracies seemed to be around the corner, and no minor Third World squabble would be allowed to spoil this moment of celebration. In the euphoric words of American academic Francis Fukuyama: 'What we may be witnessing is not just the end of the Cold War, or the passing of a particular period of post-war history, but the end of history as such: that is, the end point of mankind's ideological evolution and the universalization of Western liberal democracy as the final form of human government'.[4]

The Road to Kuwait

One person who did not share this self-congratulatory mood was Iraq's absolute ruler Saddam Hussein. In September 1980 he had taken his country to war against Iran in an attempt to deflect the lethal threat posed to his personal rule by Khomeini. When that war led to a severe economic crisis, which in his perception was bound to bring about his downfall, on 2 August 1990 he sent his troops into the oil-rich emirate of Kuwait, hoping to seize its mammoth wealth for Iraq and throwing the embryonic 'new world order' into its first major test.

Not that this should have come as a complete surprise. Though Saddam invested huge efforts to depict the end of hostilities as a shining victory, it quickly transpired that Iraq had emerged from the war a crippled nation. From a prosperous country with some $35 billion in foreign reserves in 1980 it had been reduced to dire economic straits with $80 billion in foreign debt and a need for $10 billion per annum to balance its current deficit before it could even think of reconstructing its shattered infrastructure, estimated at a whopping $230 billion.

At a pan-Arab summit meeting in Amman in February 1990, Saddam asked King Hussein of Jordan and President Hosni Mubarak of Egypt to inform the Gulf states that Iraq was not only adamant on a complete moratorium on its wartime loans but urgently needed an immediate infusion of an additional $30 billion. 'Let the Gulf regimes know', he added, 'that if they did not give this money to me, I would know how to get it,' accompanying this threat with Iraqi military manoeuvres in the neutral zone on the Kuwaiti border.[5] The message was immediately passed to Riyadh by the Jordanian monarch.

The same month, during a working visit to Kuwait, the Iraqi oil minister pressured his hosts to abide by the new oil quota set by OPEC earlier that year. Then he proceeded to Riyadh to deliver a personal message from Saddam to King Fahd demanding that the Saudis convince the rest of the Gulf states not to exceed their oil quotas. This had scant influence on Kuwait and the United Arab Emirates (UAE). Instead of reducing their oil quotas to make room for increased Iraqi production they continued to exceed their quotas by far, putting a downward pressure on the world oil market. Since Saddam was intent on pushing oil prices up without relinquishing his own plans for increased production, an immediate change in Kuwaiti and UAE policy became a matter of great urgency.[6]

Saddam himself drove the point home forcibly during discussions at the Arab summit meeting in Baghdad in May 1990. In an extraordinary closed session with the visiting heads of states, he tabled his grievances against the Gulf oil states and derided the continued violation of oil quotas by some of them as a declaration of war on Iraq: 'War is fought with soldiers and much harm is done by explosions, killing, and coup attempts – but it is also done by economic means. Therefore, we would ask our brothers who do not mean to wage war on Iraq: this is in fact a kind of war against Iraq'. 'Were it possible', he concluded, 'we would have endured. But I believe that all our brothers are fully aware of our situation … we have reached a point where we can no longer withstand pressure'.[7]

This threat failed to have the intended effect. Rebuffing several tough warnings by Baghdad, the Emir of Kuwait would neither reduce oil production nor forgive his wartime loans to Iraq nor extend Baghdad additional grants. It was only on 10 July, during a co-ordination meeting of the Gulf oil ministers in Jeddah, that Kuwait and the UAE succumbed to combined Saudi, Iranian and Iraqi pressure and agreed to abide by their oil quotas.[8] By this time, however, Saddam had come to expect far more from Kuwait. He was now determined to extract substantial grants plus a complete moratorium on war loans on top of adherence to OPEC quotas. The Kuwaiti indifference to his desperate needs amounted to 'stabbing Iraq in the back with a poisoned dagger'.[9] He had gone out of his way to plead the Iraqi case and further begging would only cause him (and, by extension, Iraq) an unendurable public humiliation.

He began to put his strategy in place. On 15 July, the buildup of armed forces began and within four days some 35,000 men from three divisions had been deployed along the Kuwaiti border. In a memorandum submitted to the Arab League's Secretary-General on 16 July, Iraqi Foreign Minister Tariq Aziz accused Kuwait not only of triggering a drop in oil prices that cost Iraq some $89 billion between 1981 and 1990, but also of stealing $2.4 billion worth of Iraqi oil by 'setting up oil installations in the southern section of the Iraqi Rumaila oil field and extracting oil from it'. In order to rectify this and to help Iraq recover from the dire economic plight it now faced due to its defence of 'the [Arab] nation's soil, dignity, honour and wealth', Aziz tabled several demands: the raising of oil prices to over $25 a barrel; the cessation of Kuwaiti 'theft' of Iraqi oil and the return of the 'stolen' $2.4 billion; a complete moratorium on Iraq's wartime loans; and the formation of 'an Arab plan similar to the Marshall Plan to compensate Iraq for some of the losses during the war'.[10]

The next day Saddam escalated further. In an address to the nation on the twenty-second anniversary of the 'Baath Revolution' he accused Kuwait and the UAE yet again of conspiring with 'world imperialism and Zionism' to 'cut off the livelihood of the Arab nation', threatening that Iraq would not be able to put up with such behaviour for much longer, since 'one would be better off dead than having one's livelihood cut off'. The two states had therefore to come 'back to their senses', he said, preferably through peaceful means. However, he cautioned, 'if words fail to afford us protection, then we will have no choice but to resort to effective action to put things right and ensure the restitution of our rights'.[11]

While the substance of the demands was not new, by stating in public what had hitherto been said behind closed doors and by backing his demands with military moves, Saddam had changed the whole character of his dispute. He had committed himself to certain objectives in such a way that any compromise on his part would have been seen as a capitulation. There was no room left for bargaining or procrastination. Kuwait had to accept his demands in full or face the grave consequences. As Kuwait rebuffed the accusations as being 'out of line with the spirit of the existing fraternal relations between Kuwait and Iraq, and [in] conflict with the most fundamental bases on which we all wish to govern our Arab relations',[12] Saddam accelerated the military buildup and on 2 August invaded the small principality.

Failing to Prevent the Invasion

American spy satellites picked up the movement of Iraqi troops to the Kuwaiti border almost immediately, but it was believed to be geared towards intimidation rather than imminent action. When Saddam made his first public threat to Kuwait on 17 July, the administration issued a public statement that it would defend its interests and friends in the region. The same message was passed to the Iraqi ambassador in Washington while the US ambassador to Baghdad, April Glaspie, informed Undersecretary of State for Foreign Affairs Nizar Hamdoon of the administration's expectation 'that disputes be settled peacefully and not by threats and intimidation'. A week later, after an internal CIA memo estimated that 'Iraq now has ample forces and supplies available for military operations inside Kuwait', State Department spokesperson Margaret Tutwiler warned that, 'Iraq and others know there is no place for coercion and intimidation in a civilized world'. She acknowledged the lack of any defence treaties and/or special defence or security commitments to Kuwait, but when pressed reaffirmed Washington's commitment to 'the individual and collective-defense of our friends in the Gulf'.

Perplexed by these somewhat mixed signals, Saddam decided to secure his 'American flank'. No sooner had Glaspie delivered Tutwiler's statement to the Iraqi foreign ministry on 25 July than she was suddenly summoned back to the ministry to meet Saddam in what was to become one of the most crucial, and controversial, milestones on Iraq's road to Kuwait.[13]

Without further ado, the Iraqi dictator treated his guest to a lengthy exposition of Iraq's economic plight and his grievances against the Gulf monarchies. Washington was supporting 'Kuwait's economic war against Iraq' at a time when it should be grateful to Baghdad for having contained Islamist Iran. Saddam then went on to threaten America with terrorist retaliation should it sustain its hostile policy against Iraq. 'You can come to Iraq with aircraft and missiles', he said, 'but do not push us to the point where we will cease to take. If you use pressure, we will deploy pressure and force. We cannot come all the way to you in the United States but individual Arabs may reach you'. To underscore his point, he observed that the Americans lacked Iraq's readiness to lose 10,000 men in a day's combat.

Ignoring Saddam's bluster, Glaspie went out of her way to assure him of Washington's goodwill. 'President Bush is an intelligent man. He is not going to declare an economic war against Iraq', she argued. On the contrary, 'I have direct instruction from the President to seek better relations with Iraq'. Not only had the administration blocked successive attempts by the Congress to impose economic sanctions on Iraq, but it fully understood Saddam's desperate need for funds; indeed, many Americans also had a stake in higher oil prices. When Saddam stated his determination to ensure that Kuwait did not cheat on its oil quota, Glaspie empathetically conceded that 'my own estimate after 25 years of serving in the area is that your aims should receive strong support from your brother Arabs'. This was an issue for the Arabs to solve among themselves, and the United States had 'no opinion on inter-Arab disputes such as your border dispute with Kuwait ... and Secretary of State Baker had directed our official spokesman to reiterate this stand'.[14] Also repeating official statements, she told Saddam that the United States 'could never excuse settlement of disputes by any but peaceful means'.[15] This message could not be backed up by any threat of American action. She had no authority to make one. If she had judged it necessary she would have had to go back to Washington for new instructions.

According to Glaspie, after Saddam's diatribe on Iraqi rights he left to take a 30-minute call from Mubarak. He returned in a more relaxed mood and told her that there was no problem because Iraq and Kuwait would meet in Jeddah the next week. He gave an 'unconditional pledge' not to use force against Kuwait, a pledge later repeated, in Glaspie's claim, by two top officials on 28 and 29 July. He appeared uninterested in her refutation of his original points and quickly closed the meeting. When Glaspie asked Saddam 'in the spirit of friendship, not of confrontation' his intentions regarding Kuwait, he reassured her of his preference for a peaceful solution to the dispute: 'We are not going to do anything until we meet with [the Kuwaitis]. When we meet and when we see that there is hope, then nothing will happen'. However, he stressed, since Kuwait's 'economic war' was depriving 'Iraqi children of the milk they drink', Baghdad could not be expected to sit idle for much longer: 'If we are unable to find a solution, then it will be natural that Iraq will not accept death, even though wisdom is above everything else'.[16]

The natural interpretation for Saddam to put on the meeting, especially in the light of his opening harangue, was that Washington was sympathetic to Iraq's plight and its pressure campaign against Kuwait. Glaspie, by contrast, was so relieved by what she believed to have heard that she told Saddam that she would revive her holiday plans – which she had shelved when the crisis had been escalating – and would return to Washington the following Monday (30 July). She reported back to Washington that 'his emphasis that he wants a peaceful settlement is surely sincere', and this relaxed assessment fitted in with the equally optimistic reports coming from the Egyptians and the Saudis. Her advice: 'Ease off on public criticism of Iraq until we see how the negotiations develop'.[17]

The view in Washington on 26 July was thus that the crisis had abated. So it was in London, which, taking its cue from its Arab allies, regarded the crisis as a tough negotiation tactic. When Mubarak sent word that there was no danger there was a general sigh of relief and return to other business. One piece of information suggested that Saddam had sent all these forces to the border area because he wanted them away from Baghdad or in the south because of internal troubles at either location. To the self-deluding British decision-makers this seemed perfectly plausible.[18]

These rosy assessments were hardly supported by developments on the ground. Intelligence reports continued to describe a rapidly expanding military buildup. By 27 July eight divisions of some 100,000 men from the best Iraqi units were poised on the joint border. Senior officials in Washington still judged this to be more consistent with intimidation than with preparations for an actual invasion, which would have required far heavier communications traffic and a more substantial artillery stock, munitions and logistics 'tail'.[19] A message was thus sent from Bush to Saddam, promising him US friendship and asking for an Iraqi quid pro quo. The administration also toned down its own remarks and heeded Arab advice to remain detached from a problem that the Arabs now intended to solve among themselves.[20]

As news filtered out that Iraq had relaxed neither its demands nor its military pressure, a handy explanation was quickly found. On 27 July, in Geneva, a meeting of OPEC ministers was beginning. There the Iraqi oil minister set out to raise the current price from $18 a barrel to $25. This went against both prevailing market conditions, in which there was still a glut, and the Saudi determination to keep the price at a 'reasonable' level which would not trigger Western inflation. Working closely now with their former Iranian adversaries, the Iraqis allowed themselves to be pulled down to a lower price only reluctantly – first to $23 and finally to $21. In return they achieved what was assumed to be a critical agreement on overall OPEC production quotas of 22.5 million barrels a day, and promises of firm enforcement.

When this agreement was achieved on 28 July it was widely assumed that the Iraqis had been rather clever in imposing some discipline on the cartel's affairs and had obtained a better OPEC agreement than they could have otherwise expected. Yet it soon transpired that Saddam had stepped up the military pressure on Kuwait by moving forward his artillery, logistics support and aircraft. This apparently indicated that he had already made up his mind to invade come what may. His readiness to continue a dialogue with Kuwait was largely a smokescreen aimed at gaining international legitimization for the impending military action. Indeed, in conversation with Arab League Secretary-General Chedli Klibi, Tariq Aziz unequivocally stated that the Kuwaiti royal family must go.

Unfortunately, this was treated in Washington with the disbelief that commonly accompanies a warning that another government is about to break a basic international rule. The prevailing view was that the Iraqi objective was still intimidation, and that if military action were taken it would probably be confined to seizing part of the disputed Rumaila oilfield or possibly the strategically located Warba and Bubiyan islands, which Iraq had long coveted. It was assumed that Saddam would pull back from Kuwait once the islands were secured. A compelling strategic case was constructed to show why Iraq badly needed the islands.

The only problem with this analysis was that this objective had never figured prominently in Saddam's public or private utterances, in which the immediate Iraqi demand was focused on cash. Nevertheless, this notion of a limited strike was critical to American policy. Had it been appreciated that the logic of Iraqi military action was to take all of Kuwait, that might have required a firm American response; the thought that it was geared only to wounding produced more reticence. Yet even if Washington had wished to take stronger action, without local support it could not send ground troops to the area and, anyway, they would take weeks to arrive.

All the ambiguities and constraints in American policy towards the Middle East and towards Iraq itself were now surfacing. The administration could not ignore the Iraqi pressure on Kuwait, yet it did not want to jettison its policy of placating Baghdad pursued since the mid-1980s. And it still wanted to get Saddam's help in opposing terrorism and promoting a moderate view on the Arab-Israeli conflict. The Iraqi leader's unpredictability and ruthlessness were recognized, yet there was hope that he would be rational in his basic calculations.

Until Iraqi forces crossed the Kuwaiti border in strength on 2 August, the administration remained hopeful that the crisis would be peacefully resolved. When on 27 July the Senate voted 80 to 16 to impose economic sanctions on Baghdad, the administration still objected. Asked on 31 July by Congressman Lee Hamilton about the administration's response to an Iraqi invasion of Kuwait, Assistant Secretary of State for South Asian and Near Eastern Affairs John Kelly refused 'to venture into the realms of hypothesis'.[21] The following day, after a phone conversation between

President Bush and King Fahd, Washington issued a statement hoping that the next meeting between Iraq and Kuwait would be more successful. Less than twenty-four hours later, Kuwait was no more.

Could the United States, and the West in general, have prevented the invasion? Probably not. The intensity of Saddam's anxiety over the future of his personal rule and his conviction that the incorporation of Kuwait's mammoth wealth into the Iraqi coffers provided the best guarantee for his political survival meant that only an unequivocal recognition that an invasion would lead to his certain undoing could have averted such a move. Since the Americans and the Europeans failed to grasp the intensity of Saddam's predicament in the first place, the need for such drastic measures did not even cross their minds, not least in view of their long-standing courtship of the Iraqi dictator which continued up to the invasion.

Yet even if they had interpreted the situation correctly, they would have still been highly dependent on their key regional allies given their inadequate military presence in the Gulf. To deploy a lightly equipped force of 40,000 men in the region, the minimum required to make some military sense, would take a few weeks; to fully implement the operational plan for this kind of contingency (Plan 1002-90) would involve sending 200,000 personnel to Saudi Arabia over a period of months and required the active co-operation of the desert kingdom. Even then, and notwithstanding the unquestioned US air superiority, this would be a defensive force, lacking a real offensive option.[22]

The administration therefore had little choice but to take its cue from those most directly involved with Arab efforts at mediation, who also failed to identify the real nature of the problem at hand. The result was an incoherent and ineffectual policy combining mild warnings to Baghdad with attempts to sustain good relations with a regime that, in the most favourable interpretation, was engaged in extortion and in opposition to a number of central US foreign policy goals. Together with the overt emphasis on the lack of any defence commitment to Kuwait, the unfortunate message this conveyed was one of American indifference and infirmity which, in turn, led Saddam to believe that he could invade Kuwait with impunity.

Failing to Induce a Peaceful Iraqi Withdrawal

Just as America's position as the 'only remaining superpower' did not deter Saddam from invading Kuwait, so it failed to induce him to withdraw peacefully from the emirate. Given the depth of Saddam's economic plight and the commitment he had made by the invasion, Iraq's peaceful withdrawal was never a viable option. It was infinitely more difficult for him to withdraw than it would have been for him not to invade. An unconditional withdrawal, or even withdrawal with a face-saving formula that did not involve the retention of the invasion's financial and economic gains, was totally unacceptable because not only would it have failed to redress the difficult economic problems which drove Saddam into Kuwait, and which were then made worse by the international sanctions against Iraq, but it would have also constituted an enormous loss of face that Saddam felt unable to afford. Only the credible threat that the retention of Kuwait would lead to his certain demise could have driven Saddam out of the emirate without war; but this was a message that the United States, as leader of a variegated international coalition, could not convey.

Nor did the various carrots offered to Saddam, some of them by the US administration itself, do the trick.[23] Four basic types of concessions were on offer: a possible change of regime in Kuwait; serious negotiations with the Kuwaitis on economic and territorial questions; progress on other regional issues, such as the Arab-Israeli conflict; and a promise that Iraq would not be attacked and that American forces would leave the region following the evacuation of Kuwait. As early as 4 September, Soviet Foreign Minister Eduard Shevardnadze argued that Israel's agreement to participate in an international peace conference could have a 'positive influence' on the crisis in the Gulf, and the idea was reiterated three weeks later by French President François Mitterrand, who went so far as to implicitly recognize the legitimacy of some of Iraq's territorial claims.[24]

Though Saddam remained totally impervious to these proposals (in his negotiations with the Kuwaitis before the invasion he made no mention of Palestine, and opted to 'Zionize' the crisis only upon realizing the firm international response to his predatory move), in the following months France would offer the Iraqi leader several ladders for a climb-down; the last such attempt was made on 15 January 1991, a few hours before the expiry of the UN ultimatum to Iraq to leave Kuwait, only to be contemptuously rebuffed by Saddam. A request by Jacques Poos, Luxembourg's foreign minister and the European Community (EC)'s rotating president, to come to Baghdad in January 1991 on behalf of the EC was similarly dismissed out of hand, as was his suggestion of meeting Foreign Minister Aziz in Algeria. An attempt by the EC's special envoy, Yugoslav diplomat Budimir Loncar, who visited Baghdad in January, to have Saddam clarify what concessions he expected from the anti-Iraqi coalition was similarly fruitless.[25]

The UN Secretary-General, Javier Pérez de Cuéllar, found no greater Iraqi flexibility, either in his meetings with Aziz in August 1990 or in a subsequent meeting with Saddam. Having arrived in Baghdad on the night of 11 January 1991, he had to wait nearly two days for his session with the Iraqi dictator. Meanwhile he was required to endure prolonged meetings with Aziz and PLO Chairman Yasser Arafat, who had eagerly joined the Iraqi bandwagon. When allowed at long last to see Saddam, there were the familiar tales of 'American-Zionist plots' and proposals for Arab solutions, but no hint of an Iraqi withdrawal from Kuwait. Leaving Baghdad in the early hours of 14 January, the despondent Secretary-General readily conceded defeat. 'You need two for tango', he said. 'I wanted to dance but I did not find any nice lady for dancing with. Saddam did not express any desire to withdraw'.[26]

Even the Americans were showing signs of flexibility. In September 1990 Undersecretary of State Robert Kimmitt hinted that Washington would not be averse to Kuwait being forced to negotiate away its differences with Baghdad once Iraq had withdrawn. Later that month, in his address to the General Assembly, President Bush stated that an Iraqi withdrawal would pave the way, among other things, for 'all the states and peoples of the region to settle the conflict that divides Arabs from Israel'. Moreover, in an about-turn in Washington's long-standing opposition to an international conference on the Middle East, on 5 December UN Ambassador Thomas Pickering indicated his government's readiness to consider such a conference, should Iraq withdraw from Kuwait.[27]

That Saddam refused these offers of concessions, and many others of the same kind, was a clear indication of both his lack of interest in a withdrawal and the weakness of the anti-Iraq international coalition. Saddam wanted a political solution all right, but only one that would allow him to retain the full financial and economic fruits of his aggression. Had the international coalition acquiesced in Iraq's complete satellization of Kuwait, Saddam might well have withdrawn, although this process would inevitably have taken an exceedingly prolonged period of time. Since this was a non-starter even for the most appeasing members of the coalition, an Iraqi withdrawal was not on the cards; the gap between the two sides was simply too wide to bridge.

A worldwide coalition thus failed to coerce a local dictator into reneging on his aggression and was forced to resort to arms to this end; and although the war ended in a resounding Iraqi defeat, its very occurrence underscored the limits of great-power influence over Middle Eastern affairs.

So was the failure to carry the war through to its logical conclusion and topple Saddam. For while the nascent 'New World Order' enabled the assembly of an extraordinarily diverse war coalition, its functioning depended on attaining the minimum working consensus among its members; and since most Arab states – especially Saudi Arabia, whose consent to deploy foreign troops on its territory was a sine qua non for the military option – were averse to a Western-orchestrated removal of a Sunni Arab government and its replacement by a Shiite regime, likely to come under Tehran's militant sway, the coalition limited its overriding goal to Iraq's unconditional withdrawal from Kuwait with a regime change in Baghdad never featuring on its agenda.

A Self-Inflicted Downfall

Though deeply shocked and humiliated by the magnitude of the Kuwait defeat (according to Saddam's long-time mistress he wept when his troops were being driven out of the emirate),[28] the Iraqi tyrant never conceded defeat to his subjects. Victory should not be judged by the number of casualties and material losses inflicted on the enemy, he told them, but rather by the ability to withstand the onslaught of an overwhelmingly superior force. In a way he was right. Not only had he survived yet again in the face of tremendous odds to outlive politically his main Western rivals – Margaret Thatcher, George Bush and François Mitterrand – but his continued hold on power helped cement Bush's 1992 electoral defeat. Instead of gliding to reelection on the crest of his war victory, the president's election campaign was dogged by allegations regarding the administration's courting of Saddam prior to August 1990, notably the 'green light' for invasion, and criticism of its failure to end the 'Saddam problem' once and for all.

Saddam's escape, however, was achieved by the narrowest of margins. As the formidable wall of fear with which he had so laboriously surrounded his subjects crumbled under the magnitude of defeat, Iraqis took matters into their own hands and rose in strength against their unelected ruler. Fortunately for Saddam, despite President Bush's appeal to the Iraqi people and military to topple their long-reigning tyrant, the international coalition did little to support the Shiite and Kurdish uprisings as they were being crushed by the Iraqi regime.[29] The most it was prepared to do when the regime's repressive campaign generated a humanitarian disaster was to offer the Kurds (and to a lesser extent the Shiites) some protection – via 'safe havens' shielded from Iraqi attacks in northern and southern Iraq.

In subsequent years Saddam survived a number of attempted coups, and although UN sanctions hurt Iraq and prevented its resurgence as a major military threat in the Gulf, they nevertheless failed to compel him to comply with a string of special resolutions obliging Baghdad to destroy, unconditionally and under international supervision, all its nuclear, chemical and biological stockpiles and research facilities. During the 1990s, the Iraqi dictator repeatedly challenged the Security Council over the implementation of these resolutions, never giving an inch strategically but always leaving enough wiggle room for last-minute tactical concessions when confronted with the threat of force.

As Saddam regained his regional preeminence, reintegrating Iraq into the fold of Arab politics and reducing the economic noose around Baghdad to virtual insignificance, his defiance of the international community became more pronounced. In the summer of 1995, following fresh revelations that Baghdad possessed a far more extensive biological weapons programme than had been hitherto known, the Iraqi government informed Rolf Ekéus, head of the UN Special Commission (UNSCOM) established in 1991 to oversee the dismantling of Iraq's weapons of mass destruction (WMD), that it had destroyed this lethal arsenal, only to have its claim rebuffed by the normally trusting Swede.[30] Three years later the Iraqis took a major step towards the brink by announcing the cessation of cooperation with UNSCOM, which they accused of acting as proxy American spies, and ordering the departure of its inspectors from Iraq. A four-day Anglo-American air campaign against Iraq's nonconventional arsenal on 16–19 December 1998 (code-named Operation Desert Fox) failed to redress the situation, with inspectors of both the International Atomic Energy Agency (IAEA) and the Verification and Inspection Commission (UNMOVIC), UNSCOM's successor organization, denied entry to Iraq.

Things came to a head after the terror attacks of 11 September 2001 on the United States. Though the administration refrained from linking Saddam directly to the atrocity, it nevertheless made the Iraqi leader, who applauded the attacks as a heroic payback for the prolonged suffering wrought by America on the entire world,[31] a central target of its 'war on terror'. In November 2002 the United Nations passed Resolution 1441, which charged Iraq with violating earlier Security Council resolutions regarding nonconventional disarmament; demanded that it provide within 30 days 'a currently accurate, full, and complete declaration' of all aspects of its WMD programmes as well as give the IAEA and UNMOVIC 'immediate, unimpeded, unconditional, and unrestricted access' to its nonconventional sites with a view to their destruction; and warned that the regime 'will face serious consequences as a result of its continued violation of its obligations'.[32] As Saddam remained defiant, grudgingly allowing the inspectors in but failing to offer them the required co-operation, in March–April 2003 a lightning attack by a US-led international coalition, codenamed Operation Iraqi Freedom (OIF), crushed the Iraqi army and toppled the Baath regime. 'We wrote 1441 not in order to go to war', Secretary of State Colin Powell told the Security Council on 3 February. 'We wrote 1441 to give Iraq one last chance. Iraq is not so far taking that one last chance.'[33]

While the swiftness and conclusiveness of the invasion afforded a striking illustration of America's military prowess, there is little doubt that Saddam's downfall was completely of his own making. Had he collaborated in good faith with the UN inspection regime and avoided taunting the American people at one of its darkest moments, no invasion would have ensued. His failure to do so and readiness to risk a total war seems all the more inexplicable given, on the one hand, his all-consuming paranoia and utter conviction that the Americans, among others, were out to get him, and on the other, the failure of the victorious powers to trace any operative nonconventional weapons programmes. If Baghdad did not actually possess this deadly arsenal, why did Saddam embark on the dangerous game of brinkmanship that led to his undoing rather than let the inspectors into Iraq and allow the whole world to see that he had nothing to hide?

One possible explanation is that Hussein maintained the façade of a non-conventionally armed Iraq, despite his awareness of its falsehood, in order to project an image of strength and invincibility, especially vis-à-vis the Islamist regime in Tehran that had been baying for his head since its inception in 1979. Another explanation could be his meagre understanding of the geostrategic circumstances in which he operated and his ignorance of how Western policymakers, especially in Washington, make decisions and stick to them. He saw things mainly in terms of the crude conclusions about human nature that he derived from his upbringing and life experience.

In the final account, however, Saddam became a victim of his own success. Having fully subordinated the Baath party to his will, sterilized its governing institutions and reduced the national decision-making apparatus to one man surrounded by a docile flock of close associates, he had no one around him who had the courage to tell him the truth about Iraq's military and strategic position, because the consequences of such truthfulness could be fatal. As Saddam told a personal guest of his shortly after assuming the presidency in the summer of 1979: 'I know there are scores of people plotting to kill me ... but I am far cleverer than they are. I know they are conspiring to kill me long before they actually start planning to do it. This enables me to get them before they have the faintest chance of striking at me'.[34]

It is highly likely, therefore, that Saddam's brinkmanship was rooted in the determination to preserve whatever was left of Baghdad's nonconventional weapons programme, which he had falsely believed to be far more advanced than it actually was. And thus it was that the same brutish worldview that had kept him in power for longer than any other ruler in Iraq's modern history also led to his undoing – at a time when he could have easily averted this fate. Yet as the Americans were to learn before long, they had opened a Pandora's box that they found impossible to close.

Democratic Delusions

In his 1 May 2003 speech aboard the USS *Abraham Lincoln* announcing the end of 'major combat operations in Iraq', President George W. Bush acknowledged that 'the transition from dictatorship to democracy will take time' but expressed his belief that 'it is worth every effort'. 'Decades of lies and intimidation could not make the Iraqi people love their oppressors or desire their own enslavement', he argued emphatically.

> Men and women in every culture need liberty like they need food and water and air. Everywhere that freedom arrives, humanity rejoices; and everywhere that freedom stirs, let tyrants fear ... We're helping to rebuild Iraq, where the dictator built palaces for himself, instead of hospitals and schools. And we will stand with the new leaders of Iraq as they establish a government of, by, and for the Iraqi people ... Our coalition will stay until our work is done. Then we will leave, and we will leave behind a free Iraq.[35]

This ambitious 'mission creep' – from the removal of the Saddam regime and the destruction of its nonconventional weapons arsenal to the substitution of democracy for the country's despotic rule – was far easier said than done. Torn by ethnic, social and religious schisms – with the dominant Arab population hopelessly polarized between Shiite and Sunni communities, each further split into rival clans, and with the Kurdish population of the north implacably opposed to Arab domination yet deeply fragmented along tribal lines – Iraq has been a ruler's ultimate nightmare. As early as the 1830s, Ibrahim Pasha, the debonair warlord who had brought the Ottoman Empire to its knees, advised his father, the legendary Egyptian governor Muhammad Ali, to shun control of Mesopotamia altogether: 'Upon my word, Baghdad ... is not worth the expenses involved in retaining it'. King Faisal, on whose behalf the modern state of Iraq was created in 1921, candidly opined that there was no such thing as an Iraqi people, only 'unimaginable masses of human beings, devoid of any patriotic idea, imbued with religious traditions and absurdities ... and prone to anarchy'.[36]

The speed and ferocity with which Iraqis turned on each other upon their deliverance from Saddam showed that little had changed in the intervening decades. As early as April 2003, while the US-led coalition was still mopping up the last remnants of Baath resistance, the prominent Shiite leader Abdel Majid Khoei, who had returned from exile in Britain following Saddam's overthrow, was murdered near the great mosque in the holy town of Najaf where Imam Ali ibn Abi Talib – the prophet Muhammad's cousin and son-in-law, fourth caliph after the prophet's death and Shiism's 'patron saint' – is buried. Four months later, on 29 August 2003, a car bomb was detonated outside the mosque, killing over a hundred people, including the influential Ayatollah Muhammad Baqir Hakim, leader of the Iranian-sponsored Supreme Council for the Islamic Revolution in Iraq (SCIRI). By early 2004 internecine strife was in full swing, led by the minority Sunni Arab community (about 20 per cent of the total population) that had ruled Iraq since its creation. For some insurgents, notably members of Saddam's regime and locality, the overriding motivation was loyalty to the fallen tyrant; to others it was anger over the loss of prestigious and lucrative jobs. There was also a deep sense of humiliation felt by those who had long considered themselves the only people capable of running the affairs of the Iraqi state. All feared and resented their possible domination by the despised Shiites and their perceived paymaster – Iran's militant Islamist regime – and all wished to regain lost power and influence.[37]

Had the coalition sought to incorporate the Sunnis into the post-Saddam political order and placed members of the former administration, the military and the security forces on its payroll, it might well have ameliorated their grievances. Instead it chose to predicate Iraq's future on the Shiites (and to a lesser extent the Kurds), as demonstrated by the prompt dissolution of the predominantly Sunni military and security forces and the uncompensated dismissal of their members. This transformed the Sunnis into a revisionist faction bent on subverting the US-led effort to democratize Iraq, driving many of the newly unemployed officers and soldiers into the insurgency.

These grievances were further exacerbated by tribal interests, values and norms. The 'Sunni Triangle' – the vast territory from Baghdad in the south to Tikrit in the north and to Ramadi in the west, comprising the four governorates of Baghdad, Anbar, Salah ad-Din and Ninawa – is a diverse mosaic of hundreds of small and medium-sized tribes and a dozen large tribal federations, notably the Dulyam and the Shammar Jarba, each comprising over a million members. Under Saddam many of these tribes had been incorporated into the regime's patronage system; with their material benefits and political prestige curtailed after the invasion, many tribesmen joined the insurrection.[38]

To make matters worse, the Triangle's location along the Syrian, Jordanian and Saudi borders made it the first port of call for jihadists and other foreign insurgents. The overall number of these infiltrators was insignificant compared to the many thousands of Iraqi insurgents, but they exerted a disproportionate impact on the course of the fighting by recruiting significant numbers of Iraqi jihadists, offering invaluable military and logistical expertise, mounting most of the mass-casualty suicide bombings, and providing much of the revolt's religious and ideological firepower.[39] Such was the tenacity of the insurrection, subsequently joined by a multitude of Shiite militias battling both their Sunni compatriots and the central government, that in September 2006 Lt Gen. Peter W. Chiarelli, commander of US and coalition forces in Iraq, questioned the ability to defeat it. 'It is our job to win', he said. 'But it is not the kind of fight that is going to be won by military kinetic action alone ... I think the real heart of [the matter] is that there are economic and political conditions that have to improve out at al-Anbar, as they do everywhere in Iraq, for us to be successful'.[40]

It was against this backdrop that in January 2007 President Bush announced the substantial increase of coalition forces in Iraq, or the 'surge' as it came to be known, which steadily slashed violence levels and civilian deaths throughout the country, decimated the al-Qaeda in Iraq (AQI) and killed its founding leader, the Jordanian-born terrorist Abu Musab

Zarqawi. Yet it is doubtful whether this could have been achieved without the support of the predominantly Sunni popular movement known as the Anbar Awakening that 'proved to be a hugely important factor in combating al-Qaeda terrorists and other Sunni insurgents' (in the words of Gen. David Petraeus, who led the surge in 2007–8).[41]

The origin of the movement dates back to the autumn of 2005, when Sunni insurgents began fighting AQI jihadists who had exploited their newly found pre-eminence to abuse the local population (so much so that Osama bin Laden and his deputy Ayman Zawahiri urged Zarqawi to mellow his murderous ways). It gained considerable momentum in the summer of 2006 when tribal leaders, disillusioned with the anarchy that had ravaged the province during the past two-and-a-half years, aligned themselves with the coalition forces. Within a year of its advent, the Awakening had dramatically changed the security situation in Anbar, with monthly attacks dropping from some 1,350 in October 2006 to just over 200 in August 2007. By now, the movement had been established on a national basis as the coalition sought to replicate its success in other parts of Iraq. It played a particularly prominent role in improving the security situation in Baghdad, helping to slash murders by 90 per cent and attacks on civilians by 80 per cent, as well as destroying numerous insurgent networks. Its contribution in other provinces was no less substantial, with al-Qaeda leaders admitting that their forces throughout Iraq had been decimated by over 70 per cent, from 12,000 to 3,500.[42]

To the coalition's dismay, its attempt to transform the Awakening from a highly efficient counterinsurgency tool into a vehicle for Sunni-Shiite reconciliation failed to win the backing of the Shiite-dominated central government. As early as the summer of 2003, while commanding the 101st Airborne Division in northern Iraq, Petraeus had been tasked with facilitating inter-communal reconciliation in the area under his control but the effort foundered against the bedrock of government opposition. Three years later, as the top US and coalition forces commander in Iraq, he found it no less difficult to overcome Prime Minister Nuri Maliki's reluctance to introduce the Awakening into Baghdad and predominantly Shiite areas, or even to persuade him that there was no alternative to the movement 'if we were to reduce the violence and divert key elements of the Sunni insurgency from their actual or tacit support for the actions of al Qaeda'. Notwithstanding this scepticism, by January 2009 Washington had invested more than $400 million in the Awakening programme, with over 100,000 fighters (including 20,000-plus Shiites) on the coalition's payroll.[43]

It was only in September 2008, two years after its onset, that the Awakening's massive contribution to Iraq's national security was officially acknowledged, when Maliki issued an executive order naming its members Sons of Iraq and stipulating their incorporation into the Iraqi state structures. Yet hardly had the ink dried on the document than it transpired that the government had no intention of abiding by its content, not least since the improving security situation in Iraq had diminished its grudging dependence on the movement, whose existence it had resented in the first place. Hence, flaunting its pledge to integrate 94,000 Sons of Iraq (from the 100,000-plus membership list provided by the Americans) into the Iraqi security forces (ISF) or other Iraqi ministries by the end of 2009, the government absorbed only 9,000 members into the ISF by July 2010 (with another 32,000 hired by non-security ministries) and 'has been repeatedly delinquent in providing their monthly salaries'.[44]

This proved a fatal mistake. Just as the peremptory dissolution of Saddam's army in May 2003 without the existence of an adequate substitute opened the door to insurgencies of all hues, so the disbanding of the social movement that had been instrumental in turning the terrorist tide of 2007–8 and the failure to incorporate its members into the security forces left a dangerous security vacuum, as starkly illustrated by the murder of some 370 people in a spate of terror attacks during the March 2010 national elections.

All Fall Down

By now George W. Bush had left the White House and his successor, while a sharp critic of the surge ('I am not persuaded that 20,000 additional troops in Iraq is going to solve the sectarian violence there', Barack Obama stated in January 2007. 'In fact, I think it will do the reverse'.[45]) swiftly capitalized on its success to promote his electoral promise to withdraw American troops from Iraq within 16 months. 'Thanks in great measure to your service, the situation in Iraq has improved', he told a military gathering a month after taking office, uttering not a word on the strategy that had brought this about. 'Violence has been reduced substantially from the horrific sectarian killing of 2006 and 2007. Al Qaeda in Iraq has been dealt a serious blow by our troops and Iraq's Security Forces, and through our partnership with Sunni Arabs. The capacity of Iraq's Security Forces has improved, and Iraq's leaders have taken steps toward political accommodation'.

Obama acknowledged that the country had yet to turn the corner and promised to provide the necessary help for creating 'an Iraq that is sovereign, stable, and self-reliant'. Yet he insisted that since 'America can no longer afford to see Iraq in isolation from other priorities', it would have to adopt a new and less ambitious exit strategy that would not let 'the pursuit of the perfect stand in the way of achievable goals'. 'We cannot rid Iraq of all who oppose America or sympathize with our adversaries', he reasoned.

> We cannot police Iraq's streets until they are completely safe, nor stay until Iraq's union is perfected. We cannot sustain indefinitely a commitment that has put a strain on our military, and will cost the American people nearly a trillion dollars. America's men and women in uniform have fought block by block, province by province, year after year, to give the Iraqis this chance to choose a better future. Now, we must ask the Iraqi people to seize it.

By way of enabling Iraqis to seize this 'better future' the US would end its combat mission and withdraw all fighting brigades from the country by 31 August 2010. The remaining forces would then concentrate on 'supporting the Iraqi government and its Security Forces as they take the absolute lead in securing their country', with a view to completing the transition process and bringing all US troops home by the end of 2011. 'You are a great nation, rooted in the cradle of civilization', Obama sought to convince Iraqis of the merits of this strategy.

> The United States pursues no claim on your territory or your resources. We respect your sovereignty and the tremendous sacrifices you have made for your country. We seek a full transition to Iraqi responsibility for the security of your country. And going forward, we can build a lasting relationship founded upon mutual interests and mutual respect as Iraq takes its rightful place in the community of nations.[46]

Though this strategy was not as original as the newly inaugurated president would have liked his audience to believe – he was actually walking down the road taken by his much maligned predecessor, who in November 2008 had negotiated a status of forces agreement (SOFA) setting the end of December 2011 as the deadline for the completion of US withdrawal – Obama's eagerness to implement his electoral promise come what may exposed his policy before too long for what it actually was:

a rushed extrication from an unpopular international undertaking in total disregard of its likely detrimental consequences.

Indeed, as the August 2010 deadline loomed over the horizon Iraq was in the throes of renewed anarchy, with parliament failing to form a government in the wake of the March elections, near-daily terror attacks exacting scores of fatalities, and dilapidated public services stirring widespread restiveness. 'Right now, if you ask any Iraqi: what do you think of democracy? They will say it's blood, stagnation, unemployment, refugees, cheating', lamented former (Shiite) Prime Minister Ayad Allawi, whose Sunni-backed, predominantly Shiite *Iraqiya* beat Maliki's ruling party by a slim margin to become Iraq's largest parliamentary bloc. 'If democracy does not succeed in Iraq and tyranny is replaced by another tyranny, there will be no legacy'.[47]

Ignoring this grim reality, Obama went out of his way to present the imminent drawdown as a shining success, holding several events to honour the returning soldiers and reminding Americans time and again of his determination to abide by his election promise. 'As a candidate for president, I pledged to bring the war in Iraq to a responsible end', he told a convention of the Disabled American Veterans. 'I made it clear that by 31 August 2010, American combat mission in Iraq would end. And that is exactly what we are doing – as promised and on schedule'.[48]

He reiterated the same theme a year later as the last troops were about to leave Iraq, describing the withdrawal as a 'powerful reminder' of the 'renewed American leadership in the world'.[49] 'Today, I've come to speak to you about the end of the war in Iraq', he told a large gathering at the Fort Bragg military camp on 14 December 2011, a day before the formal end of America's military presence in Iraq.

> As your Commander-in-Chief, I can tell you that it will indeed be a part of history. Those last American troops will move south on desert sands, and then they will cross the border out of Iraq with their heads held high. One of the most extraordinary chapters in the history of the American military will come to an end. Iraq's future will be in the hands of its people. America's war in Iraq will be over.

'Iraq is not a perfect place', he conceded.

> It has many challenges ahead. But we're leaving behind a sovereign, stable and self-reliant Iraq, with a representative government that was

elected by its people. We're building a new partnership between our nations. And we are ending a war not with a final battle, but with a final march toward home ... The war in Iraq will soon belong to history.[50]

A few years earlier President Bush had come under scathing criticism for prematurely announcing the end of 'major combat operations in Iraq'. Now that Obama had officially and unequivocally relegated the Iraq war to the annals of history, no similar storm ensued as much of the media was still enamoured with the first African American president; yet his wilful substitution of wishful thinking for the unpalatable facts on the ground set in train a process of fragmentation and mayhem that quickly brought Iraq to the verge of disintegration.

In fairness to Obama, the dissonance between rhetorical flair and actual performance that was to become his main foreign policy hallmark was also at work here. As he tirelessly glorified the imminent disengagement, he was quietly exploring the possibility of having 8,000–10,000 troops remain in Iraq (a figure deemed far too low by the Pentagon). In April 2011 four US officials, including outgoing Secretary of Defense Robert Gates and Chairman of the Joint Chiefs of Staff Admiral Mike Mullen, visited Baghdad in an attempt to persuade the Iraqis to allow US troops to stay after the December deadline – only to be flatly rebuffed. 'Most Iraqis wanted us gone', Gates wrote in his memoirs. 'It was a regrettable turn of events for our future influence in Iraq and our strategic position in the region. And a win for Iran'.[51]

This observation proved prescient. Contrary to Obama's end-of-the-war speech, the Maliki government was anything but a 'representative government that was elected by its people'. Rather it was a sectarian and oppressive regime that retained power through underhand methods in the face of an electoral defeat and used this power to restore the all-too-familiar pattern of one-man rule characterizing Iraqi politics from the early days of statehood; and since there was no more formidable obstacle to this goal than the continued US military presence in Iraq, the authoritarian prime minister was no less keen than his American counterpart to have it ended without delay.

Nor was Iraq the 'sovereign, stable and self-reliant' state as claimed by the US president. Quite the contrary: as Maliki intensified the drive to subjugate Iraq's political system and state institutions to his will, the roiling cauldron calmed by the surge erupted again. As early as April 2012 the country's deepening sectarian schisms were glaringly exposed when a US-sponsored survey revealed that 59 per cent of Shiites considered Iraq a 'real democracy' while 75 per cent of Sunnis believed it was not; that two-thirds of Shiites viewed Iraq as going in the right direction while similar numbers of Sunnis and Kurds thought it was headed in the wrong direction; and that two out of three Shiites viewed the prime minister favourably while Sunnis disapproved of his performance by more than two to one and Kurds by almost nine to one.[52]

This polarization came to a head on 23 July 2012, when over 100 people were murdered and another 250 injured in Iraq's worst day of violence since 2010. A similar number of people were killed on 9 September in retribution for the death sentencing of the exiled Sunni Vice President Tariq Hashemi (tried and convicted in absentia of operating death squads during the surge). Three months later a raid on the residence of Finance Minister Rafi Issawi over the same allegation sparked mass protest throughout Anbar. Seen as part of a devious government ploy to marginalize and repress the Sunni community and its leaders, the persecution of the highly respected minister of finance and the foremost remaining Sunni member of cabinet sent shockwaves across neighbouring provinces. By the time Issawi resigned his influential post in March 2013, having taken shelter in the compound of a former leader of the Anbar Awakening to avoid arrest, the Sunni Triangle was mired in protest with tens of thousands taking to the streets every Friday to voice their grievances. Meanwhile, the president of the Kurdistan Regional Government (KRG), Massoud Barzani, implemented a series of measures (e.g., passing a separate budget, separating the region from the national electricity grid, independently exporting oil through Turkey and establishing relations with foreign countries) that significantly enhanced Kurdistan's autonomy and edged it towards statehood.[53]

To make matters worse, a number of jihadist groups, notably the Islamic State of Iraq and Greater Syria (ISIS, sometimes translated as the Islamic State of Iraq and the Levant, or ISIL), capitalized on the swelling protest to style themselves as protectors of the oppressed Sunnis. Established in October 2006 by AQI as an umbrella network of several jihadist groups, the Islamic State in Iraq (ISI), as it was initially called, played an active role in the Sunni uprising before going into remission during the surge and rebounding in grand style after the completion of the US withdrawal. On 21 July 2012 its leader, Abu Bakr Baghdadi, proclaimed the 'Breaking Down the Walls' campaign aimed at undermining the Maliki government, freeing imprisoned terrorists and laying the groundwork for joint Iraqi-Syrian governance. By the time the campaign ended a year later with the release of 500 al-Qaeda terrorists in attacks on the Abu Ghraib and the Taji prisons, the organization had carried out two dozen bombing waves throughout Iraq and had broken into eight prisons, freeing scores of terrorists.[54]

When on 23 April 2013 Iraqi security forces killed some 50 Sunni protestors near the northern town of Kirkuk, Sunni militants retaliated with a string of car bombings and suicide attacks that killed dozens of people. With Shiite militias responding in kind, 963 civilians were killed and another 2,191 injured in May alone – the deadliest month since 2008. This grizzly record was quickly broken when more than a thousand people were murdered during the holy month of Ramadan (9 July–10 August). By the time 2013 ended, some 7,800 civilians had been murdered and another 18,000 were wounded, making it Iraq's bloodiest year since 2008.[55]

The escalating violence in Iraq was greatly compounded by the internecine strife in Syria. For one thing, Maliki's fear that a Sunni triumph in Syria would spill over into Iraq drove him to intensify the suppression of Sunni protest, which in turn exacerbated the deepening Iraqi malaise.[56] For another, the Syrian conflict enabled the resurgent Islamist groups to gain invaluable combat experience that would prove critical in their future confrontation with the Iraqi security forces.

Having sent a contingent of ISI fighters to Syria in 2011 under the banner of *Jabhat al-Nusra* ('Victory Front'), Baghdadi sought to capitalize on its military successes, notably the March 2013 conquest of the northeastern town of Raqqa, and on 8 April changed the organization's name to ISIS to reflect the extension of its ambitions to include Greater Syria (*ash-Sha'm*). To his dismay, his man in Syria – Nusra commander Abu Muhammad Jawlani – would not have his increasingly prominent group reabsorbed into its parent organization, instead swearing allegiance to al-Qaeda's new leader Ayman Zawahiri.

For nearly a year Zawahiri attempted to mediate an agreement between the two estranged groups, whose relations descended into heavy fighting that claimed thousands of jihadist lives, before announcing (on 3 February 2014) that ISIS 'is not a branch of the al-Qaeda group ... does not have an organizational relationship with it and [al-Qaeda] is not the group responsible for their actions'. As Baghdadi remained unimpressed, Zawahiri implored him to leave Syria and concentrate his efforts on Iraq. 'Heed my words for the sake of sparing the blood of Muslims, unifying their ranks and achieving their victory over their enemy, even if you consider it an injustice', he wrote. 'You must stand up to the enemies of Islam in Iraq where they need your efforts and this will end the sedition among Muslims and bring back the bond of brotherhood between them. Rely on God and take this decision and you will find in all your mujahedeen brothers and the supporters of jihad the support and sustenance you need'.[57]

He pleaded to no avail. As early as January 2014 ISIS had captured Anbar's capital of Ramadi (though parts of it were subsequently retaken by the government) and the key city of Fallujah, where US forces had fought two bitter battles a decade earlier, launching a major offensive in northern and western Iraq five months later alongside a sustained effort to reclaim lost Syrian territories. On 9 June the group conquered Mosul, Iraq's second largest city, with the Iraqi armed forces fleeing in fear, and two days later captured Tirkit, Saddam Hussein's hometown. By the end of the month ISIS had established control over much of the Sunni Triangle and the Syrian northeastern province of Deir Ezzour, proclaimed a caliphate headed by Baghdadi, 'commander of the faithful' (i.e., leader of Muslims everywhere), and changed its name to the Islamic State (IS) to reflect its claim to leadership of the worldwide Muslim community (*umma*). 'Rush O Muslims to your state', the self-styled caliph urged his would-be subjects. 'Those who can immigrate to the Islamic State should immigrate, as immigration to the house of Islam is a duty … If you hold to it you will conquer Rome [i.e., Christianity] and own the world, if Allah wills'.[58]

With thousands of Muslims from all over the world answering the call, and its coffers swelling with revenues from the oilfields under its control, IS escalated the fighting in Syria and Iraq, making substantial territorial gains in both countries and triggering mass flight of conquered populations. When in early August 2014 US fighters bombed IS targets in northern Iraq as part of newly authorized 'targeted airstrikes' to prevent 'genocide of minority groups', the organization responded by posting a YouTube video (on 19 August) showing the decapitation of a captured US journalist with his purported executioner, speaking in a plainly British accent, threatening further executions in the event of continued air attacks before slitting his hapless victim's throat.

IS made good its threat on 2 September, posting a decapitation video of yet another US journalist followed 11 days later by a video depicting the beheading of a British aid worker – apparently carried out by the same masked executioner. Yet while this ghastly PR exercise enticed further European Muslims into IS's ranks and drove the CIA to concede that the group 'mustered between 20,000 and 31,500 fighters across Iraq and Syria' (rather than the 10,000 as previously believed),[59] it failed to achieve its intended deterrent goal as the international revulsion sparked by the beheadings drove the grudging administration to declare that 'the US is at war with ISIL in the same way the US is at war with al-Qaeda'. 'We will degrade, and ultimately destroy, ISIL through a comprehensive and sustained counterterrorism strategy', Obama pledged in a special address to the nation on 10 September. 'But I want the American people to understand how this effort will be different from the wars in Iraq and Afghanistan. It will not involve American combat troops fighting on foreign soil. This counterterrorism campaign will be waged through a steady, relentless effort to take out ISIL wherever they exist, using our air power and our support for partner forces on the ground'.[60]

And so it was that three years after triumphantly announcing the end of the Iraq war, the president who had made disengagement from the conflict a key promise of his election campaign and the hallmark of his first term in office found himself sucked into the Iraqi quagmire towards the end of his second tenure. And while Obama has thus far managed to avoid putting American boots on the ground while somewhat degrading IS's military capabilities (killing scores of militants and some of its top leaders), the air campaign has neither dimmed IS's appeal to Western Muslims nor prevented it from making substantial gains in Iraq that may well force Washington to deepen its military intervention (e.g., in late October 2014 the US army had to use Apache helicopters to prevent IS from occupying Baghdad's international airport).[61]

7. THE LIMITS TO POWER

No regional dispute has attracted a longer and more sustained international intervention than the Arab-Israeli conflict, and few conflicts have been more impervious to outside influence than this century-long feud. As early as the 1920s and 1930s Arab violence frustrated the League of Nations' decision to establish a Jewish national home in Palestine and drove Britain, the foremost world empire of the day and the League's appointee to facilitate this goal, not only to abdicate this obligation but to become a foremost opponent of Jewish statehood. It did the same in November 1947 when the League's successor, the United Nations, voted to partition Palestine into two states – one Jewish the other Arab; rejecting this solution, the Arab nations resolved instead to destroy the state of Israel at birth and gain the whole for themselves. 'The invasion of Palestine by the Arab states was the first armed aggression which the world had seen since the end of the [Second World] War', Trygve Lie, the first UN Secretary-General, wrote in his memoirs. 'The United Nations could not permit that aggression to succeed and at the same time survive as an influential force for peaceful settlement, collective security, and meaningful international law'.[1] Neither did successive international peacemaking efforts – from the 1949 UN-sponsored Lausanne conference to the 1955 Anglo-American Alpha Project, to the Geneva and Madrid peace conferences of 1973 and 1991 – come anywhere near bridging the wide divide between Arabs and Jews.

The handful of breakthroughs (or seeming breakthroughs) towards mutual reconciliation was a result of direct negotiations between Israel and its Arab adversaries, with the great powers remaining conspicuously absent. Just as the seeds of the March 1979 Egyptian-Israeli peace treaty were planted in secret talks between Foreign Minister Moshe Dayan and

Deputy Prime Minister Hassan Tohami, so the September 1993 Israel–PLO Declaration of Principles (DOP) was reached in secret negotiations in the Norwegian capital of Oslo at a time when the formal and highly publicized US-sponsored peace process launched at the 1991 Madrid conference was virtually deadlocked. Not only did the US administration take no part in the Oslo talks; it was barely aware of their existence, just as seventeen years earlier it had been ignorant of the secret Israeli-Egyptian contacts.

Slide to War

The fact of the matter is that from the very beginning the Arabs' primary instrument for opposing Jewish national aspirations was violence, and no amount of foreign interference has been able to change this reality. Rather it was the relative success or failure of the use of that instrument in any given period that determined Arab politics and diplomacy. When violence backfired spectacularly in 1948, inter-Arab politics in the subsequent two decades were driven by an attempt to undo the consequences of that defeat (or *al-Nakba*, 'the catastrophe', as it is called in Arab parlance) and to bring about the Jewish state's demise. This culminated in June 1967 in yet another major Arab-Israeli war.

It is true that, as we have seen, the crisis preceding the 1967 war was sparked by false Soviet warnings (on 13 May) of an imminent Israeli attack on Syria. Yet it is no less true that from the very beginning the Soviets went out of their way to reassure the Americans that they 'would not wish [the] Arabs to force confrontation with Israel which could escalate into open hostilities',[2] and that upon realizing the full escalatory potential of the crisis sparked by these warnings they strove to induce their Arab allies to step back from the brink. As Prime Minister Kosygin told Egyptian Minister of War Shams Badran at the end of May, 'You have obtained a big political victory. Now we must work to calm the situation.'[3]

These calming words had little effect on Egyptian President Nasser. Viewing the initial Soviet warning as a golden opportunity to reassert his fledgling pan-Arab prestige, he placed his army on the highest state of alert and ordered two armoured divisions into the Sinai Peninsula, formally demilitarized since the 1956 Suez war. Having learned from his chief of staff, whom he sent to Damascus the same day to get a first-hand impression of the military situation, that there were no Israeli concentrations along the Syrian border,[4] Nasser quickly raised the ante and demanded the removal of the United Nations Emergency Force (UNEF), deployed on Egyptian (but not on Israeli) territory after the 1956 war as a buffer between the two states. As the UN observers were quickly withdrawn and replaced by Egyptian forces, the president escalated his activities still further and announced the closure of the Strait of Tiran at the southern mouth of the Gulf of Aqaba, a vital economic lifeline of the Jewish state, to Israeli and Israel-bound shipping. 'Now with our concentrations in Sinai, the chances of war are fifty-fifty', he told his cabinet on 21 May, during a discussion on the move's possible consequences. 'But if we close the Strait, war will be a one hundred percent certainty'.[5]

The die was cast. Having manoeuvred himself into the driver's seat of inter-Arab politics, with his erstwhile Arab rivals standing in line to rally behind his banner, Nasser could not climb down without risking a tremendous loss of face. In a widely publicized article in Egypt's foremost newspaper, *al-Ahram* (on 26 May), editor-in-chief and Nasser's mouthpiece Muhammad Hassanein Heikal explained why war was inevitable and dared Israel to attack Egypt. A week later, at a meeting with the armed forces' supreme command, Nasser predicted an Israeli strike against Egypt within forty-eight to seventy-two hours at the latest. 'The Arabs are sniffing blood', read a CIA memorandum on 3 June. 'So fast and far does Nasir's [*sic*] band-wagon seem to be rolling that even the Iranian government, long friendly to Israel and bitterly hostile to Nasir, has been compelled to issue a statement mouthing phrases about Muslim solidarity'.[6]

Yet for all his militancy, Nasser had weighty reasons to forgo a first strike at this particular timing. His war preparations had not been completed: the Egyptian forces in Sinai were still digging in, an Arab expeditionary force designed to deploy in Jordan had not yet arrived, and coordination of the operational plans of the newly assembled Arab war coalition required more time. No less important, Nasser feared that an Egyptian attack would trigger an Anglo-American military response that might neutralize the perceived Arab political and military superiority over Israel gained by the most remarkable demonstration of pan-Arab unity since the 1948 war.[7]

Nasser's fears of American intervention were compounded by the nature of the Egyptian operational plan, which envisaged deep thrusts into Israel's territory. An armoured division was to break out of the Gaza Strip and capture some border villages inside Israel, while another armoured division was to cut off the southern Negev from the rest of Israel, thereby achieving the long-standing Egyptian objective of establishing a land bridge with Jordan.[8] Given Nasser's belief in US commitment to Israel's territorial integrity, indeed in an American-Israeli plot to provoke Egypt into a military confrontation that would lay the ground to the restoration of UNEF,[9] such plans could hardly be implemented if Cairo were to take the military initiative. Their execution as an act of self-defence in response to an Israeli attack was a completely different matter, however. Not only was such a scenario certain to put Moscow, which by now was quietly pressuring its Arab allies to de-escalate, squarely behind Cairo, but it could also weaken the extent of international support for Israel given the lack of appetite in the Western capitals for a new Arab-Israeli war, as evidenced by Washington's tireless efforts to defuse the crisis; the appeals by America's Middle Eastern embassies to throw the 'unviable client state' of Israel under the bus; and the ultimatum by President Charles de Gaulle of France, then Jerusalem's foremost military supplier, against launching a pre-emptive strike. President Johnson might not have been as blunt as his French counterpart, but in a meeting with Israeli Foreign Minister Abba Eban on 26 May he emphasized that Jerusalem must not 'be the one to bear the responsibility for any outbreak of war' and that 'Israel will not be alone unless it decides to go alone' – an assertion interpreted by Eban (and the US special team dealing with the crisis) as a warning against a pre-emptive strike.[10]

This explains Nasser's pretence to play the political card, notably his readiness to meet Vice President Hubert Humphrey in Cairo and to send his own deputy, Zakaria Muhieddin, to Washington. He had no intention whatsoever of giving ground; the move was aimed at cornering Israel and making it more vulnerable to Arab pressure and, eventually, war. In his letter to Johnson (on 2 June) acquiescing in the above visits, Nasser made it eminently clear that the conflict was not about the presence of UN forces on Egyptian soil or freedom of navigation in the Gulf of Aqaba, let alone the supposed Israeli threat to Syria; rather it revolved around 'the rights of the Arab people of Palestine' and the persistent denial of their 'established right of return and life in their homeland' – the standard Arab euphemism for Israel's destruction through demographic subversion. And as if there remained any doubts about his strategic goal, Nasser reverted to another favourable metaphor of Israel's destruction, publicly styling himself as the new Saladin: 'During the crusaders' occupation, the Arabs waited seventy years before a suitable opportunity arose and they drove away the crusaders … recently we felt that we are strong enough, that if we were to enter a battle with Israel, with God's help, we could triumph'.[11]

Towards an Egyptian-Israeli Peace

If the outbreak of the 1967 war underscored the limits of great-power ability to prevent an undesirable regional deterioration, its outcome has irretrievably changed the course of Middle Eastern history. Instead of destroying the 'neo-crusading Zionist entity', Nasser saw his air force destroyed on the ground within three hours of the outbreak of hostilities, and his army crushed and expelled from Sinai over the next three days. As Syria, Jordan and Iraq attacked Israel, their armies were similarly routed. By the time the war was over, after merely six days of fighting, Israel had extended its control over vast Arab territories about five times its own size, from the Suez Canal, to the Jordan River, to the Golan Heights.

The glaring dissonance between the prewar euphoria and the magnitude of the defeat punctured the sterile bubble of denial and suggested to the Arabs that military force had its limits. Even Nasser seemed to recoil from the pan-Arab ideals he had preached for so long. A few days before the outbreak of hostilities on 5 June he had proudly prophesied that 'the battle will be total and our basic aim will be the destruction of Israel'. A month later he rejected a Syrian proposal to merge the two states on the grounds that the liberation of the occupied territories constituted a more pressing need than Arab unity.[17] For a person who had built himself into the living symbol of pan-Arab unity this was a major reordering of priorities. So was his begrudging acceptance of UN Security Council Resolution 242 of November 1967, which recognized Israel's right to secure existence. 'You issue statements, but we have to fight', he told an all-Arab summit in Cairo in September 1970. 'If you want to liberate, then get in line in front of us ... but we have learnt caution after 1967, and after the Yemenis dragged us into their affairs in 1962, and the Syrians into war in 1967'.[13]

Yet it is doubtful whether this disillusionment would have culminated in Arab-Jewish reconciliation had Nasser lived longer. Shortly before his sudden death on 28 September 1970, he confided in Jordan's King Hussein that since the Arabs were in no position to destroy Israel by force of arms in the foreseeable future they should adopt a phased strategy that would first regain the territories lost in the 1967 war before launching the final drive to total victory. 'I believe that we now have a duty to remove the aggressor from our land and to regain the Arab territory occupied by the Israelis', he said. 'We can then engage in a clandestine struggle to liberate the land of Palestine, to liberate Haifa and Jaffa'.[14]

It was thus left to Nasser's successor to give these revanchist dreams a ceremonial burial. While paying homage to his predecessor's pan-Arab legacy (in April 1971 he even announced the formation of an Egyptian-Syrian-Libyan federation), from his first moments in power Anwar Sadat adopted an 'Egypt first' approach, which subordinated pan-Arab considerations to the Egyptian national interest. In December 1970 he expressed readiness to recognize Israel 'as an independent state' within internationally agreed and secure borders on the basis of a complete withdrawal from Egyptian lands – not from the other Arab territories occupied in the 1967 war.[15] Two months later, in a written response to UN special envoy Gunnar Jarring, he confirmed that 'Egypt will be ready to enter into a peace agreement with Israel' in return for a complete Israeli withdrawal from its territory, as well as the Gaza Strip. He reiterated this position at a Cairo meeting with US Secretary of State William Rogers, going so far as to tell his distinguished guest of his 'full understanding for Israel's problems', including its 'need for security'.[16] When these moves failed to achieve the desired outcome, Sadat sought to buttress his leadership credentials in the Arab world and to force Israel to take him seriously by launching a surprise attack together with Syria's President Hafez Assad.

Like the June 1967 conflict, the October 1973 war was a watershed in Middle Eastern history. It was the first all-out war in which the Arabs managed to score impressive military gains. Although the end of hostilities found the Israeli army closer than ever to Damascus and Cairo, the initial Arab successes shattered Israeli self-confidence. The line of defence along the Suez Canal, the embodiment of military prowess in the minds of many Israelis, collapsed like a house of cards. The Golan Heights, the shield of northern Israel, proved no barrier to a surprise Syrian attack. Consequently, the Israel that emerged from the war was a different nation: sober, mellowed, permanently scarred. It was still distrustful of its neighbours, yet better tuned to signs of regional moderation; highly apprehensive of the security risks attending territorial concessions, yet aware that land could not buy absolute security, as evidenced by the steady growth in public support for the 'territory for peace' formula.

Already in December 1973 an international peace conference was convened in the Swiss town of Geneva, for the first time since the late 1940s, with the participation of Israel and some of its Arab neighbours. A month later Egypt and Israel signed an agreement on the disengagement of forces along the Suez Canal and the establishment of a buffer zone between the two armies supervised by a United Nations Emergency Force (UNEF), which enabled Egypt to retain a military presence on the east bank of the canal – a significant psychological and economic achievement. This was followed in September 1975 by a far more ambitious accord containing a mutual recognition that 'the conflict between them and in the Middle East shall not be resolved by military force but by peaceful means' and a commitment to the peaceful pursuit of a comprehensive settlement on the basis of Security Council Resolution 338 of 22 October 1973 (a follow-up to Resolution 242) that ended the October war. Israel agreed to withdraw its forces to the eastern side of the Mitla and Gidi passes, some thirty miles east of the canal, and to return the oilfields on the southwestern coast of the Gulf of Suez, while Egypt agreed to the passage of 'non-military cargoes destined for or coming from Israel' through the Suez Canal (something that four years earlier Sadat had made conditional on the resolution of the Palestinian problem).[17]

The significance of this agreement could not be overstated. Here was the largest and most powerful Arab state, which had spearheaded the fight against Israel during the past two-and-a-half decades, agreeing in all but name to end the state of belligerency with the Arab world's nemesis. By committing itself to peace with Israel on the basis of Resolutions 242 and 338, Egypt effectively recognized its right to existence, something that was anathema to most Arabs. By precluding the use of force in the quest for a settlement, Cairo distanced itself from the pan-Arab struggle against Israel. What Sadat seemed to be telling his fellow Arabs was that the old way of thinking on the conflict was passé. There was no military solution to this historic feud, only a political one. Israel was in the Middle East to stay and the Arabs had better disavow their unrealistic dream of a unified regional order and follow Egypt's lead in rolling Israel back to the 1967 borders. And if there remained any doubts about the Egyptian president's determination to sway the Arab world from war to peace with Israel, they were completely dispelled in November 1977 when he made his historic visit to Jerusalem and, some eighteen months later, concluded a fully fledged peace treaty with the Jewish state.

This was no personal whim of a capricious president. In charting his daring course Sadat tapped into the growing disenchantment among Egyptians with pan-Arab ideals in general, and the Palestinian cause in particular. After four bitter wars and untold human and material losses, doubts had begun to surface as to whether the 'full liberation of Palestine from Zionist occupation' was at all feasible, and whether it justified such an exorbitant price. Egyptians looked around and felt betrayed and exploited.

While their Arab brothers had offered little more than fiery rhetoric and meagre financial contributions, they had served as pan-Arabism's sacrificial lamb. Military expenditure topped a quarter of the national income while revenues were rapidly drying up. The Suez Canal was closed, its once-thriving cities turned into ghost towns by the war of attrition waged during Nasser's last years (1969–70). Many of Egypt's best and brightest were drawn away from the economy into military service, while hard-currency earnings were down as tourists kept away.

Capitalizing on this growing disenchantment, in the wake of the 1973 war Sadat embarked on a sustained attempt to demolish Nasser's domestic and international legacy, with intellectuals, journalists and political victims lining up to expose the dark and hitherto undisclosed side of his regime. Egyptians learned that Nasser's socialist programmes had been ill-conceived and poorly managed, bankrupting the state and its citizens alike. They were informed of the repressive nature of the Nasserite police state, where paralyzing fear ensured submission and where arbitrary arrests, imprisonment without trial, torture and execution were common practice. Nasser's pan-Arabism came under heavy fire for having substituted one imperial master for another by making Egypt fully subservient to Soviet expansionist designs. It was only Sadat's expulsion of the Soviet forces from Egypt in July 1972 and, even more so, the 1973 crossing of the Suez Canal that had made Egypt the true master of its own fate. 'We do not know exactly how much they cost us either in thousands of lives or in thousands of millions of Egyptian pounds', the renowned novelist Tawfiq Hakim lamented the human and material costs of the military catastrophes wrought by Nasser.

> However, according to what has been mentioned and published, our losses in the recent wars alone are evaluated at about four billion pounds … had this amount been spent on the villages of Egypt, which number about four thousand, the share for each village would have been a million pounds. Such a sum would completely re-create the villages and raise them to the level of the villages of Europe. But our Egyptian villages have remained in their sad condition, and our poor peasants in their ignorance, disease, and poverty.[18]

It was this unique convergence of Egyptian and Israeli disillusionment with the continuation of the conflict, rather than any external influences, that enabled Sadat and Prime Minister Begin, who won a surprise electoral victory in May 1977 after nearly three decades of failed attempts, to end the long-standing enmity between their states.

To be sure, Secretary of State Henry Kissinger quickly capitalized on Sadat's anti-Soviet sentiments and his conviction that the key to Israeli concessions lay in Washington to ingratiate the administration with the Egyptian president by applying heavy pressure on Jerusalem, including the suspension of weapons supplies when negotiations on the second disengagement agreement were temporarily stalled (March–September 1975). Yet it is doubtful whether the American 'reassessment' (as this extended pressure was euphemistically known), or the substantial political and economic inducements attending the agreement (which, among other things, set Cairo on the road to becoming the largest recipient of US foreign civilian aid), would have been remotely as effective without the profound disillusionment process triggered by the October war. Indeed, notwithstanding the deep enmity between Prime Minister Yitzhak Rabin and Defence Minister Shimon Peres, which constrained Israel's negotiating position, and Rabin's predilection for co-ordination with the US developed during his Washington ambassadorship (1968–73), the Israeli government was not deterred from fighting back the American pressure. This was most vividly illustrated on 21 May 1975, when, at the initiative of the American-Israel Public Affairs Committee (AIPAC), 76 senators sent a strongly worded letter to President Ford urging a greater responsiveness to 'Israel's economic and military needs' since 'a strong Israel constitutes the most reliable barrier to the domination of the area by other parties'. A week later, in yet another unmistakable signal to the administration to ease the pressure on Jerusalem, the Senate blocked the sale of Hawk anti-aircraft missiles to Jordan. Meanwhile, successive public opinion polls showed most Americans convinced of Israel's genuine interest in reaching an agreement.[19]

Likewise, notwithstanding the Carter administration's help in papering over recurrent disagreements between Begin and Sadat, most notably during the Camp David summit of September 1978 that delineated the broad contours of the crystallizing peace accord, these efforts would have amounted to little had it not been for the two leaders' determination to make peace.

Anxious to redeem his extremist image dating to his 1940s anti-British struggle, Begin appointed the former Labourite minister of defence, Moshe Dayan, as his foreign minister (instead of the obvious candidates from his right-wing Likud party), promptly sending him on a string of regional secret missions to explore the possibility of peacemaking, while he himself visited Romanian dictator Nicolae Ceausescu, who enjoyed close relations with many Arab regimes. This culminated in mid-September 1977 in the Dayan–Tohami secret meeting in Morocco, and the road from there to Jerusalem was short.

Not only were the Americans not informed of these contacts (with Tohami suggesting that Washington be kept in the dark until Egypt and Israel reached a general agreement),[20] but the administration's frenzied efforts to orchestrate negotiations between Israel and a unified Arab delegation within the Geneva framework only served to catalyse the nascent Israeli-Egyptian secret channel.

Had it been up to Carter, Sadat would have never come to Jerusalem. The American president believed that Kissinger's step-by-step approach had outlived its usefulness and that his efforts to exclude Moscow from the Arab-Israeli peace process had been equally misconceived. Hence, rather than encourage a direct Egyptian-Israeli dialogue, Carter sought to reactivate the peace process on a multilateral basis and in cooperation with the Soviet Union. Matters came to a head on 1 October 1977, following the issuance of a joint US-Soviet statement urging the reconvening of the Geneva conference within three months and outlining some general principles for a settlement which, by Carter's account, 'neither the Israelis nor the Arabs were ready to accept'.[21]

This backfired in no time. Keenly aware of the reverse correlation between the state of global détente and small states' manoeuvrability (i.e., the warmer the superpower relations the narrower the local actors' freedom of action), Sadat and Begin viewed Carter's courtship of Moscow with deep suspicion. Having agreed during his mid-July first official meeting with Carter to participate in an international peace conference on the basis of Security Council resolutions 242 and 338, and to territorial compromise on the Egyptian and Syrian fronts,[22] Begin was getting cold feet. Shown an advance copy of the US-Soviet declaration, he told Ambassador Sam Lewis 'in most unequivocal terms that Israel would not attend [the] Geneva Conference if any, repeat, any PLO members took part'; meanwhile Dayan sought to convince Secretary of State Vance that 'a United Arab Delegation would tie Egypt's hands completely'. Saying nothing of his Morocco meeting two weeks earlier, he argued that there might be a way for Israel to reach an agreement with Egypt – but not in Geneva. 'Of course, what is agreed upon could be signed in Geneva', he sought to reassure Vance. 'But if Egypt is bound by a United Arab Delegation we won't be able to make any progress'. The Secretary of State would have nothing of this. '[H]e did not think that Israel could negotiate a separate treaty with Egypt without there at least being a Geneva Conference', he said. 'The Egyptians could not do it without Geneva'.[23]

This line of thinking was not only completely unfounded but the inverse of the truth. Far from seeking Geneva's blessing for an Egyptian-Israeli deal, Sadat viewed the conference as an insurmountable barrier to such an agreement (which is precisely why Syria, despite its total rejection of peace, agreed to attend). Having no appetite for a collision with the hyperactive Carter, he feigned acquiescence in his efforts to revive the conference while trying to dilute its most detrimental aspects; once the administration seemed to be on the same wavelength as his Soviet nemesis, however, Sadat decided to confront it with a fait accompli by bringing his secret contacts with Israel to a dramatic and irreversible fruition.

While plotting his Jerusalem visit, however, he gave the US president a last chance to rethink Geneva by proposing the immediate convocation of an international conference in East Jerusalem to discuss 'the essentials of peace'. Each participant would come alone rather than within a unified delegation, and the conference would hold its deliberations even if some invitees failed to arrive. As Carter dismissed the idea, wondering whether Sadat 'was not losing his sense of reality', the Egyptian president swiftly raised the ante and in a speech to the Egyptian parliament on 9 November expressed his readiness 'to go to the ends of the earth ... to go to their house, the Knesset itself, to debate them'.[24]

Yet even this bombshell, which tantalized the entire world, failed to disabuse the administration of its Geneva delusions. Judging the statement as proof of the 'dramatizing lengths to which he [is] prepared to go to achieve peace [within the Geneva framework], not as a serious possibility', Cairo Ambassador Herman Eilts recommended that Sadat's 'hand will be strengthened if gambit succeeds and cosponsors able to convene Geneva in relatively near future'. Two days later, after Begin issued an official invitation to Sadat to come to Jerusalem, Carter informed the Egyptian president that 'the coming days will be crucial to our effort to bring about an early reconvening of the Geneva Conference'. As late as 18 November Vance implored Carter to impress upon Begin and/or Dayan, prior to Sadat's arrival in Israel the next day, that 'we are counting on their agreeing to [the Geneva] approach since it is the only way we see to maintain the momentum that will be created by Sadat's visit'.

The president duly complied. 'We fully recognize that the substantive issues of territory, the Palestinian problem and the nature of peace cannot be resolved in the short time allotted for President Sadat's visit', he wrote to Begin. 'A step of historic proportions could however be accomplished if the visit could close with the way cleared for Israel and all the Arab parties to reconvene at Geneva in December or shortly thereafter'. 'It also occurs to us that a constructive step that would make Syria's agreement to Geneva easier – and strengthen Sadat's position – would be Israel's agreement to Syria's being included as a member of the working group that would deal with the West Bank and Gaza', Carter added. 'I hope you can make such a proposal to President Sadat'. At the same time he urged the Egyptian president 'to obtain Begin's agreement to include Syria, in addition to Egypt, Jordan, Israel and the Palestinians, in the conference working group that would be set up to discuss the West Bank and Gaza'. Nothing of course could have been further from the two leaders' minds than making their budding understanding captive to pan-Arab whims, and no sooner had Sadat returned from Jerusalem than he told Eilts that 'after his visit to Israel, the Geneva Conf is really not needed any longer.'[25]

The Festering Palestinian Problem

Carter was no more insightful of the mindset of the PLO, designated in October 1974 by the Arab League as the 'sole legitimate representative' of the Palestinian people, than he was of that of Sadat and Begin (and, for that matter, the rest of the Arab leaders).

The first US president to declare the establishment of a 'Palestinian homeland' a condition for regional peace (in contrast to the received wisdom at the time whereby the West Bank, or most of it, would be returned to Jordan), Carter tirelessly toiled to incorporate the PLO, whose hallowed founding document, the Palestinian Charter, devoted about two-thirds of its 33 articles to the need to destroy Israel, into the political process.[26] Since by way of facilitating the 1975 disengagement agreement the Ford administration had given Israel a written pledge that the United States 'will not recognize or negotiate with the PLO as long as the PLO does not recognize Israel's right to exist and does not accept Security Council Resolutions 242 and 338', both Prime Minister Rabin, who met Carter on 4–5 April 1977, and Begin were taken aback by the president's courtship of the Palestinian group. Yet for all the administration's efforts, including its readiness to acquiesce in a diluted acceptance of 242 that emptied the resolution of its original intent (i.e., its misrepresentation as implying

Palestinian self-determination at a time when the Palestinians weren't even mentioned), the PLO would not budge from its open commitment to Israel's destruction. 'Edward, I want you to tell Vance that we're not interested', Yasser Arafat told Arab-American academic Edward Said, who liaised between the administration and the PLO. 'We don't want the Americans. The Americans have stabbed us in the back. This is a lousy deal. We want Palestine. We're not interested in bits of Palestine. We don't want to negotiate with the Israelis. We're going to fight'.[27]

It was only in November 1988, eight years after Carter's electoral defeat by Ronald Reagan and more than two decades after the passing of Resolution 242, that an extraordinary session of the Palestine National Congress, the PLO's 'parliament', convened in Algiers, declared the establishment of an independent Palestinian state and accepted the UN document; and like most other regional developments, the impetus for this decision came from a number of indigenous events rather than external influences, first and foremost the Israeli invasion of Lebanon in June 1982 and the expulsion of the PLO from the country.

On the face of it, the Israeli move should have unified the Arabs against their old nemesis. In reality, as on numerous past occasions, the confrontation only served to confirm the hollowness of pan-Arab solidarity since none of the Arab states came to the rescue of the Palestinians. Even Syria, which was also on the receiving end of the Israeli invasion, failed to co-operate with the PLO and instead used the war as a means to make the Palestinian organization fully subservient to its will. When Arafat failed to play the role assigned to him by Assad, he was summarily expelled from Damascus and confronted with an armed revolt against his authority by pro-Syrian elements within the PLO. In November 1983, having returned to Lebanon with some of his troops, Arafat and his loyalists found themselves besieged by the Syrian army in the northern town of Tripoli. A month later, a humiliating exodus of PLO forces from Lebanon took place – for the second time in a year – only this time from Tripoli rather than from Beirut, and under Syrian, rather than Israeli, pressure. As a result, Arafat saw no choice but to seek Egyptian protection. In December 1983, shortly after his second expulsion from Lebanon, he arrived in Cairo, for the first time in six years, for a dramatic meeting with Hosni Mubarak, who had assumed the presidency in October 1981 after Sadat's assassination by an Islamist zealot. This was a diplomatic and public relations coup for Egypt, which would gradually become the PLO's main patron, shielding it from Syrian pressure and providing a vital channel to the US administration.

An equally important impetus for the Algiers decision was the Palestinian uprising, or *intifada*, which broke in the West Bank and the Gaza Strip in December 1987. Doing more to redeem Palestinian dignity and self-esteem than decades of PLO terrorism, this popular insurrection pushed the Palestine problem to the forefront of the Arab-Israeli conflict and boxed Arafat into a corner. Were he to fail to seize the moment, the PLO's claim to championship of the 'armed struggle', let alone to exclusive representation of the Palestinian people, might be largely discredited. The intifada was as much an act of protest against the PLO's failure as it was a revolt against the Israeli occupation; and with a young and dynamic leadership rapidly developing in the West Bank and Gaza, and new political groups making significant inroads into Palestinian society, Arafat feared that any indecision on his part would result in the loss of the influence the PLO had built in the territories during the 1970s and 1980s. He therefore moved quickly to assert control over the unexpected uprising, while at the same time striving to achieve a political and diplomatic breakthrough that would convince the local populace that its sacrifices had not been in vain.

Yet while the Algiers decision led to the opening of the US–PLO dialogue the Carter administration had failed to produce, Palestinian leaders went out of their way to reassure their Arabic-speaking constituents that this was merely a tactical ploy aimed at enhancing the organization's international standing and, as a consequence, its ability to achieve the ultimate goal of Israel's destruction. In the words of Salah Khalaf (aka Abu Iyad), Arafat's second in command: 'We vowed to liberate Palestine before 1967. We will restore Palestine step by step and not in one fell swoop, just as the Jews had done. We are learning from them and there is nothing wrong in this ... The establishment of a Palestinian state on any part of Palestine is but a step toward the [liberation of the] whole of Palestine'.[28]

Given this mindset, it was hardly surprising that the PLO leapt upon the Iraqi occupation of Kuwait in the summer of 1990 to shed its feigned moderation. Arafat had been striving for decades to entangle the Arab states in a war with Israel on the Palestinians' behalf. Now that the most powerful Arab state presented its predatory move as the first step towards 'the liberation of Jerusalem' the temptation was too great for Arafat to resist, even if the price was the sacrifice of the ruling Kuwaiti family or the potential elimination of Kuwait as an independent state. As he put it in a Baghdad rally, the Palestinians were 'in the same trench with the Iraqi people to confront the US-Zionist-Atlantic buildup of invading forces, which are desecrating Arab lands'.[29]

This folly cost the PLO dearly. The Gulf monarchies were neither forgiving nor forgetful. As the primary financiers of the Palestinian cause they felt betrayed by their beneficiaries; as hosts to a large population of Palestinian workers they felt threatened. As a result, not only did the PLO lose the $133 million in annual contributions as the vengeful Gulf states suspended their financial support, but following the liberation of Kuwait most of the 400,000 Palestinians who had been living and working in the emirate were expelled, creating a major humanitarian crisis and denying the PLO the substantial income regularly received from the earnings of those workers. With the additional loss of funds and investments in Kuwaiti banks, the total amount forfeited by the PLO as a direct result of the Gulf crisis was in excess of ten billion dollars, bringing the organization to the verge of bankruptcy.

Starved of financial resources, ostracized by its Arab peers and increasingly overpowered in the West Bank and Gaza by Hamas, the PLO was desperate for political rehabilitation (in an Arab League summit in mid-1991 the organization was not even allowed to raise the Palestinian issue) – and Arafat for a personal comeback. Fortunately for the Palestinian leader, a lifeline was suddenly offered from the least expected source: the Israeli government headed by Rabin.

Brought to power in July 1992 for the second time in 20 years on a straightforward peace platform, the seventy-year-old Rabin, who as chief of staff had masterminded Israel's 1967 victory, was well aware that this was his last chance to go down in history as Israel's greatest peacemaker, and was therefore prepared to secure his legacy regardless of the costs, even if this meant breaking the taboo to which all Israeli governments had long subscribed: negotiating directly with the PLO without the organization first abandoning its formal commitment to Israel's destruction. This led in short order to the Oslo talks, which culminated on 20 August 1993 in the signing of a draft peace agreement at the Norwegian government's guesthouse. Three weeks later, in a festive ceremony on the White House lawn shown in real time throughout the world, Foreign Minister Peres and Mahmoud Abbas (alias Abu Mazen), Arafat's second in command since Abu Iyad's assassination in 1991, signed a bilateral Declaration of Principles on Interim Self-Government Arrangements, providing for Palestinian self-rule in the entire West Bank and the Gaza Strip for a transitional period of up to five years in which Israel and the Palestinians would negotiate a permanent peace settlement. During this interim period the territories would be administered by a Palestinian council, to be freely and democratically elected after the withdrawal of Israeli military forces from both the Gaza Strip and the populated areas of the West Bank.

As with the Egyptian-Israeli talks, the US administration had no inkling of the Oslo secret channel. When news of the agreement broke, Secretary of State Warren Christopher was stunned – just as he had been 17 years earlier, as deputy Secretary of State, on the occasion of Sadat's visit to Jerusalem – while President Clinton, fresh into his first tenure, capitalized on this unexpected breakthrough to boost his popularity by hosting the signing ceremony.

Nor did Washington have greater success in steering the peace process to fruition. Notwithstanding Clinton's exceedingly close relationship with Arafat – the most frequent foreign visitor to the Oval Office during his presidency – he failed to persuade the Palestinian leader to abide by his contractual peace obligations, notably to disarm the Hamas and Islamic Jihad terror groups or to desist from building up the PLO's own terrorist infrastructure, and was repeatedly duped by Arafat on crucial aspects of the peace process such as the PLO's tacit approval of terror attacks on Israelis and its failure to abolish those clauses in its charter calling for Israel's destruction, a key foundation of the Oslo process. When in September 1996 Arafat exploited the opening of a new entrance to an archaeological tunnel in old Jerusalem to unleash a tidal wave of violence, in which 15 Israelis and 58 Palestinians were killed, the administration failed to see this cynical ploy for what it was and refrained from vetoing an anti-Israel Security Council resolution.

Likewise, when in November 1997 Washington threatened Saddam Hussein with punitive action if he continued to obstruct UN attempts to trace and dismantle his remaining weapons of mass destruction, huge demonstrations in support of Iraq were held in Palestinian towns with Arafat sending his public 'blessings to the brotherly Iraqi people and its leadership'. Hafez Barghouthi, editor of the Palestinian Authority's largest newspaper, *al-Hayat al-Jadida*, claimed that, 'History will not remember the United States, but it will remember Iraq, the cradle of civilization, and Palestine, the cradle of religions'.[30]

Clinton's extraordinary indulgence of Arafat faced its foremost moment of truth during the July 2000 summit, convened under his auspices in the presidential retreat of Camp David, when the PLO chairman rejected Israel's offer to establish an independent Palestinian state in 92 per cent of the West Bank and the entire Gaza Strip, with East Jerusalem as its capital.[31] 'If the Israelis can make compromises and you can't, I should go home',

Clinton told Arafat just before the end of the summit. 'You have been here fourteen days and said no to everything. These things have consequences; failure will mean the end of the peace process'.[32] In public the president was more diplomatic yet no less pointed as to who was culpable for the summit's failure. 'Prime Minister Barak showed particular courage, vision, and an understanding of the historical importance of this moment', he told a White House news conference announcing the end of the talks. 'The prime minister moved forward more from his initial position than Chairman Arafat, particularly surrounding the question of Jerusalem'. A few days later, in a special interview on Israeli television, Clinton elaborated:

> I kept telling the Palestinians, and I will say again to the world that you cannot make an agreement over something as important as a city that is the holiest place in the world if it is required of one side to say: 'I completely defeated the interest of the other side'. If either side gets to say that at the end, there won't be an agreement. There can't be.[33]

This impassioned plea failed to impress Arafat. Two months after the summit, on 29 September, he launched an all-out war of terror (euphemized as the al-Aqsa Intifada) that pitted Palestinians and Israelis in their bloodiest struggle since the 1948 war. Yet instead of triggering a global outrage, Arafat's deliberate use of violence served to reaffirm his international stature as it had on numerous past occasions. At the end of the 1960s, as PLO terrorism was rapidly spreading, the UN General Assembly adopted a resolution recognizing the 'inalienable rights' of the Palestinian people. In November 1974, on the heel of a string of deadly terror attacks on Israeli civilians including the murder of 11 Israeli athletes during the 1972 Munich Olympics, Arafat became the first non-state leader to address the General Assembly. In September 1996, as noted above, Arafat's unflinching sacrifice of dozens of Palestinians seriously undermined Prime Minister Benjamin Netanyahu's domestic and international standing. Now that he unleashed a total war of terror on his peace partner who had just raised the spectre of Palestinian statehood – for the first time since the November 1947 partition resolution – a diverse cohort of international apologists was busy exonerating him of any wrongdoing and pointing an accusatory finger at Israel. 'After the collapse of the Camp David summit in July, [Arafat] is said to have concluded that the Palestinians no longer had "a partner for peace"', wrote the influential *Economist* magazine, as if it had been the Israeli prime minister rather than the Palestinian leader who had turned his back on a generous peace offer. 'He has little faith in Mr Barak, whose skill at expanding Jewish settlements, while receiving diplomatic accolades from America and Europe, has long infuriated him. And he is believed to be greatly disillusioned with President Clinton, whom Mr Arafat had believed to be genuinely "sensitive" to the Palestinian cause'.[34]

While it is doubtful whether Clinton concurred with this outlandish prognosis, he nevertheless felt obliged to appease the Palestinian leader. On 23 December 2000, a month before leaving office, he proposed a new peace plan that envisaged additional Israeli concessions, including an increase in the territory of the prospective Palestinian state to 94–6 per cent of the West Bank and the award of Israeli territory adjoining Gaza to make up for the 4–6 per cent that would be annexed to the Jewish state. Yet Arafat dragged his feet for over a week before giving his response to Clinton in person on 2 January 2001. According to Dennis Ross, presidential special envoy to the Middle East who attended the meeting, the PLO chairman rejected 'every single one of the things he was supposed to give', including Israeli sovereignty over the Wailing Wall, Judaism's holiest site:

> He rejected the idea on the refugees. He said we need a whole new formula, as if what we had presented was non-existent. He rejected the basic ideas on security. He wouldn't even countenance the idea that the Israelis would be able to operate in Palestinian airspace. You know when you fly into Israel today you go to Ben-Gurion. You fly in over the West Bank because you can't [fly any other way] – there's no space through otherwise. He rejected that. So every single one of the ideas that was asked of him he rejected.[35]

Arafat was no more responsive to George W. Bush's forthright approach than he had been to his predecessor's indulgence. When Secretary of State Colin Powell visited Ramallah at the end of February 2001, a month after the new administration's inauguration, to demand an end to Palestinian violence, operatives of Force 17 – Arafat's praetorian guard that secured Powell during the visit – shot and wounded a number of Israelis. Even during the visit a huge anti-American demonstration, in which effigies of the Secretary of State were burned, marched through the city centre a few minutes after Powell had passed by, managing to make a point without interfering with the convoy.[36]

In the coming months Arafat repeatedly tested the administration's patience both by doing nothing to reduce the level of violence (in April and May 2001 there were over 1,200 terror attacks, including seven suicide bombings) and by misleading US officials about his actions and intentions. And while the 9/11 attacks and the attendant war on terror drove Arafat into feigned solidarity with the American people in an attempt to disguise the mass celebration of the attacks in Palestinian towns and cities (in a macabre coincidence, on 9/11 *al-Hayat al-Jadida* lauded 'the [October 1983] Lebanese suicide bombers who taught the US marines a tough lesson [killing 241 of them])',[37] Palestinian violence not only continued unabated but shot to new heights in October, making it the fourth most violent month in the then 13-month-long terror war.

By the end of the year Bush had come to consider Arafat the main obstacle to peace,[38] and relations between the two reached breaking point in early 2002 when the PLO chairman denied, in a personal letter to the president, any knowledge of the PA-owned *Karine A* vessel, loaded with some 50 tons of Iranian weapons, ammunitions and explosives, that was intercepted by the Israeli navy en route to Gaza. In a phone conversation with Mubarak, Bush vented his frustration with the Palestinian-Iranian arms deal 'because I was led to believe [that Arafat] was willing to join us in the fight on terror. I took him at his word'. (As late as June 2002 Arafat denied that the PA had anything to do with the smuggling attempt, arguing that the weapons were destined for Lebanon's Hezbollah organization.)

Vice President Dick Cheney echoed this sentiment in public. 'We don't believe him', he said, brushing aside Arafat's feigned innocence. 'Based on the intelligence we've seen, the people that were involved were so close to him it's hard to believe that he wasn't'. Cheney added:

The really disturbing part of this, of course, is that there are a lot of places he could go in the Arab world if he were looking for support and sustenance or for help in moving the peace process forward. Clearly, he hasn't done that. What he's done is gone to a terrorist organization, Hezbollah, and a state that supports and promotes terrorism, that's dedicated to ending the peace process, Iran, and done business with them.[39]

In these circumstances, Bush was quietly sympathetic to Israel's harsh response to the March 2002 terror offensive, in which 126 Israelis were murdered (more than twice the relative fatality toll of 9/11), and it was only on 4 April, about a week after the start of Operation Defensive Shield against the West Bank's terror infrastructure, that he publicly urged Israel to 'halt incursions into Palestinian areas [and to] begin the withdrawal from the cities it has occupied'. Yet this call, which he repeated with a greater sense of urgency a couple of days later, was merely a means to deflect international criticism of the administration's alleged aloofness vis-à-vis the Palestinian-Israeli crisis, as was Powell's dispatch to the region to try to negotiate a ceasefire. Having lost all trust in Arafat, Bush was deeply sceptical about the mission's success. 'You're going to have to spend some political capital', he told Powell. 'You have plenty. I need you to do it'.[40]

No sooner had Powell returned empty-handed than harsh voices began to emanate from Washington. In his meetings with US officials during Operation Defensive Shield, former Prime Minister Netanyahu was repeatedly asked why Israel failed to exploit the operation in order to get rid of Arafat. On 5 May, during a visit by Prime Minister Ariel Sharon to Washington in which he tried to convince his hosts to sever all ties with Arafat and start cultivating a new generation of Palestinian leaders, National Security Adviser Condoleezza Rice publicly called for the PA's reform since Arafat had failed to meet his leadership responsibilities. The Palestinian Authority must be 'democratic, transparent, and non-corrupt', she told the Fox News Sunday programme. '[This is] what we ask of every government in the world. And we are going to start demanding [that] of the Palestinian leadership'.[41]

Though the State Department sought to promote a ceasefire by pressuring Israel rather than the PA, Bush was increasingly won over to the idea of a drastic Palestinian reform. 'A Palestinian state will never be created by terror', he stated in a long-awaited speech on 24 June 2002. 'My vision is two states, living side by side, in peace and security. There is simply no way to achieve that peace until all parties fight terror ... Peace requires a new and different Palestinian leadership, so that a Palestinian state can be born. I call on the Palestinian people to elect new leaders, leaders not compromised by terror'.[42]

Yet even at this stage, with Arafat confined by Israel to his Ramallah compound, there was little the leader of the free world could do to enforce his two-state vision and he was forced to watch helplessly as Mahmoud Abbas, his own preferred candidate, was unceremoniously restrained by his boss, who maintained tight control of the PLO and the PA to his dying day on 11 November 2004.

As it was, Bush was to be similarly disillusioned with Abbas, who proved to be warp and woof of the same fabric as his more flamboyant predecessor: a dogmatic PLO veteran who had never eschewed his commitment to Israel's destruction and who viewed the 'peace process' as the continuation of his lifelong war by other means. As late as July 2002 Abbas described Oslo as 'the biggest mistake Israel ever made', enabling the PLO to get worldwide acceptance and respectability while hanging fast to its own aims. In his address of the Palestinian Legislative Council shortly after Arafat's death he swore to 'follow in the path of the late leader Yasser Arafat and … work towards fulfilling his dream … We promise you that our hearts will not rest until the right of return for our people is achieved and the tragedy of the refugees is ended'.

Abbas made good his pledge. In a televised speech on 15 May 2005, on the occasion of Israel's Independence Day, he described the proclamation of the Jewish state as an unprecedented historic injustice and vowed his unwavering refusal to ever 'accept this injustice'.[43] Two-and-a-half years later, at the US-sponsored peace conference in Annapolis, Abbas rejected Prime Minister Ehud Olmert's proposal of a Palestinian Arab state in 97 per cent of the West Bank and the entire Gaza Strip and dismissed out of hand the request to recognize Israel as a Jewish state alongside the would-be Palestinian state (as stipulated by the partition resolution of November 1947, which the PLO had pretended to accept in 1988), insisting instead on the full implementation of the 'right of return' – the Palestinian and Arab euphemism for Israel's destruction. He was quickly followed by his supposedly moderate colleagues – from Oslo negotiator Ahmad Qurei to chief peace negotiator Saeb Erekat, to Prime Minister Salam Fayad – while the PA's television broadcast an information clip produced by the Palestinian Authority Central Bureau of Statistics showing a map in which Israel was painted in the colours of the Palestinian flag, symbolizing its transformation into a Palestinian Arab state.[44] In Abbas's words: 'A Jewish state, what does that suppose to mean? You can call yourselves as you like, but I don't accept it and I say so publicly'.[45]

8. CLUELESS IN ARABIA

Transforming America's relations with the Islamic world was perhaps the foremost foreign policy issue through which Barack Obama sought to set his presidency apart from that of his immediate predecessor. Having long downplayed his Muslim roots – going so far as to disguise not only his middle name, Hussein, but also to substitute the Arabic-originated Barack with the less conspicuous Barry[1] – Obama embraced them with a vengeance since taking office in an attempt to underscore his (supposed) intimate familiarity with Islam. As he explained in his celebrated June 2009 address to the Muslim World in Cairo:

> I'm a Christian, but my father came from a Kenyan family that includes generations of Muslims. As a boy, I spent several years in Indonesia and heard the call of the azaan at the break of dawn and at the fall of dusk. As a young man, I worked in Chicago communities where many found dignity and peace in their Muslim faith ... So I have known Islam on three continents before coming to the region where it was first revealed. That experience guides my conviction that partnership between America and Islam must be based on what Islam is, not what it isn't.[2]

By way of educating Americans on 'what Islam isn't', the Obama administration went out of its way to deny, ignore, euphemize and whitewash anything smacking of Islamic violence, radicalism or expansionism. Federal agencies purged counter-terrorism training materials of references to Islam, presidential advisors extricated such terms as 'jihad' and 'Islamic extremism' from the central document outlining the US national security strategy, and NASA was instructed 'to reach out to the Muslim world and engage much more with dominantly Muslim nations to help them feel good about their historic contribution to science, math and engineering.'[3]

When in November 2009 Palestinian-American military psychiatrist Nadal Hassan murdered 13 people and wounded 43 others in a Texas military base to the shouts of 'Allahu Akbar',[4] a Department of Defense report treated the massacre as workplace violence. 'Each year, more than one million people in the US are harmed by workplace violence, and an estimated 17,000 take their own lives in the place of employment' it read, as if the murderer was a disgruntled employee haggling about working conditions rather than an Islamist zealot with proven connections to al-Qaeda. Even when fleetingly discussing the motivations for domestic terrorism, the report relegated 'religious causes' to the bottom of the list behind such factors as 'animal rights, environmentalism, nationalism, [and] white supremacy'.[5] Small wonder that when in August 2014 Hassan wrote to the self-styled caliph Abu Bakr Baghdadi, shortly after his jihadist group had publicly beheaded an American journalist, requesting 'formally and humbly' to be made a citizen of his self-proclaimed Islamic State (IS),[6] the administration remained conspicuously mute. It was similarly aloof vis-à-vis the January 2015 Paris massacres, where Islamist terrorists affiliated with al-Qaeda and IS murdered 15 people in attacks on a newspaper office and a Jewish food shop, with Obama describing the perpetrators as 'a bunch of violent, vicious zealots who ... randomly shoot a bunch of folks in a deli in Paris'.[7]

Queried about this incredible assertion, White House Press Secretary Josh Earnest provided the equally mind-boggling explanation that 'the point that the president was trying to make is that these individuals were not specifically targeted. These were individuals who happened to randomly be in this deli and were shot while they were there'.[8] The administration would not fall into the trap of 'legitimizing what we consider to be a completely illegitimate justification for this violence' by amplifying the perpetrators' 'warped view of Islam', Ernest further argued, but would rather describe precisely what happened: 'These are individuals who are terrorists. And what they did was they tried to invoke their own distorted deviant view of Islam to try to justify them. And I think that is completely illegitimate. And what we should do is we should call it what it is. And it's an act of terror, and it's one that we roundly condemn'.[9]

The press secretary was merely echoing his president, who spared no effort to dismiss the religious credentials of radical leaders and groups operating in the name of Islam and to dissociate their actions from that faith. Osama bin Laden 'was not a Muslim leader' but 'a mass murderer of Muslims' whose demise 'should be welcomed by all who believe in peace and human dignity'; IS was anything but Islamic since 'no religion condones the killing of innocents, and the vast majority of [its] victims have been Muslim'.[10] Even the Muslim Brotherhood – the world's foremost Islamist organization committed to the creation of a worldwide caliphate, and the bedrock of some of today's most murderous terror groups – was described as 'largely secular'.[11] As such, these groups' extremism had nothing to do with the faith they pretended to represent but was rather a misguided, if not wholly inexplicable, overreaction to the arrogant and self-serving Western policies. 'The relationship between Islam and the West includes centuries of coexistence and cooperation, but also conflict and religious wars', Obama argued in his Cairo speech.

> More recently, tension has been fed by colonialism that denied rights and opportunities to many Muslims, and a Cold War in which Muslim-majority countries were too often treated as proxies without regard to their own aspirations ... Violent extremists have exploited these tensions in a small but potent minority of Muslims ... [culminating in] the attacks of September 11, 2001 and the continued efforts of these extremists to engage in violence against civilians.[12]

This depiction of Muslims as hapless victims of the aggressive encroachments of others, too dim to be accountable for their own fate, is not only completely unfounded but the inverse of the truth. (Indeed, two years later Obama would chastise Middle Eastern leaders for using the same 'post-colonial' rhetoric and casting the West 'as the source of all ills, a half-century after the end of colonialism' in an attempt 'to direct their people's grievances elsewhere'.)[13] Far from a function of its unhappy interaction with the West, the story of Islam has been the story of the rise and fall of an often astonishing imperial aggressiveness and, no less important, of never quiescent imperialist dreams that have survived the fall of the Ottoman Empire to haunt Islamic and Middle Eastern politics into the twenty-first century; and even as these dreams have repeatedly frustrated any possibility for the peaceful social and political development of the Arab-Muslim world, they have given rise to no less repeated fantasies of revenge and restoration and to murderous efforts to transform fantasy into fact. If, today, America is reviled in the Muslim world, it is not because of its specific policies but because, as the pre-eminent world power, it blocks the final realization of this same age-old dream of regaining the lost glory of the caliphate.

This in turn means that, contrary to Obama's wishful thinking, in the historical imagination of many Arabs and Muslims bin Laden is not a 'mass murderer' but the new incarnation of Saladin, defeater of the Crusaders and conqueror of Jerusalem – a true believer who courageously stood up to today's neo-Crusaders. That much is clear from the overwhelming support for the 9/11 attacks throughout the Arab and Islamic worlds, the admiring evocations of these murderous acts during the 2006 crisis over the Danish cartoons, and the glaring lack of enthusiasm about bin Laden's demise. In the words of the then Palestinian Prime Minister Ismail Haniyeh: 'We condemn the assassination and the killing of an Arab holy warrior. We ask God to offer him mercy with the true believers and the martyrs. We regard this as a continuation of the American policy based on oppression and the shedding of Muslim and Arab blood.'[14] Indeed, bin Laden's ability to live for years in plain sight outside the Pakistani capital of Islamabad, a stone's throw from the army's military academy, leaves little doubt that, for all their public denials, the Pakistani authorities had sheltered him from their American allies precisely because he was an admired 'Muslim leader'.

Nor has IS's extroverted brutality detracted one iota from its religious credentials, as evidenced by the influx of thousands of young Muslim men (and women) from all over the world to participate in its self-proclaimed jihad. With far more Muslims killed throughout history by their co-religionists than by non-Muslims, these volunteers can see no doctrinal or moral impediments to fighting their 'deviant' co-religionists, not least since the group's bloodletting has thus far been insignificant by regional standards (suffice it to mention the 250,000 fatalities of the ongoing Syrian civil war, where most of the killing has been done by Bashar Assad's 'infidel' Alawite regime).

Even the gruesome public beheadings, which enticed the reluctant Obama administration into anti-IS military action, are hardly a rarity in the contemporary Middle East, let alone in Islamic history, all the way to the prophet Muhammad who oversaw the beheading of the entire man-folk of the Jewish tribe of Quraiza. Saudi Arabia, to note a prominent example, beheads people as a matter of course for a range of 'offences' including adultery, sorcery and apostasy (in the month preceding IS's beheading of two US journalists, at least 19 people were officially beheaded by the desert kingdom).[15]

It is the failure to recognize this state of affairs that accounts for the total breakdown of Obama's Middle Eastern policies. For all his appeasing outreach to Arabs and Muslims – from the avowed 'new way forward' in his inaugural speech, to awarding his first major presidential interview to the *al-Arabiya* TV network and making his first foreign speech at the Turkish parliament, to blaming the West for the region's pervasive malaise, to submissively bowing to Saudi King Abdullah in their April 2009 London meeting – Obama has failed to win the quiescence, let alone the respect and admiration of these societies. On the contrary, in line with bin Laden's gloat after the 9/11 attacks that 'when people see a strong horse and a weak horse, by nature, they will like the strong horse',[16] the president's professed humility and chest beating were viewed not as the goodwill gestures they purported to be but as shows of weakness, leading to a downward spiral of his prestige from his first days in office.

By the time of his re-election campaign in 2012, approval of Obama's policies in Muslim-majority states had plummeted, with most Middle Easterners opposed to his return to the White House (e.g., 76 per cent in Egypt, 73 per cent in Jordan, 62 per cent in Lebanon). Indeed, fewer Muslims and Arabs had a favourable opinion of the United States at the end of his first term in office than in George W. Bush's last year: 48 per cent in Lebanon (compared to 51 per cent under Bush), 19 per cent in Egypt (compared to 22 per cent) and 12 per cent in Jordan and Pakistan (compared to 19 per cent respectively under Bush).[17] That this decline took place despite Obama's greater likeability among Arabs and Muslims spoke volumes about their general disillusionment with the wide gap between his hyped rhetoric and actual performance. In the words of a Saudi academic, who had been formerly smitten with the first African American president: 'He talks too much'.[18]

Bamboozled by the Mullahs

Take Iran's quest for nuclear weapons, perhaps the foremost threat to Middle Eastern stability, if not to world peace, in the foreseeable future. In a sharp break from the Bush administration's attempts to force Tehran to abandon its nuclear weapons programme, which culminated in five UN Security Council resolutions imposing a string of escalating economic sanctions,[19] Obama opted for the road of 'engagement that is honest and grounded in mutual respect'.[20]

In his *al-Arabiya* interview, a mere week after inauguration, the new president promised that if the Iranians agreed 'to unclench their fist, they will find an extended hand from us'. Two months later, in a videotaped greeting on the occasion of the Iranian New Year, he reassured the mullahs of his absolute commitment 'to diplomacy that addresses the full range of issues before us', claiming that this 'new beginning' would win Iran substantial gains, most notably worldwide acceptance of the legitimacy of the Islamic regime derided by the Bush administration as a central plank of the 'Axis of Evil'. This, however, could only be achieved 'through peaceful actions that demonstrate the true greatness of the Iranian people and civilization. And the measure of that greatness is not the capacity to destroy, it is your demonstrated ability to build and create'.[21]

In his Cairo address, Obama amplified this message. While warning that Tehran's nuclear ambitions might trigger 'a nuclear arms race in the Middle East that could lead this region and the world down a hugely dangerous path', he made no allusion to the possibility of coercion, going out of his way to empathize with Iran's supposed sensitivities. 'I understand those who protest that some countries have weapons that others do not', he said.

> No single nation should pick and choose which nation holds nuclear weapons. And that's why I strongly reaffirmed America's commitment to seek a world in which no nations hold nuclear weapons. And any nation – including Iran – should have the right to access peaceful nuclear power if it complies with its responsibilities under the nuclear Non-Proliferation Treaty [NPT]. That commitment is at the core of the treaty, and it must be kept for all who fully abide by it. And I'm hopeful that all countries in the region can share in this goal.[22]

The framing of Iran's nuclear weapons program within the NPT context was totally misconceived since the matter at hand was one of international security rather than legality. Even if Tehran were not a signatory to the NPT, and hence legally free to develop nuclear weapons, it would still be imperative for the international community to prevent this eventuality for the simple reason that the existence of the deadliest weapons at the hands of a militant regime driven by messianic zeal and committed to the worldwide export of its radical brand of Islam would be a recipe for disaster.

To make matters worse, Obama's eagerness to demonstrate his even-handedness and goodwill to a regime that viewed the world in zero-sum terms cast him as weak and indecisive, an image that was further reinforced by the administration's kneejerk response to the Islamist regime's brutal suppression of popular protest over the rigging of the June 2009 presidential elections. That the US president, who had made a point in his inaugural address to dismiss 'those who cling to power through corruption and deceit and the silencing of dissent' as being 'on the wrong side of history', and who in his Cairo speech lectured Muslim regimes throughout the world on the duty to rule 'through consent, not coercion',[23] remained conspicuously aloof in the face of the flagrant violation of these very principles did not pass unnoticed by the mullahs. President Mahmoud Ahmadinejad demanded an American apology for its supposed meddling in the elections while Iran's supreme leader, Ayatollah Ali Khamenei, ridiculed Obama for privately courting Tehran while censuring it in public. 'The US President said that we were waiting for the day when people would take to the streets', he stated in a Friday sermon. 'At the same time they write letters saying that they want to have ties and that they respect the Islamic Republic. Which are we to believe?'[24]

Khamenei was not the only one to be baffled by Obama's double talk. In a secret memorandum to top White House officials (on 4 January 2010), Defense Secretary Robert Gates warned that 'the United States does not have an effective long-range policy for dealing with Iran's steady progress toward nuclear capability'. He was particularly alarmed by the absence of an effective strategy to prevent Tehran from amassing all the major parts of a nuclear bomb – fuel, designs and detonators – while stopping just short of assembling a fully operational weapon, thus remaining within the bounds of the NPT while becoming a 'virtual' nuclear power. 'If their policy is to go to the threshold but not assemble a nuclear weapon, how do you tell that they have not assembled?' he amplified this concern in a nationwide TV interview. 'I don't actually know how you would verify that'.[25]

Gates was similarly troubled by the lack of contingency planning for different scenarios, notably an Israeli preventive strike on Iran's nuclear facilities: 'would we help Israel, hinder it, take no action, or conduct follow-up operations (especially if Israel failed to destroy the nuclear sites)? If Iran retaliated against Israel, would we come to Israel's defense? If Iran were to hit US troops, facilities, or interests in retaliation after an Israeli strike, how would we respond?' A discussion at the White House failed to allay these concerns. 'I was put off by the way the president closed the meeting', he recalled. 'To his very closest advisors, he said, "For the record, and for those of you writing your memoirs, I am not making any decisions about Israel or Iran. Joe [Biden], you be my witness"'.[26]

It was only at the end of December 2011, following Tehran's rebuff of yet another UN resolution (1929, of 6 June 2010) and the voicing of 'serious concerns regarding possible military dimensions to Iran's nuclear program' by the International Atomic Energy Agency (IAEA), that Obama authorized harsh US sanctions that effectively crippled Tehran's oil-exporting capabilities. Yet he did so with the utmost reluctance, under heavy congressional pressure, and with the Damoclean sword of an Israeli preventive strike hovering over his head;[27] and although the European Union (EU) followed suit with similar measures that further afflicted the Iranian economy, Obama refrained from carrying the sanctions to their logical conclusion, instead offering the mullahs an olive branch upon his re-election. 'I will try to make a push in the coming months to see if we can open up a dialogue between Iran and not just us, but the international community, to see if we can get this thing resolved', he told a White House press conference. 'I can't promise that Iran will walk through the door that they need to walk through, but that would be very much the preferable option ... we want to get this resolved and we're not going to be constrained by diplomatic niceties or protocols.If Iran is serious about wanting to resolve this, they'll be in a position to resolve it'.[28]

Of course Iran had never been 'serious' about resolving the nuclear issue in a way that was remotely acceptable to the Western nations. Had this been the case, it wouldn't have poured billions of dollars into its nuclear weapons programme for decades at the expense of the economic wellbeing of ordinary Iranians and the cost of sustained international isolation. For the mullahs in Tehran, Obama's idyllic vision of a nuclear-free world meant nothing. Since their nuclear ambitions emanated from imperialist rather than defensive or prestige-related considerations, the disarmament of other nuclear powers (notably Israel) could only whet their appetite by increasing the relative edge of these weapons for the Islamic Republic's ceaseless quest for regional hegemony, if not the world mastery envisaged by its founding father, Ayatollah Ruhollah Khomeini. As he put it in his day: 'The Iranian revolution is not exclusively that of Iran, because Islam does not belong to any particular people ... We will export our revolution throughout the world because it is an Islamic revolution. The struggle will continue until the calls "there is no god but Allah and Muhammad is the messenger of Allah" are echoed all over the world'.[29]

This is not to say that the most militant and ideologically extreme regimes are not susceptible to bouts of pragmatism (not to be misconstrued for moderation!) whenever this suits their needs, and the Islamic Republic has been no exception to this rule. Hitler expanded Germany's frontiers through non-violent means for years before shedding his façade and triggering World War II by invading Poland. Stalin espoused the theory of 'socialism in one country' to help consolidate his hold on the levers of power, while Khomeini famously drank from 'the poisoned chalice' and agreed to end the eight-year Iran–Iraq war despite failing to unseat the heretic Baath regime in Baghdad.

The August 2013 inauguration of Hassan Rouhani as president clearly corresponded to this pattern. Here was a man well versed in Western thinking and ways of life (he holds a law doctorate from Glasgow Caledonian University) yet a consummate insider of the Islamist regime and its world-conquering agenda; negotiator of Iran's first nuclear accord with the West (in November 2004) who had no qualms about feigning full suspension of uranium enrichment to the international community while reassuring his constituents that 'while we were talking to the Europeans in Tehran, we were installing equipment in Isfahan'.[30]

In his address to the UN General Assembly on 24 September 2013, Rouhani continued this doublespeak. He reiterated the peaceful nature of Iran's nuclear programme while insisting on its right to continue uranium enrichment – the foremost indicator of Tehran's nuclear weapons ambitions; he lauded a final accord on Iran's nuclear programme as 'a global message of peace and security' yet conditioned its attainment on the avoidance of 'excessive demands in the negotiations by our counterparts' – the standard euphemism for international insistence on the dismantling of Tehran's enrichment programme; and he threatened that failure to reach an agreement on Tehran's terms would be detrimental to 'the economy and trade of the other parties as well as the development and security prospects of our region'. 'The people of Iran are devoted to certain principles and values at the apex of which are independence, development and national pride', he argued. 'If this obvious national fact is not understood by our negotiating partners and they commit grievous miscalculations in the process, a historic and exceptional opportunity will be lost'.[31]

For Obama, however, this was good enough. Ignoring the real gist of the speech, let alone its anti-Western invective (blaming 'the strategic blunders of the West' for transforming the Middle East 'into a haven for terrorists and extremists', Rouhani demanded a sweeping apology 'not only to the past but also to the next generation'), he promptly offered to meet the Iranian president in New York during the General Assembly's annual session. When the proposal was declined, the two leaders held a 15-minute phone conversation on 27 September – the first such high-level contact since the 1979 Islamic revolution – described by Obama as laying the 'basis for resolution' of the Iranian nuclear problem. 'President Rouhani has indicated that Iran will never develop nuclear weapons', he told reporters at the White House. 'While there will surely be important obstacles to moving forward and success is by no means guaranteed, I believe we can reach a comprehensive solution'.[32]

The nuclear talks between Iran and the P5+1 (France, Germany, Britain, Russia, China and the United States) were thus resumed in Geneva and on 24 November the two sides reached an interim nuclear agreement known as the Joint Plan of Action (JPOA), whereby Tehran agreed to curb some of its nuclear activities for a period of six months (e.g., stop enriching uranium beyond 5 per cent) so as to facilitate 'a mutually agreed long-term comprehensive solution that would ensure [that] Iran's nuclear program will be exclusively peaceful', in return for some $7 billion in sanctions relief.[33]

No sooner had the ink dried on the accord than it transpired that for the Islamist regime it was but a clever ploy to loosen the economic noose around Tehran while holding fast to its nuclear ambitions. 'In this agreement, the right of [the] Iranian nation to enrich uranium was accepted by [the] world powers', Rouhani told his subjects in a nationwide television broadcast. 'With this agreement … the architecture of sanctions will begin to break down'. This theme was echoed by numerous Iranian officials, notably Foreign Minister Mohammed Javad Zarif, Iran's chief Geneva negotiator, who insisted that while 'the structure of the sanctions and the [hostile] atmosphere that existed have collapsed, the structure of Iran's nuclear programme is preserved, and we can resume enriching uranium to 20 per cent within less than 24 hours'. '[The] Iranian enrichment program will continue and will be a part of any agreement, now and in the future', he vowed emphatically.[34]

As the JPOA was about to come into effect on 20 January 2014, after two more months of haggling during which Tehran introduced a new advanced centrifuge despite its pledge to suspend uranium enrichment, Rouhani described the accord as 'big-power surrender to the great Iranian nation' and pledged to defend Iranian rights and interests in the ensuing negotiations over the country's nuclear future.[35] And while Western commentators and diplomats whitewashed this assertion as a ploy to deflect domestic criticism, Tehran did not moderate its stance regarding the permanent settlement, thus forcing the extension of the designated negotiating period by another four months – to 24 November 2014.

And why should it have acted differently at a time when the Western powers were bending over backwards to reach an agreement even if this failed to address the problem it was designed to solve? This was evidenced inter alia by the administration's obstruction of congressional legislation authorizing new sanctions in the event of noncompliance with the JPOA; by the rapid breakdown of both Iran's diplomatic isolation and economic strangulation;[36] and by the apparent readiness to leave substantial parts of Tehran's nuclear infrastructure intact, thus allowing it to resume its nuclear weapons drive at will.[37]

Above all, despite its lip service to leaving 'all options on the table', the Obama administration not only showed a distinct lack of appetite for the military option – the ultimate catalyst of Iranian concessions – but went out of its way to forestall a preventive Israeli strike, especially in 2010–12 when it seemed to be on the cards. Later Israeli attempts to pressure the Western powers to stick to their guns in the final settlement talks by implying that the military option remained very much on the table were derisively dismissed by the administration. 'The feeling now is that Bibi's bluffing', scoffed an unnamed senior official, referring to the Israeli prime minister, Benjamin Netanyahu, by his nickname. 'It's too late for him to do anything. Two, three years ago, this was a possibility. But ultimately he couldn't bring himself to pull the trigger. It was a combination of our pressure and his own unwillingness to do anything dramatic. Now it's too late.'[38]

That a month before the lapse of the deadline for nuclear negotiations the military option could so cavalierly be dismissed sent an unmistakable message of the administration's desperation for a deal that would allow it to feign success while effectively passing the nuclear hot potato to its successor. Indeed, at a time when Netanyahu was derided as a 'coward' by unnamed White House officials and Israeli Defence Minister Ya'alon was denied audience with Vice President Biden and Secretary of State Kerry during a Washington visit, the mullahs in Tehran were reportedly mulling over an American proposal that would allow them to keep many of their enrichment centrifuges intact in return for a reduction in their stockpile of low-enriched uranium, thus prolonging the time needed for building a nuclear weapon but not eliminating this possibility altogether as demanded by the Israelis and the US president himself for that matter.[39]

And as if to dispel any doubts about his appeasing intentions, in mid-October 2014, without telling any of America's regional allies, Obama wrote a secret letter to Iran's Supreme Leader Khamenei proposing US-Iranian military collaboration against IS after the conclusion of a nuclear agreement and pledging that American military operations in Syria would not target the Tehran-propped Assad regime whose overthrow the US president had repeatedly urged – this at a time when the IAEA's director-general warned that 'we cannot provide assurance that all material in Iran is in peaceful purposes' and that 'in order to provide that assurance, Iran has to clarify the issues relating to possible military dimensions and implement the additional protocol'.[40]

The Iranian response to this overture was swift and derisive. Parliamentary speaker and former top nuclear negotiator Ali Larijani blasted Obama as a hypocrite who 'uses bullying words against Iran when he speaks to the media, but picks up a very friendly and kindly tone when he writes a letter'; a senior Rouhani advisor dismissed him as 'the weakest president the US has ever had', whose desperation for a deal had to be exploited for concluding an agreement on Tehran's terms; while Ali Shamkhani, secretary of Iran's Supreme National Security Council (SCNC), said that Khamenei informed Obama 'of the Islamic Republic's clear, transparent and firm positions on the nuclear issue and told him that Iran will not accept having an [uranium] enrichment programme that is nominal or decorative'.[41] Small wonder that the November 2014 negotiations deadline had to be extended yet again, this time for a longer period of seven months – to 24 June 2015.

Losing Turkey

Obama was no more successful in his outreach to Turkey – the other large non-Arab state and former imperial master of the Middle East – which he had made a major cornerstone of his engagement strategy. 'This is my first trip overseas as President of the United States', he told the Turkish parliament on 6 April 2009:

> I've been to the G20 summit in London, and the NATO summit in Strasbourg, and the European Union summit in Prague. Some people have asked me if I chose to continue my travels to Ankara and Istanbul to send a message to the world. And my answer is simple: Evet – yes. Turkey is a critical ally ... And Turkey and the United States must stand together – and work together – to overcome the challenges of our time.[42]

Having praised Turkey's 'strong, vibrant, secular democracy', Obama voiced unequivocal support for the country's incorporation into the European

Union – a highly contentious issue among the organization's member states. 'Let me be clear', he said:

> The United States strongly supports Turkey's bid to become a member of the European Union. We speak not as members of the EU, but as close friends of both Turkey and Europe. Turkey has been a resolute ally and a responsible partner in transatlantic and European institutions. Turkey is bound to Europe by more than the bridges over the Bosphorus. Centuries of shared history, culture, and commerce bring you together. Europe gains by the diversity of ethnicity, tradition and faith – it is not diminished by it. And Turkish membership would broaden and strengthen Europe's foundation once more.

'I know there are those who like to debate Turkey's future', he continued.

> They see your country at the crossroads of continents, and touched by the currents of history ... They wonder whether you will be pulled in one direction or another. But I believe here is what they don't understand: Turkey's greatness lies in your ability to be at the center of things. This is not where East and West divide – this is where they come together.[43]

As with his Cairo speech, Obama's reading of the historic Turkish-Western interaction and its attendant implications was disastrously flawed. Far from being a bridge between East and West, the Ottoman Empire was an implacable foe that had steadily encroached on Europe and its way of life. It is true that the nineteenth century saw numerous instances of Ottoman-European collaboration; but this was merely pragmatic manoeuvring aimed at arresting imperial decline and holding on to colonial possessions that did not prevent the Muslim empire from unleashing a prolonged orgy of bloodletting and mayhem on its rebellious European subjects – from the Greek civil war of the 1820s to the Crimean War, to the Balkan crisis of the 1870s, to the Armenian genocide of World War I.

As the twentieth century's first comprehensive ethnic cleansing and a source of inspiration for future mass murderers ('Who speaks today of the extermination of the Armenians?' Hitler famously asked his generals days before beginning World War II),[44] the Armenian genocide has become a major obstacle to Ankara's accession to the EU, as the Turkish government not only failed to acknowledge its very occurrence as demanded by the European organization but misrepresented it as a natural act of self-defence against a disloyal subject population. In the words of Yusuf Hikmet Bayur, doyen of Turkish historians: 'It's one thing to say that the Turks killed the Armenians spontaneously, and another to say that, when the Armenians revolted, the Turks, who were locked in a life or death struggle, used excessive force and killed a good many people'.[45]

In his 2008 election campaign, Obama stated that 'America deserves a leader who speaks truthfully about the Armenian Genocide and responds forcefully to all genocides. I intend to be that President'. '[T]he Armenian Genocide is not an allegation, a personal opinion, or a point of view, but rather a widely documented fact supported by an overwhelming body of historical evidence', he further argued. 'As a senator, I strongly support passage of the Armenian Genocide Resolution (H.Res.106 and S.Res.106), and as President I will recognize the Armenian Genocide'.[46]

No sooner had the presidential hopeful taken his oath of office than this pledge was all but forgotten. In his above address to the Turkish parliament Obama made no mention of genocide. Instead, putting victim and perpetrator on a par, he urged both Turks and Armenians to work 'through the past in a way that is honest, open and constructive'.[47] A year later the administration made a spirited effort to block a (nonbinding) congressional resolution branding the Armenian massacres as 'genocide', only to watch it pass by the slimmest of margins.[48] In the coming years the president continued to flaunt his election pledge. He paid the customary lip service to Armenian suffering and vowed to ensure that 'such dark chapters of human history are never again repeated'.[49] Yet he refrained from urging the Turkish government to own up to its tragic past, let alone from fulfilling his own pledge to 'recognize the Armenian genocide'.

Obama was of course not the first US president to betray the Armenians: he was actually following in the precise footsteps of his immediate predecessor, George W. Bush, whose legacy he constantly besmirched.[50] Yet his carefully contrived image as a shining human rights champion (his close confidante-made-UN-representative Samantha Power earned her stripes through a Pulitzer Prize-winning indictment of America's failure to confront genocide)[51] and the messianic euphoria attending his election (which made him the first and only person to have won the Nobel Prize on the basis of future promise rather than actual achievement) helped underscore his betrayal and dent his initial aura. Most importantly, if past presidents had shunned the Armenian issue as a quid pro quo to Turkish contribution to Western interests, Obama pandered to a regime that was openly and defiantly positioning itself in opposition to American values and interests, which in turn made his exercise in appeasement not only futile but also counterproductive.

Indeed, by the time Obama addressed the Turkish parliament, the country's 'strong and secular democracy', which he lauded as the foremost and most enduring legacy of the republic's founding father Mustafa Kemal (Atatürk), was well and truly under siege. In the seven eventful years since it won the November 2002 general elections, the Islamist Justice and Development Party (Adalet ve Kalkınma Partisi, AKP) and its hugely ambitious leader, Recep Tayyip Erdoğan, had transformed Turkey's legal system, suppressed the independent media, sterilized the political and military systems, and incarcerated hundreds of opponents and critics on the flimsiest and most dubious charges. When in June 2013 thousands of Turks took to the streets to protest their dissatisfaction with the regime, the authorities heavy-handedly suppressed the unrest, with demonstrators prosecuted for attempting to overthrow the government. Several months later the exposure of massive AKP corruption, reaching as high as cabinet ministers and Erdoğan's son, led to the purge of thousands of police officers for an attempted 'judicial coup' alongside scores of opponents in the media, parliament and the justice system.[52]

This process was not confined to the domestic front. Turkey's growing Islamization has been accompanied by an aggressive blend of anti-Western sentiments and a resurgent Neo-Ottoman hegemonic ambition to 'reintegrate the Balkan region, Middle East and Caucasus ... together with Turkey as the centre of world politics in the future' (in the words of foreign-minister-turned-prime-minister Ahmet Davutoğlu).[53] Hence the denial of Turkish territory to the 2003 Iraq invasion and to anti-IS operations eleven years later; hence Turkey's projection as a role model for Middle Eastern and Islamic societies and the championship of worldwide Islamic causes as exemplified by Erdoğan's urging of German Turks to avoid assimilation in their adoptive society and to found 'Turkish-language educational institutions throughout Germany;[54] hence Ankara's worsening relations with Greece and the bullying of Cyprus against exploiting its newly found natural gas deposits in the eastern Mediterranean; and hence the alignment with anti-Western states and organizations from Russia to Syria, to Iran, to Hamas and Hezbollah (defined by the US and the EU as terror groups).

Evolving into the staunchest international backer of its Islamist counterpart in Tehran (though the relationship was to sour when the two parties found themselves on the opposing sides of the Syrian civil war), Ankara mounted a spirited defence of the Iranian nuclear ambitions with

Erdoğan telling all nuclear weapons powers to dispense with their own arsenals before pressuring Tehran to eschew such weapons. Meanwhile, burgeoning Turkish-Iranian trade relations (which shot from $1 billion in 2000 to $10.4 billion in 2009) helped Tehran loosen the international economic noose, and in May 2010 Ankara sought to undermine the sanctions regime altogether by signing (with Brazil) a nuclear fuel swap deal that would have provided for the dispatch of low-enriched Iranian uranium to Turkey in return for fuel for one Iranian nuclear reactor.[55]

Similarly evocative has been the AKP's systematic demolition of Turkey's longtime multifaceted relationship with Israel. As early as 2004 Erdoğan accused Jerusalem of practising 'state terrorism' and two years later his wife publicly endorsed *Valley of the Wolves*, a ferociously anti-American and anti-Semitic Turkish movie. Matters came to a head between December 2008 and January 2009 when Israel, seeking to end years of rocket and missile attacks on its population centres from the Hamas-controlled Gaza Strip, launched a large-scale military operation against the terror group. In late January Erdoğan stormed out of a panel discussion with Israeli President Shimon Peres at the international economic conference in the Swiss town of Davos, having derided Israel as 'child killer', before arriving to a hero's welcome in Istanbul as 'Conqueror of Davos'.[56] Four months later bilateral relations plunged to their lowest ebb after the interception of a Turkish-sponsored flotilla attempting to break the naval blockade of Hamas (deemed legal by a UN inquiry committee)[57] under the pretence of transferring aid to Gaza's civilian population. When nine Islamist militants were killed in violent clashes with Israeli forces boarding the *Mavi Marmara* flagship, Ankara downgraded its diplomatic relations with Israel and cancelled all military co-operation with Jerusalem; the Turkish navy was ordered to 'ensure freedom of navigation' in the eastern Mediterranean at the risk of confrontation with the Israeli navy; and the Turkish air force began installing a new identification friend or foe (IFF) system on its fighting aircraft, replacing the built-in system that automatically designated Israeli jets or ships as friendly.[58]

By the time Israel and Hamas clashed again in the summer of 2014, Erdoğan had openly and habitually reverted to vile ant-Semitic rhetoric (despite an Obama-brokered official Israeli apology for the *Mavi Marmara* incident), comparing Israel's policies (indeed its raison d'être as a Jewish state) to the Nazi attempt 'to create a pure Aryan race in Germany' and threatening Turkish Jews with retribution for the supposed crimes of their coreligionists:

They kill the women so that they will not be able to give birth to Palestinian babies. They kill the babies so that they will not be able to grow up to be men. They kill the men so that they will not be able to defend their homeland. They are even afraid of babies in cribs … Rest assured that the more they kill, the more they will be afraid. The more they shed blood, the more they will drown in the blood that they shed. No cruelty lasts forever.[59]

While Ankara's growing domestic oppressiveness and foreign policy aggressiveness have attracted the odd criticism by US officials,[60] by the end of his first term in office Obama still counted Erdoğan as one of his five closest international friends and allies (alongside Germany's Merkel, Britain's Cameron, India's Singh and South Korea's Myung-bak); and it was only after the Syrian civil war had raged for over two years that he chided the Turkish leader for 'letting arms and fighters flow into Syria indiscriminately and sometimes to the wrong rebels, including anti-Western jihadists'.[61]

His pleading was to no avail. Ignoring Washington's growing frustration, Erdoğan sustained his support for the Islamist fight against the regime of his former-friend-turned-nemesis Bashar Assad (whose 2004 visit to Ankara was the first for a Syrian president in 68 years), even as IS emerged as the pre-eminent member of the anti-Assad coalition. Thus, for example, not only did the Turkish government remain conspicuously aloof vis-à-vis the slaughter of Syrian Kurds in the town of Kobane in the autumn of 2014 (though it eventually allowed some Kurdish forces to come to the aid of their brothers), but Erdoğan criticized the US for airdropping military and humanitarian supplies to the besieged Kurds.[62]

When in October 2014 Vice President Biden revealed that Erdoğan had privately conceded to erring in allowing IS-allied foreign jihadists to cross into Syria, the prime minister exploded. 'I have never said to him that we had made a mistake, never. If he did say this … then he has to apologize to us', he retorted before threatening that the vice president would become 'history for me' if he did not apologize. Biden was thus forced to offer a mea culpa in a special phone call to his 'old friend' in Ankara. 'The Vice President made clear that the United States greatly values the commitments and sacrifices made by our Allies and partners from around the world to combat the scourge of ISIL, including Turkey', read a statement issued by his office. 'The two leaders reaffirmed the importance of Turkey and the United States working closely together to confront ISIL'.[63]

Exacerbating the Arab-Israeli Conflict

If there were any illusions that the Palestinian-Israeli conflict would be the arena where Obama would be able to vindicate his Nobel Peace Prize, they were swiftly dashed as the fresh laureate seemed to be doing his utmost to make the intractable conflict truly irresolvable. By the time he took office in January 2009 Israel and the PLO had been engaged in 15 years of negotiations in the framework of the Oslo process. Within months of his inauguration the Palestinian leadership, buoyed by his sustained pressure on Israel, dropped all pretences of seeking a negotiated settlement in favour of forcing a complete Israeli withdrawal from the disputed territories without a peace agreement.

While in his 2008 election campaign the presidential hopeful went out of his way to pander to Israeli sensitivities, going so far as to endorse Jerusalem as Israel's undivided capital to the alarm of Arabs and Muslims,[64] no sooner had he entered the White House than he revealed where his true sympathies lay. In his first meeting with Prime Minister Netanyahu, three weeks before making his Cairo speech, Obama stated in plain view of the world media that the 'settlements have to be stopped in order for us to move forward', while Secretary of State Hillary Clinton clarified that the president wanted 'to see a stop to settlements – not some settlements, not outposts, not "natural growth" exceptions'. Two months later Obama dismissed the suggestion by Jewish American leaders that Israel would be more prone to risk-taking if assured of US backing and support. 'Look at the past eight years', he argued. 'During those eight years, there was no space between us and Israel, and what did we get from that? When there is no daylight, Israel just sits on the sidelines, and that erodes our credibility with the Arab states'.[65]

By way of putting the maximum daylight between his administration and Israel, Obama not only snubbed Netanyahu as a matter of course (as in a March 2010 White House meeting when he abruptly walked out on the prime minister 'to have dinner with Michelle and the girls', disallowing any photographs of the meeting and refusing a joint statement at its end),[66] but often exploited blatant anti-Israel activities, notably the international chorus of condemnation attending the May 2010 *Mavi Marmara* incident, to tighten the political noose around Jerusalem.

When on 14 June 2009 Netanyahu broke with Likud's ideological precept and agreed to the establishment of a Palestinian state provided it recognized Israel's Jewish identity, the administration did nothing to disabuse the Palestinian leadership of its adamant rejection of the idea of Jewish statehood – the root cause of the decades-long failure of the two-state solution – and instead pressured the Israeli government for a complete freeze of building activities in the West Bank and East Jerusalem. This culminated in an Israeli imposition (on 24 November 2009) of a ten-month construction freeze with a view to facilitating 'meaningful negotiations to reach a historic peace agreement that would finally end the conflict between Israel and the Palestinians'.[67]

If Netanyahu hoped that this unprecedented move would cut Israel some slack with the administration, let alone entice the Palestinian Authority (PA) into serious negotiations, he was to be bitterly disappointed. Watching the deepening schism in US-Israeli relations with undisguised glee in anticipation of substantial (and unreciprocated) concessions, the Palestinian leadership dismissed Netanyahu's acceptance of the two-state solution out of hand. Chief peace negotiator Saeb Erekat announced that the prime minister 'will have to wait 1,000 years before he finds one Palestinian who will go along with him', while Fatah, the PLO's largest constituent organization and PA President Mahmoud Abbas's alma mater, reaffirmed its longstanding commitment to the 'armed struggle' as 'a strategy, not tactic ... in the battle for liberation and for the elimination of the Zionist presence. This struggle will not stop until the Zionist entity is eliminated and Palestine is liberated'.[68]

Nor did Abbas have any qualms about walking away from the negotiating table upon the expiry of the construction moratorium in September 2010 in defiance of Obama's buoyant prediction earlier that month that peace could be achieved within a year. Asked by Netanyahu to reconsider, in return for a renewed settlement freeze and recognition of Israel as a national home for the Jewish people, the PA president reiterated his refusal to ever sign 'an agreement recognizing a Jewish state' and threatened a unilateral declaration of statehood were the talks to remain stalled.[69]

He made good on his threat in September 2011 when, in open rebuff of Jerusalem and Washington and in flagrant violation of the 1990s PLO-Israel accords that envisaged the attainment of peace through direct negotiations between the two parties, he sought to face Israel with a fait accompli by gaining UN recognition of Palestinian statehood. Having failed to garner sufficient support at the Security Council, in November 2012 Abbas obtained General Assembly recognition of Palestine as a 'non-member observer state', to the undisguised dismay of the administration which condemned the move as 'counterproductive' and an obstacle 'in the path [to] peace'.[70]

The stark warning by John Kerry, who took over from Clinton as Obama's second-term Secretary of State, that 'the window for a two-state solution is shutting … we have some period of time – a year to year-and-a-half to two years, or it's over' made no impression on the Palestinians.[71] To be sure, in apparent deference to Kerry's tireless efforts to jumpstart the stalemated talks they agreed to return to the negotiations at the end of July 2013; yet this was a rather transparent ploy to drive a wedge between Israel and the administration, which appeared to have recognized the futility of its first-term strategy and adopted a seemingly more conciliatory tone towards Jerusalem, and to lay the international groundwork for a renewed unilateral drive for UN recognition of Palestinian statehood.

This strategy bore the desired fruit before too long. When at the end of April 2014 Abbas walked out of the talks yet again, having rallied the Arab League behind his 'absolute and decisive rejection to recognizing Israel as a Jewish state' and formed a 'unity government' with Hamas, the administration blamed Israel for the debacle while the EU indicated the possible boycott of Israeli entities that operated beyond the 1967 lines.[72]

Netanyahu's acceptance of Kerry's proposal to free another 400 convicted terrorists and halt new construction activities in the West Bank as a quid pro quo for the extension of the talks for another nine months did little to redeem his tarnished image in Washington. When in July 2014 he was grudgingly drawn into a new war with Hamas that subjected most of Israel's population to constant rocket and missile attacks for seven full weeks, he was cold-shouldered by the administration, which collaborated with Hamas's foremost patrons – Turkey and Qatar – in an attempt to organize a ceasefire amenable to the terror group; endorsed the suspension of US flights to Israel, thus triggering an avalanche of suspensions that left the Jewish state briefly cut off from the rest of the world; and withheld certain weapons supplies in an attempt to rein in Israel's military operations. 'The thing about Bibi is, he's a chickenshit', complained an anonymous senior White House official. '[H]e won't do anything to reach an accommodation with the Palestinians or with the Sunni Arab states. The only thing he's interested in is protecting himself from political defeat. He's not [Yitzhak] Rabin, he's not [Ariel] Sharon, he's certainly no [Menachem] Begin. He's got no guts'.[73]

Appeasement of one's enemies at the expense of friends whose loyalty can be taken for granted is a common – if unsavoury – human trait, yet Obama seems to have taken it to unprecedented heights. So much so that during a January 2015 visit to Saudi Arabia, Qatar and Israel, a leading

US senator was told that 'it's better to be America's enemy than her friend, because she seems to respect her enemies more'.[74]

What makes this state of affairs all the more galling is that while his persistent snub of America's longest and most loyal Middle Eastern ally has bought Obama the distrust of most Israelis (at the end of the 2014 Gaza war only 4 per cent of them found him more pro-Israel than pro-Palestinian, compared to 31 per cent upon his ascension),[75] his tireless pandering to the Palestinians ('You will never have an administration as committed ... as this one', he told Abbas)[76] failed to buy him their sympathy and appreciation. On the eve of the 2012 elections a mere 9 per cent of Palestinians believed that his re-election would have a positive impact and nearly four times as many thought it would have adverse implications. And as if to add insult to injury, a comprehensive 2013 survey found Palestinians more hostile to America than any other national group, with 76 per cent considering it an enemy (compared to 1 per cent of Israelis) and only 4 per cent viewing it as a partner.[77]

So much for the ballyhooed 'new beginning between the United States and Muslims around the world'.

9. THE SPRING THAT NEVER WAS

In the early afternoon of 19 May 2011 Barack Obama made a foreign policy speech at the State Department's headquarters in Washington, D.C., in full view of the world media. Three weeks earlier the administration had killed its decade long Public Enemy No. 1, al-Qaeda founding leader Osama bin Laden, and the president was keen to tie this success to the tidal revolutionary wave that had swept across the region since December 2010, toppling in rapid succession the long-reigning Tunisian and Egyptian autocrats, Zine El Abidine Ben Ali and Hosni Mubarak, and kindling euphoric talk in the West of an 'Arab Spring' that would usher in an era of regional democratization.

'For six months, we have witnessed an extraordinary change taking place in the Middle East and North Africa', Obama effused. 'Square by square, town by town, country by country, the people have risen up to demand their basic human rights. Two leaders have stepped aside. More may follow. And though these countries may be a great distance from our shores, we know that our own future is bound to this region by the forces of economics and security, by history and by faith'.[1]

According to Obama, as inevitable corollaries of the Middle East's perennial malaise and persistent disregard of ordinary people's 'cries for a better life', these momentous events 'should not have come as a surprise'. But they did, and not only to the US administration and the Western chancelleries but also to longtime observers of the region and, indeed, to Middle Easterners themselves – both ruled and rulers. At the end of January 2011 President Bashar Assad confidently explained why the Tunisian and Egyptian upheavals would not spread to Syria, and this prognosis was echoed by the US ambassador to Damascus who asserted that 'Assad is no Qaddafi. There is little likelihood of mass atrocities. The Syrian regime will answer challenges aggressively but will try to minimize the use of lethal force'.[2] As is well known, it didn't take long for the Syrian popular protest to spiral into one of the bloodiest civil wars in the region's modern history.

The truth of the matter is that, from the outbreak of the Tunisian upheaval, Washington was reduced to the role of a hapless spectator as local demonstrations over the self-immolation of a disgruntled small town vegetable vendor snowballed into nationwide restiveness; by the time Obama condemned (on 14 January 2011) 'the use of violence against citizens peacefully voicing their opinion in Tunisia' and urged 'all parties to maintain calm and avoid violence', the crisis had blown over and Ben Ali had fled the country.[3]

Obama's impact on the subsequent Egyptian crisis was not much greater. Since the mass protest that swept the 82-year-old Mubarak from power was the culmination of long-simmering domestic problems and grievances that had little to do with extra-regional influences, there was little the US president could do beyond reacting to the rapidly unfolding events while attempting to have it both ways: to avoid being 'on the wrong side of history', a favourite Obama quip that his White House staffers never tired of repeating,[4] without alienating America's autocratic Arab allies, first and foremost the Saudi royal family. According to PA President Abbas, on 25 January, the first day of the Egyptian protests, he was contacted by Secretary of State Clinton, who asked him to phone Mubarak (whom he had met the previous day) and persuade him to step down.[5]

True or not, on 28 January Obama capitalized on Mubarak's public announcement of far-reaching reforms to reveal that he called the Egyptian president after his speech to remind him of his 'responsibility to give meaning to those words, to take concrete steps and actions that deliver on that promise' and to warn against any attempt to suppress the protest since 'all governments must maintain power through consent, not coercion'. At the same time he sought to maintain a semblance of even-handedness, pledging US commitment 'to working with the Egyptian government and the Egyptian people – all quarters – to achieve … a future that befits the heirs to a great and ancient civilization' and urging protestors 'to express themselves peacefully [since] violence and destruction will not lead to the reforms that they seek'.[6]

Four days later, however, the gloves came off. As the Egyptian president announced that he wouldn't seek re-election upon the expiry of his term in eight months' time, Obama prodded him to step down so as to initiate a 'meaningful' and 'peaceful' transition process. 'After his speech tonight,

I spoke directly to President Mubarak', he read in a televised statement from the White House.

> He recognizes that the status quo is not sustainable and that a change must take place … Through thousands of years, Egypt has known many moments of transformation.The voices of the Egyptian people tell us that this is one of those moments; this is one of those times. Now, it is not the role of any other country to determine Egypt's leaders. Only the Egyptian people can do that. What is clear – and what I indicated tonight to President Mubarak – is my belief that an orderly transition must be meaningful, it must be peaceful, and it must begin now.[7]

While this abrupt and very public betrayal of one of America's staunchest regional allies at a critical moment in his quest for survival was to come under scathing criticism, especially after the Egyptian revolution failed to meet Western expectations of democratization, it was effectively little more than a quintessential Obama grandstanding aimed at taking credit for events he had not set in train and over which he had no control. As Zbigniew Brzezinski, President Carter's National Security Advisor and onetime Obama foreign affairs mentor, put it: 'I greatly admire his insights and understanding. I don't think he really has a policy that's implementing those insights and understandings. The rhetoric is always terribly imperative and categorical: "You must do this", "He must do that", "This is unacceptable" … [But] he doesn't strategize. He sermonizes'.[8]

Sermonizing was very much in evidence in Obama's 19 May speech. While stressing the need for 'a sense of humility' given that 'it's not America that put people into the streets of Tunis or Cairo – it was the people themselves who launched these movements, and it's the people themselves that must ultimately determine their outcome', he had no qualms about lecturing local leaders how to conduct themselves in the face of the regional turbulence. 'The Syrian people have shown their courage in demanding a transition to democracy', he categorically stated, as if the Damascus dictator was taking his marching orders from Washington. 'President Assad now has a choice: He can lead that transition, or get out of the way. The Syrian government must stop shooting demonstrators and allow peaceful protests. It must release political prisoners and stop unjust arrests. It must allow human rights monitors to have access to cities like Dara'a; and start a serious dialogue to advance a democratic transition'.[9]

In the coming years Obama was to reiterate this refrain ad nauseam while at the same time shunning real measures to facilitate its implementation. Time and again he warned Assad that the use of chemical weapons against the civilian population or the transfer of such weapons to 'the wrong people' (i.e. Hezbollah) would constitute a 'red line' that could trigger a harsh American military response, only to be repeatedly rebuffed.[10] Even after the regime's gassing to death of over 1,000 of its rebellious subjects forced Obama to announce (on 31 August 2013) his intention to seek congressional authorization for a punitive air strike he went out of his way to clarify that the move was not aimed at toppling the Syrian dictator. 'This would not be an open-ended intervention', he stated. 'We would not put boots on the ground. Instead, our action would be designed to be limited in duration and scope. But I'm confident we can hold the Assad regime accountable for their use of chemical weapons, deter this kind of behavior, and degrade their capacity to carry it out'.[11] And although Assad's acceptance of a Russian proposal for the dismantling of Syria's chemical weapons arsenal allowed Obama to call off the strike while claiming victory, the incident not only ensured the survival of the Syrian regime for as long as it feigned compliance with the Russian deal but it effectively gave Assad carte blanche to continue slaughtering his citizens so long as this was done with conventional (but not chemical) weapons. Indeed, with US-Soviet relations ebbing sharply over the 2014 Ukraine crisis, and IS becoming the foremost international scourge after its public execution of a few Western hostages, the ongoing Syrian bloodbath has fallen off the Western radar, allowing Assad to resume chemical attacks on its subjects with impunity, and with Secretary of State Kerry expressing readiness to talk with the Syrian dictator to stem the violence.[12]

Libyan Intervention

The glaring discrepancy between Obama's hyped rhetoric and actual timidity was also on display during the Libyan crisis of 2011. While on 3 March, a fortnight after the eruption of Libyan violence, the president stated with his usual 'imperative and categorical' pomp that 'Muammar Gaddafi has lost the legitimacy to lead and he must leave',[13] he left it to his Paris and London peers to orchestrate the international intervention on behalf of the fledgling uprising with Washington 'leading from behind'. Those were the euphoric days of the 'Arab Spring' and Western leaders expected Qaddafi to follow in the footsteps of his ill-fated counterparts in Tunis and Cairo without delay. When the colourful Libyan dictator would not act the script and step down, British Prime Minister David Cameron and French President Nicolas Sarkozy exploited Obama's hesitancy to organize the first – and only – Western military attempt to sway the 'Arab Spring' in its desired direction. This expanded, in a classic case of mission creep, from a UN-sanctioned arms embargo (26 February 2011) to the establishment of a no-fly zone for Libyan military aviation (17 March), to a massive bombing campaign 'to defend the lives of the Libyan people', to a straightforward effort to topple Qaddafi.[14] As Obama, Cameron and Sarkozy put it in a joint *New York Times* article: 'Our duty and our mandate under U.N. Security Council Resolution 1973 is to protect civilians, and we are doing that. It is not to remove Qaddafi by force. But it is impossible to imagine a future for Libya with Qaddafi in power … It is unthinkable that someone who has tried to massacre his own people can play a part in their future government … It would be an unconscionable betrayal'.[15]

Lost in this self-righteous interventionist craze (which, incidentally, was strongly opposed by Vice President Biden, Chairman of the Joint Chiefs-of-Staff Mullen and Defense Secretary Gates, who even thought of resigning over the issue)[16] was the realization that its very occurrence indicated that Libyans were far less keen to see the back of their unelected ruler than were their Tunisian and Egyptian counterparts. For it was not the regime's military and security prowess – a far cry from many of its Arab/Muslim counterparts – that enabled it to crush the uprising and withstand the assault of a vastly superior international coalition for a full eight months. Rather, it was its solid grounding in Libya's tribal society and the opposition's lack of sufficient popular support. Indeed, for all its eccentricities, Qaddafi's rule had been rather benign by Middle Eastern standards, with regime-occasioned deaths ranging in the thousands rather than the hundreds of thousands; even the affable and thoroughly westernized King Hussein of Jordan, internationally acclaimed for his peaceable and moderate conduct, slaughtered more people in the course of a single month ('Black September' 1970) than Qaddafi probably did during his entire 42-year rule.

Nor for that matter did the Western-supported rebels espouse greater respect for human rights or compassion for their compatriots than the regime they strove to supplant. On the contrary, from the outset the uprising was marred by wholesale abuse of the population it was supposed to liberate, including extrajudicial executions, mass detentions, systematic torture and rape, lynching, beheadings and looting. Men, women and children were snatched from their homes, workplaces and checkpoints or simply from the streets; many were beaten with sticks and rifle butts, kicked, punched and insulted, at times while blindfolded and handcuffed.

Black Libyans and Sub-Saharan Africans were singled out for special persecution. Many victims were found with hands tied behind their backs and bullets through their skulls; others had been burned alive. Entire cities and towns were ethnically cleansed of their black population; some 500,000 African migrant workers fled the country.[17] This was accompanied by pervasive manifestations of anti-Semitism, with rebel propaganda and literature employing classic anti-Semitic themes and images in an attempt to magnify the uprising and depict Qaddafi as a 'Zionist stooge'. When an exiled Libyan Jewish doctor, who had treated rebels suffering from post-traumatic stress disorder during the uprising, attempted after the fall of the regime to reopen Tripoli's synagogue as a prelude to a historic reconciliation between the country's exiled Jewish community and its former compatriots, demonstrations broke out in Tripoli and Benghazi with an angry mob storming his hotel to demand his immediate deportation.[18]

That these atrocities passed virtually unmentioned by the international community reflected the coalition's reluctance to concede the false premise not only of its military intervention, designed as it was to protect Libyans from a repressive leader rather than deliver them to new predatory rulers, but also of the underlying ideal of the 'Arab Spring'. For if anything, the events in Libya followed a pattern of militant Islamization that was to become the norm in countries affected by the popular upheavals. Millions of television viewers throughout the world could see hordes of Libyan rebels kneeling in prayer before rushing to battle to the chants of 'Allahu Akbar', religious insignia adorning their combat vehicles; yet journalists, politicians, state officials and intellectuals kept insisting, against all available evidence, on the revolt's secular, democratic nature.

Qaddafi's repeated warnings of the uprising's predominantly Islamist impetus were thus dismissed; displays of religious zealotry among rebels, notably the Libyan Islamic Fighting Group (LIFG) with its history of combat in Afghanistan and close al-Qaeda collaboration, were wilfully ignored, as were reports of the transfer of captured weaponry to Islamist terror groups outside Libya (e.g., Hamas in Gaza); and the rebellion's endorsement by Islamist groups, including al-Qaeda, was thoroughly whitewashed.[19] When in February 2011 the Muslim Brotherhood's spiritual guide, Yusuf Qaradawi, issued a fatwa obliging Libyan soldiers to assassinate Qaddafi, CNN reassured its audience that 'there is little or no overt presence of the

Brotherhood in Benghazi'; that 'in the end, the reach of the Brotherhood may be most limited by the emergence of secular forces at the forefront of the rebel movement'; and that even this limited influence was not to be feared since, 'like their counterparts in Egypt, they would embrace multiparty democracy'.[20]

As it would transpire before too long, the Muslim Brothers had no intention whatsoever to embrace multiparty democracy. To be sure, having emerged from decades of Nasserite repression as a regular parliamentary opposition group rather than a revolutionary movement, they left the violent quest for an Islamic order to their non-Egyptian branches as well as to splinter Egyptian militant groups such as *al-Takfir wa-l-Hijra* (Excommunication and Hijra), *al-Gamaat al-Islamiya* (the Muslim Associations) and *Tanzim al-Jihad* (Organization of the Jihad), which on 6 October 1981 assassinated President Sadat and made an abortive attempt to trigger a nationwide revolt by capturing the southern town of Asyut. Yet this pragmatism meant no ideological moderation. No sooner had the Brothers won the post-Mubarak 2012 presidential elections than they embarked on an ambitious effort to Islamize Egyptian society and its political system, with President Muhammad Mursi plotting far-reaching constitutional reforms giving the head of state sweeping powers. And while Mursi was overthrown in a widely supported military coup on 3 July 2013, after a mere year in power, his downfall reflected popular disenchantment with his crass, impatient and incompetent leadership rather than disillusionment with the Islamist ideal, let alone a drift to secularization or Western-type democratization. Indeed, Field Marshal Abdel Fattah Sisi, the coup's perpetrator and subsequently elected Egyptian president, is a deeply devout person (despite his brutal suppression of the Muslim Brotherhood and public outburst against radical Islam), as was Anwar Sadat and many of the officers who had run the country since their 1952 'revolution'.[21]

At any rate, the expectations of Egypt's swift democratization were reduced to grudging acquiescence in the continuation of the decades-long military dictatorship and its ruthlessly enforced stability. Even the Obama administration, which stubbornly stuck to the ill-fated Muslim Brotherhood's regime, condemned its overthrow and demanded that the Egyptian military 'move quickly and responsibly to return full authority back to a democratically elected civilian government as soon as possible',[22] was quickly brought into line by Sisi, who rebuffed its military and economic pressures and indicated his readiness to mend relations with Moscow, Cairo's foremost international ally until the mid-1970s.

Springtime Delusions

Reluctant to concede that the upheavals had never been the celebrated 'Arab Spring' they were taken for, Western observers massively downplayed the significance of this Islamist surge, whether by denying its very occurrence (as with the administration's astounding mischaracterization of the Muslim Brotherhood as 'largely secular,'[23] which perhaps helps explain its warm endorsement of their rule) or by attributing it to the Islamists' organizational superiority and the secularists' failure to provide compelling alternatives at both the ideological and personal levels, or by predicting the Islamists' inevitable moderation due to their newly assumed governing responsibilities.[24]

In his 19 May speech, Obama portrayed the 'Arab Spring' as a regional antithesis to Islamism in general, and to the militant brand offered by Osama bin Laden and his ilk in particular. 'Bin Laden and his murderous vision won some adherents,' he argued. 'But even before his death, al-Qaeda was losing its struggle for relevance, as the overwhelming majority of people saw that the slaughter of innocents did not answer their cries for a better life. By the time we found bin Laden, al-Qaeda's agenda had come to be seen by the vast majority of the region as a dead end, and the people of the Middle East and North Africa had taken their future into their own hands.'[25] Small wonder, then, that when a year later al-Qaeda affiliates attacked the US consulate in the Libyan city of Benghazi on the eleventh anniversary of 9/11, killing Ambassador J. Christopher Stevens and three other Americans, the administration responded with customary obfuscation. Ignoring both the attack's deliberate timing and a Libyan forewarning of its imminence,[26] UN Ambassador Susan Rice described the incident as a spontaneous protest over a US-made anti-Muslim video clip that spun out of control, while White House Press Secretary Jay Carney argued that 'we don't have and did not have concrete evidence to suggest that [the attack] was not in reaction to the film'. Obama tacitly amplified this misrepresentation a day after the attack ('We reject all efforts to denigrate the religious beliefs of others. But there is absolutely no justification to this type of senseless violence'), becoming more explicit in a UN address a fortnight later: 'I have made it clear that the United States government had nothing to do with this video ... [Yet] there is no video justifying an attack on an Embassy'.[27]

Likewise, when the Libyan rebels' interim leader announced upon Qaddafi's demise that the country's legislative and banking systems would be governed by Islamic law (or *Sharia*), French philosopher

Bernard-Henry Lévy, perhaps the most vociferous proponent of the international intervention, quickly downplayed the significance of this statement. 'There is sharia, and then there is sharia', he argued. 'And the whole problem amounts to knowing what … is included in this term: the stoning of adulteresses, as in Iran? The amputation of thieves' limbs, as in Saudi Arabia? Or rather a sum of moral precepts one strives to combine with the Napoleonic Code, as is the case in Egypt? … France went through the Terror, the Restoration, two Empires and several blood baths before it was able to embody the republican ideal of 1789, and after that the ideal of a secular society', he reasoned. 'And we expect Libya, itself, to pass from a dark night into light?'[28]

Of course the enshrinement of the Sharia as Egypt's 'main source of all state legislation' has had nothing to do with the desire to combine Islamic moral precepts with 'the Napoleonic Code'. Quite the reverse, in fact: it has sought to keep the country's millenarian Islamic legacy at arm's length from Western corrupting influences, of which the Napoleonic invasion – one of the most ostentatious modern-day Western encroachments on Muslim lands – is a potent symbol. And just there, no doubt, lay the crux of the matter. For Western observers, the passage 'from a dark night into light' that was the 'Arab Spring' meant transition to a liberal, secular democracy.[29] For Middle Easterners it meant a return to the Islamic sociopolitical order that had underpinned the region for over a millennium as the schizophrenic state system established in its place after World War I failed to fill the void left by its destruction.

With Islam making no distinction between temporal and religious powers, and Muslim populations unaffected by the secularization and modernization processes undergone by their Western counterparts since the late 1700s, Middle Eastern societies (and for that matter, Muslim communities throughout the world) have remained deeply devout to this very day. So much so that the avowedly secularist doctrine of pan-Arabism, which dominated inter-Arab relations for most of the twentieth century, was inextricably linked with Islam, the religion that the Arabs had given to the world and had practised for longer than anyone else. In the words of a prominent pan-Arab ideologue and practitioner: '[Arab] "nationalism" springs from the Muslim feeling of brotherhood enjoined on them by the Prophet Muhammad in his last public speech'.[30] Hence the introduction of religious provisions into the Syrian and Iraqi constitutions by the secularist, pan-Arab Syrian and Iraqi Baath parties and hence the enshrinement of Islam as 'the official religion in Palestine' and of the Sharia as 'the main source of legislation' by the PLO's 2003 draft constitution of the prospective

Palestinian state.[31] Even the constitution of post-Saddam Iraq, drafted under the watchful eye of the occupying American forces, established Islam as the state religion and 'a fundamental source of legislation', prohibiting any laws contradicting 'the established provisions of Islam'.[32]

Nor has this phenomenon been confined to the Arab states. In Afghanistan, the Taliban are poised to regain power after the withdrawal of foreign forces despite a decade-and-a-half-long US-led military, economic and political effort to prevent such an eventuality. In Iran, the clerics became key political players already in the Safavid Empire (1501–1722) and the process reached its apogee under the Qajar dynasty (1795–1925), where they controlled the religious, judicial and educational institutions, cultivated ties with bazaar merchants and artisans, and exploited the collapse of the powerful group of local administrators (*sayyeds*) to amass fabulous wealth. The clerics suffered a major setback under the Pahlavi dynasty (1925–79), which sought to turn Iran into a modern secularized state, yet they quickly monopolized the January 1979 revolution that overthrew Shah Mohammed Reza Pahlavi, transforming Iran in short order into an Islamic republic. And while the Islamist regime has apparently lost much of its popular appeal over the years, as evidenced by the mass protests on the thirtieth anniversary of the takeover of the American embassy in Tehran, this has mostly to do with such factors as its oppressive ruling style, economic mismanagement, and political corruption and cronyism (the rigging of the June 2009 presidential elections triggered the mass protests) rather than a yearning for Western-style secular democracy.

Even Turkey, which has gone further than any of its Middle Eastern counterparts to secularize and westernize its sociopolitical system, has remained effectively Islamic in its ethos. Although the 1923 constitution stipulated the equality of all Turks before the law and while the Turkish Republic's founding father, Mustafa Kemal (Atatürk), went to great lengths to extricate the country from its Islamic past – including the abolition of the caliphate and non-designation of Islam as state religion, the ending of the millet system that had regulated the lives of non-Muslims in the Ottoman Empire, and the prohibition of the public wearing of religious attire – modern Turkish nationalism has remained as ethnically and religiously exclusionary as before. In the words of historian Bernard Lewis, 'One may speak of Christian Arabs – but a Christian Turk is an absurdity and a contradiction in terms. Even today, after thirty-five years of the secular Republic, a non-Muslim in Turkey may be called a Turkish citizen, but never a Turk'.[33]

Non-Muslims thus found themselves as inferior in Atatürk's secularist republic as they had been under Ottoman imperial rule. Lacking institutionalized legal standing, they face numerous difficulties: from obtaining places and freedom of worship designated and registered by the government, to running their own affairs, asserting (expropriated) property rights and ownership, training their clergy, and educating their followers and children (Turkish legislation provides no private higher religious education for non-Muslims, and there are no such opportunities in the public education system).[34] And this unhappy state of affairs has taken a distinct downward turn over the past decade with the AKP's systematic dismantling of Atatürk's secularist state and international vision.[35] So much so that a January 2015 survey found 55 per cent of Turks (66 per cent among AKP voters) convinced that Islam was still the target of Crusades, with 20 per cent of them supportive of the use of violence in the name of Islam. Asked who the real victims of the *Charlie Hebdo* terror attack were, only one in five said it was the murdered Frenchmen while three out of four claimed it was Muslims – in Europe and throughout the world.[36]

Against this backdrop, it was only natural for the toppled pan-Arab autocracies to be supplanted by Islamists of all hues and colours, and not only in Egypt and Tunisia, which saw the advent (and subsequent decline) of elected Islamist governments. In Morocco, Islamists won the largest number of parliamentary seats in the November 2011 elections, nearly twice as many as their main rivals; in Syria, not only have Islamists played the key role in the anti-Assad revolt (as they did against his father in the late 1970s and early 1980s), but the struggle has quickly snowballed into a religious war (that has partly spilled over to Lebanon) between the minority Alawite regime and its Shiite backers, Tehran and its Lebanese sidekick Hezbollah, and a Sunni rebel coalition supported by Turkey and the Gulf monarchies and spearheaded by a myriad of militant Islamist groups;[37] and in Yemen, where President Ali Abdullah Saleh stepped down in February 2012 after 33 years in power, Islamist violence, including by al-Qaeda, has become a commonplace with the Islamic Republic of Iran making substantial inroads into the country's sociopolitical fabric through political outreach and arms shipments to Shiite rebel groups, notably the Houthis, who by early 2015 had captured the capital of Sanaa, toppled the central government, dissolved parliament and announced the formation of a new government.[38]

Even Libya has been a far cry from the showcase Western-propped democratized society it was supposed to become, as the collapse of the

Qaddafi regime that had skilfully kept the country's disparate components intact for 42 years gave way to general anarchy with a multitude of (mainly Islamist) militias controlling various parts of the country and vying for power with the central government. This deteriorated in the summer of 2014 into a fully fledged civil war as the Islamists contested the army's dissolution of parliament (which had enforced sharia law in December 2013) and the elections for the successor legislature in which they suffered a crushing defeat. Deriding the new parliament as dominated by Qaddafi loyalists, in early July 2014 the Islamists launched a major assault, codenamed Operation Libya Dawn, on the country's two foremost cities, capturing Benghazi by the end of the month and seizing Tripoli, the national capital, a few weeks later, convening their own legislature there.[39] And while the government had regained control of much of Benghazi by the end of the year, it has yet to enforce its authority throughout the province, where IS has reportedly established a firm foothold,[40] let alone the entire country. But even in the unlikely event that it did, this will hardly mean a shift to democracy as the National Forces Alliance, which defeated the Islamist Justice and Construction Party in the February 2012 elections to become Libya's largest parliamentary faction (before being eclipsed by the Islamists a year later), had promised to make sharia 'the main inspiration for legislation' and went out of its way to rebut the liberal label attached to it by Western observers. In the words of its spokesman: 'The concepts of "liberal" and "secular" simply don't exist in Libyan society'.[41]

And so it goes. Four years after invading Libya under the pretext of saving lives and putting the country on the road to democracy, the Western powers have been reduced (yet again) to passive spectators of the country's descent to greater savagery, higher death toll and pervasive anarchy. With neighbouring Egypt under the same autocratic rule as it had been prior to the 2011 revolution; Yemen overtaken by Islamist Shiite militants; Syria fragmented into several sub-states and Iraq on the verge of disintegration; the Islamist regime in Tehran as committed as ever to its world-conquering agenda and the attainment of nuclear weapons; Islamist Turkey bent on renewed imperial glory; and a string of militant Islamist groups controlling vast tracts of land throughout the region, the Western pipedream of 'a massive opportunity to spread peace, prosperity, democracy and vitally security' (to use Prime Minister Cameron's description of the 'Arab Spring')[42] has been replaced by the grim realization that, if anything, the region is sprinting Back to the Future and there is absolutely nothing the Western nations can do to reverse it.

EPILOGUE

Whether they would admit it or not – and Middle Easterners have always found it easier to blame others for their misfortunes – the main culpability for the region's endemic malaise lies with the local players. That Arabs have been fighting Jews, Iranians, Kurds and fellow Arabs for decades has had nothing to do with external intervention and everything to do with a host of indigenous factors, from religious militancy to ethnic cleavages, to economic and territorial greed, to hegemonic ambitions. Violence was not imported to the Middle East as a by-product of foreign imperialism but has rather been an integral part of the region's millenarian political culture.

In a widely covered address (in February 2015) Barack Obama derided the Islamic State (IS), the militant group that had conquered vast tracts of Iraq and Syria and proclaimed itself a caliphate, as 'a brutal, vicious death cult that, in the name of religion, carries out unspeakable acts of barbarism'. Yet he cautioned his fellow Americans that 'lest we get on our high horse and think this is unique to some other place, remember that during the Crusades and the Inquisition, people committed terrible deeds in the name of Christ'.[1]

What the president forgot to mention, however, is that while the numerous atrocities committed in the name of Christianity throughout the ages were antithetical to that faith's doctrinal precepts, Islam has been inextricably linked with violence from the outset. For although Christianity's universal vision is no less sweeping than that of its great monotheistic rival, its universalism was conceived in purely spiritual terms that made a clear distinction between God and Caesar. Islam, by contrast, has never distinguished between temporal and religious powers, which were combined in the person of Muhammad.

Having fled his hometown of Mecca to Medina in 622 CE to become a political and military leader rather than a private preacher, the prophet spent the last ten years of his life fighting to unify Arabia under his rule. Indeed, he devised the concept of jihad, 'exertion in the path of Allah', as a means of enticing his local followers to raid Meccan caravans, instantaneously transforming a common tribal practice into a supreme religious duty and the primary vehicle for Islam's millenarian expansion. As he stated in his farewell address: 'I was ordered to fight all men until they say, "There is no god but Allah"'.[2]

If Christendom was slower than Islam in marrying religious universalism with political imperialism, it was faster in shedding both notions. By the eighteenth century the West had lost its religious messianism, and by the midtwentieth century had lost its imperial ambitions. Islam has retained its imperialist ambitions to date. The last great Muslim empire may have been destroyed and the caliphate left vacant, but the longing for unfettered suzerainty, though tempered and qualified in different places and at different times, has never disappeared, and has resurfaced in our own day with a vengeance.

Nor is this world-conquering vision confined to such extremist groups as the Islamic State, al-Qaeda, Hezbollah or Hamas. To this day, many Muslims and Arabs unabashedly pine for the restoration of Muslim Spain and consider their 1492 expulsion from the country a grave historical injustice, as if they were Spain's rightful owners and not former colonial occupiers of a remote foreign land, thousands of miles from their ancestral homeland. Indeed, as immigration, conversion and higher rates of childbirth have greatly increased the number of Muslims within Europe itself over the past several decades, Islamists have increasingly envisaged the continent's looming surrender to the House of Islam. In the words of Yusuf Qaradawi, a spiritual guide of the Muslim Brotherhood and one of today's most influential Islamic thinkers, whose views are promulgated to millions of Muslims worldwide through the media and the internet: 'Islam will return to Europe as a conqueror and victor, after being expelled from it twice – once from the South, from Andalusia, and a second time from the East, when it knocked several times on the door of Athens'. And the late Zaki Badawi, a doyen of interfaith dialogue in Britain, set his sights much higher: 'Islam is a universal religion. It aims to bring its message to all corners of the earth. It hopes that one day the whole of humanity will be one Muslim community'.[3]

This grandiose agenda continues to meet with condescension and denial on the part of Western decision-makers and public opinion shapers, and none more so than the US current administration – the would-be leader of the 'free world'. The subtler, but infinitely more significant plank of the agenda – the gradual takeover of Western societies through demographic growth and steady conversion by 'an army of preachers and teachers who will present Islam in all languages and in all dialects' (to use Qaradawi's words) – has been virtually ignored. Its more militant version, though massively acknowledged at times (e.g., 9/11, the 2005 London bombings, the 2015 Paris and Copenhagen attacks), has been euphemized as 'violent extremism' stemming from socioeconomic and political grievances rather than from a millenarian religiously based political legacy. Hence the US administration's stubborn adherence to the anachronistic term the Islamic State of Iraq and the Levant (ISIL), long after its substitution by the Islamic State (IS), in an attempt to disguise the real scope of the group's ambitions and its conformity with Islam's fundamental precept of unifying the worldwide community of believers (*umma*). As President Obama put it: 'Al-Qaeda and ISIL and groups like it are desperate for legitimacy. They try to portray themselves as religious leaders – holy warriors in defense of Islam. That's why ISIL presumes to declare itself the "Islamic State".'[4]

Of course the Islamic State is hardly the sole Middle Eastern entity identifying as such. Israel excepted, all regional states are legally, politically, culturally and socially Islamic, while some are straightforward theocracies. Saudi Arabia, to mention a prominent example, is predicated on the extremist Wahhabi doctrine (the wellspring of numerous 'violent extremist' groups), preaching a return to the 'unspoiled' Islam of the seventh century, while Iran is an Islamic Republic avowed to the world-conquering vision of its founding father, Ayatollah Ruhollah Khomeini, which hasn't hesitated to sacrifice hundreds of thousands of its subjects on this altar or to spend tens of billions of dollars on the acquisition of nuclear weapons designed to promote this goal.

To deny this reality is the height of folly, and to imagine that it can be appeased or deflected through such magic potions as 'more democracy', 'a global effort against corruption' or investment in 'the education and skills and job training that our extraordinary young people need' (to use Obama's words)[5] is to play into its hands. It is only when the Western chancelleries break out of their delusional bubble and acknowledge the Manichean and irreconcilable nature of the challenge posed by their Islamist adversaries that their policies will stand the slightest chance of success. Until that happens, not only will Middle Eastern and Muslim societies remain as impervious to external influences as they have been for generations, but their impact on European societies will correspondingly grow.

NOTES

Introduction

1   'Kerry aides checked by security at Egyptian presidential palace', Reuters, 22 July 2014; 'Egyptian media applaud tough security check on John Kerry', BBC News, 23 July 2014.

2   The White House, Office of the Press Secretary, 'Statement by the Press Secretary on the Conviction of Journalists in Egypt', 23 June 2014; 'John Kerry "wanded" by security guards at Egypt's presidential palace', *Guardian*, 24 July 2014; 'Joe Biden Apologizes For Saying Turkey Admitted To Border Security Failures In ISIS Fight', *Huffington Post*, 4 October 2014.

3   Yehuda Blanga, 'Should Washington Withhold Aid to Egypt?' *Middle East Quarterly*, autumn 2014; The White House, Office of the Press Secretary, 'Readout of the President's Call with Egyptian President al-Sisi', 10 June 2014; Jay Solomon, 'John Kerry Voices Strong Support for Egyptian President Sisi', *Wall Street Journal*, 22 June 2014.

4   See, for example, Pew Research Global Attitudes Project, 'Global Opinion of Obama Slips, International Policies Faulted', 13 June 2012.

Chapter 1

1   L. Carl Brown, *International Politics and the Middle East* (London: Tauris, 1984), p. 5.

2   See, for example, George Antonius, *The Arab Awakening* (London: Hamish Hamilton, 1938); Arnold Toynbee, 'The Present Situation in Palestine', *International Affairs*, January 1931, p. 40; Barbara Tuchman, *The Guns of August* (New York: Dell, 1962), p. 161; Bernard Lewis, *The Middle East: 2000 Years of History from the Rise of Christianity to the Present Day* (London: Weidenfeld & Nicolson, 1995), pp. 342–3; Albert Hourani, *A History of the Arab Peoples* (London: Faber, 1991); George Lenczowski, *The Middle East in World Affairs*, 4th ed. (Ithaca: Cornell University Press, 1980), pp. 58–9, 79–87; Roger Owen, *State, Power and Politics in the Making of the Modern Middle East* (London: Routledge, 1992), especially chapters 1 and 4; David Fromkin, *A Peace to*

End All Peace: The Fall of the Ottoman Empire and the Creation of the Modern Middle East (New York: Avon, 1990), pp. 17, 19, 565; Edward W. Said, *Orientalism: Western Conceptions of the Orient*, reprinted with a new afterward (London: Penguin, 1995), p. 220; Amin Said, *al-Thawra al-Arabiyya al-Kubra* (Cairo: Isa al-Babi al-Halabi, 1951); Suleiman Musa, *al-Haraka al-Arabiyya: Sirat al-Marhala al-Ula li-l-Nahda al-Arabiyya al-Haditha, 1908–1924* (Beirut: Dar al-Nahar, 1970); Zeine N. Zeine, *The Emergence of Arab Nationalism with a Background Study of Arab-Turkish Relations in the Near East*, 2nd rev. ed. (Beirut: Khayat's, 1966); Abu Khaldun Sati Husri, *Yawm Maisalun: Safha min Tarikh al-Arab al-Hadith*, rev. ed. (Beirut: Dar al-Ittihad, 1964); Zaki Hazem Nuseibeh, *The Ideas of Arab Nationalism* (Ithaca: Cornell University Press, 1956); Zeine N. Zeine, *The Emergence of Arab Nationalism with a Background Study of Arab-Turkish Relations in the Near East*, 2nd rev. ed. (Beirut: Khayat's, 1966).

3   The discussion in this chapter draws on Efraim Karsh and Inari Karsh, *Empires of the Sand: the Struggle for Mastery in the Middle East 1789–1923* (Cambridge: Harvard University Press, 1999).

4   For general studies of the Eastern Question see: M.S. Anderson, *The Eastern Question 1774–1923* (London: Macmillan 1966); J.A.R. Marriott, *The Eastern Question: An Historical Study in European Diplomacy*, 2nd rev. ed. (Oxford: Clarendon Press, 1918); A.L. Macfie, *The Eastern Question 1774–1923* (Essex: Longman Group UK, 1989); Edouard Driault, *Question d'Orient depuis ses origines jusqu'à nos jours*, 4ième éd. refondue (Paris: Felix Alcan, 1909); Albert Sorel, *La Question D'Orient au XVIIIe siècle* (Paris: E. Plon et Cie, 1878); Allan Cunningham, *Anglo-Ottoman Encounters in the Age of Revolution & Eastern Questions in the Nineteenth Century*, ed. Edward Ingram (London: Frank Cass, 1993).

5   Dufferin to Granville, 24 June 1882, FO 78/3397, No. 168; Granville to Dufferin, 25 June 1882, FO 78/3395, No. 302; Dudley W.R. Bahlman (ed.), *The Diary of Sir Edward Walter Hamilton, 1880–1885* (Oxford: Clarendon Press, 1972), vol. 1, pp. 208, 212, 297.

6   A.J.P. Taylor, *The Struggle for Mastery in Europe 1848–1919* (Oxford: Oxford University Press, 1971), p. 90.

7   See, for example, Ronald Robinson and John Gallagher, with Alice Denny, *Africa and the Victorians: The Official Mind of Imperialism* (London: Macmillan, 1981), p. 159; Hourani, *A History of the Arab Peoples*, p. 283.

8   Karsh and Karsh, *Empires of the Sand*, chapter 4.

9   Michael B. Oren, *Power, Faith and Fantasy: America in the Middle East 1776 to the Present* (New York: Norton, 2007), p. 325. For earlier versions of this misconception see, for example: Feroz Ahmad, 'The Late Ottoman Empire', in Marian Kent (ed.), *The Great Powers and the End of the Ottoman Empire* (London: Frank Cass, 1996), p. 15; Elie Kedourie, *Politics in the Middle East* (Oxford: Oxford University Press, 1992), p. 93; Malcolm Yapp, *The Making of the Modern Middle East 1792–1923* (London: Longmans, 1987), p. 266; Howard M. Sachar, *The Emergence of the Middle East 1914–1924* (London: Allen Lane, 1970), p. 32; Fromkin, *A Peace to End All Peace*, pp. 48–50; John DeNovo, *American Interests and Policies in the Middle East 1900–1939* (Minneapolis: University of Minnesota Press, 1963), p. 90.

10 Grey to Beaumont, 16 August 1914, 'Correspondence Respecting Events Leading to the Rupture of Relations with Turkey, Presented to Both Houses of Parliament by Command of His Majesty', November 1914, Cmd. 7628, no. 17, p. 5; Grey to Mallet, 18 August 1914, *ibid.*, no. 21, p. 7; Mallet to Grey, 21 August 1914, *ibid.*, no. 27, p. 9; Sazonov to Giers, 23 August 1914, in *Ministère des Affaires Étrangères, Recueil de Documents Diplomatiques, Négociations ayant précédé la guerre avec la Turquie 19 juillet (1 août) – 19 octobre (1 novembre) 1914* (Petrograd, 1915), no. 34.

11 Arnold Toynbee, *Turkey: A Past and a Future* (New York: George Dorn, 1917), pp. 28–9.

12 Yusuf Hikmet Bayur, *Türk Inkilabi Tarihi* (Istanbul: Maarif Matbaari, 1953), vol. 3, p. 198; further addenda to 'Report of an inhabitant of Athlit', circulated on 2 November 1916 under no. 7977, FO 371/2783/225831, 10 November 1916.

13 'Report of the Committee on Asiatic Turkey', 30 June 1915, CAB 27/1.

14 'Correspondence between Sir Henry McMahon, His Majesty's High Commissioner at Cairo, and the Sherif of Mecca July 1915–March 1916, presented by the Secretary of State for Foreign Affairs to Parliament by Command of His Majesty', Cmd. 5957, London, 1939, p. 3 (hereafter 'Hussein–McMahon Correspondence').

15 Eliezer Tauber, *The Emergence of the Arab Movements* (London: Cass, 1993), chapter 28.

16 Ernest Dawn, 'The Origins of Arab Nationalism', in Rashid Khalidi, Lisa Anderson, Muhammad Muslih and Reeva S. Simon (eds), *The Origins of Arab Nationalism* (New York: Columbia University Press, 1991), p. 13.

17 T.E. Lawrence, 'Syria: the Raw Material' (written early in 1915 but not circulated), *Arab Bulletin*, no. 44, 12 March 1917, FO/882/26.

18 'Intelligence Report', 28 December 1916, FO 686/6, p. 176; *Arab Bulletin*, 23 June 1916, p. 47 and 6 February 1917, pp. 57– 8, FO 882/25; McMahon to Grey, 20 October 1915, FO 371/2486/154423.

19 Lawrence, 30 July 1917, FO 686/8; Mark Sykes, 'Notes on Conversations with the Emirs Abdullah and Faisal', 1 May 1917, FO 882/16, p. 233.

20 *T.E. Lawrence to his Biographers Robert Graves and Liddell Hart* (London: Cassell, 1963), p. 101.

21 Martin Gilbert, *Churchill, Vol. IV: 1916–1922* (London: Heinemann, 1975), p. 596.

22 Fromkin, *A Peace to End All Peace*, pp. 17, 19.

23 CO 732/3, fols. 409–12; 'Sherifian Policy in Mesopotamia & Trans-Jordania', CO 732/3/10127, fols. 418–22; Churchill to Lloyd George, received at the Colonial Office at 8.30 p.m., 14 March 1921, CO 732/4/17976, fol. 167. For discussion of the episode see Karsh and Karsh, *Empires of the Sand*, chapter 20.

24 'Sherifian Policy in Mesopotamia & Trans-Jordania', 25 February 1921, CO 732/3, fols. 420–1.

25 'First Conversation on Trans-Jordania, Held at Government House, Jerusalem, March 28, 1921', FO 371/6343, fols. 99–101.

26 'Second Conversation on Trans-Jordania', 'Third Conversation on Trans-Jordania', *ibid.*, fols. 101–2.

27 'Letter from Mr. Churchill to Sir Herbert Samuel, at Sea', 2 April 1921, *ibid.* fols. 102–3.

28 William Armstrong, 'After Sykes–Picot: Britain, France, and the struggle for the Middle East', *Hurriyet Daily News*, 4 December 2014.

29 Antonius, *The Arab Awakening*, pp. 248–9.

30 Said, *al-Thawra al-Arabiyya*, vol. 1, pp. 110–11; Musa, *al-Haraka al-Arabiyya*, pp. 52–3. Hussein also demanded the release of political prisoners and the granting of autonomy to Syria.

31 Abdullah ibn Hussein, *Mudhakkirati* (Jerusalem: Matbaat Bait al-Maqdis, 1945), pp. 105–7; Said, *al-Thawra al-Arabiyya*, vol. 1, p. 111; *idem, Asrar al-Thawra al-Arabiyya al-Kubra wa Masat al-Sharif Hussein* (Beirut: Dar al-Katib al-Arabi, 1960), pp. 52–3.

32 Djemal to Faisal, November 1917, FO 371/3395/12077; Wingate to Balfour, 25 December 1917, FO 371/3395/12077; Suleiman Musa (ed.), *al-Murasalat al-Tarikhiyya 1914–1918: al-Thawra al-Arabiyya al-Kubra* (Amman: Matbaat al-Quwat al-Musallaha, 1973–5), pp. 154, 156, 158–9; *Arab Bulletin*, 24 December 1917, pp. 402–3 & 3 January 1918, p. 521.

33 T.E. Lawrence, *Seven Pillars of Wisdom: A Triumph* (Garden City: Doubleday, 1935), pp. 554–5.

34 B.H. Liddell Hart, *T.E. Lawrence to his Biographer* (London: Cassell, 1962), p. 142 (recording a conversation with Lawrence on 1 August 1933).

35 Faisal to Djemal, 11 June 1918, FO 371/3881/146256.

36 Bonn State Archives, IA Türkei 165 43 Pera Telgram 22 August 1918, 'Secret: Report by the German Ambassador on a conversation with Talaat Pasha'; Musa, *al-Murasalat*, p. 210.

37 Albert Hourani, *The Emergence of the Modern Middle East* (London: Macmillan, 1981), pp. 209–210.

38 For the text of the Sykes–Picot Agreement, as well as a memorandum by its two authors accompanying the draft agreement, see CAB 42/11/9. See also E.L. Woodward & R. Butler (eds), *Documents on British Foreign Policy 1919–1939*, First Series (London: Her Majesty's Stationery Office, 1960), vol. 4, pp. 241–51 (hereinafter – DBFP).

39 Elie Kedourie, *In the Anglo-Arab Labyrinth: The McMahon–Husayn Correspondence and Its Interpretations 1914–1939* (Cambridge: Cambridge University Press, 1976), p. 155.

40 Sykes to War Office, 30 April 1917, FO 882/16. For Picot's report of the meeting see his telegram of 2 May 1917, MAE, Guerre 1914–18, vol. 877.

41 For accounts of these meetings see: Wingate to Foreign Office, 7 May 1917, reporting
    Sykes's telegram from Jeddah of the previous day, FO 371/3054/93335; *Arab Bulletin*,
    no. 50, 13 May 1917, p. 207; Sykes's telegram of 24 May 1917, FO 371/3054/104269;
    'Note by Sheikh Fuad El Khatib taken down by Lt Col. Newcombe', FO 882/16; Picot's
    telegram of 24 May 1917, MAE, Guerre 1914–18, vol. 877.

42 Memorandum by Sir Mark Sykes, June 1918, FO 371/3381/107379; 'Note by Sheikh
    Fuad El Khatib'.

43 McMahon to Grey, 26 October 1915, FO 371/2486/163832.

44 McMahon to Hussein, 24 October & 24 December 1915, 'Hussein–McMahon
    Correspondence', pp. 8, 14.

45 McMahon to Hussein, 24 October 1915, *ibid.*, p. 8.

46 H.W. Young, 'Foreign Office Memorandum on Possible Negotiations with the Hedjaz',
    29 November 1920, FO 371/5066/14959, especially paragraphs 9–12.

47 'Report of Conversation between Mr. R.C. Lindsay, C.V.O., representing the Secretary
    of State for Foreign Affairs, and His Highness the Emir Feisal, representing the King of
    the Hedjaz' (held at the Foreign Office on Thursday, 20 January 1921), CO 732/3, fol
    366. Faisal's reasoning was incorporated into Antonius's *The Arab Awakening*, p. 178,
    almost verbatim.

48 CO 732/3, fol. 366. For further discussion of this issue see Karsh and Karsh, *Empires
    of the Sand* pp. 238–41.

49 'Hussein–McMahon Correspondence', p. 8.

50 McMahon to Grey, 26 October 1915, FO 371/2486/163832.

51 'Report of the Committee on Asiatic Turkey', p. 3.

52 Hussein to McMahon, 5 November 1915, Hussein–McMahon Correspondence, p. 8.

53 David Lloyd George, *Memoirs of the Peace Conference* (New Haven: Yale University
    Press, 1939), vol. 2, pp. 650, 664–5.

54 3 April 1917, CAB 24/9, fos. 306–8.

Chapter 2

1 'Draft Resolutions in Reference to Mandatories', *Foreign Relations of the United States,
    Paris Peace Conference 1919* (Washington, D.C.: Government Printing Office, 1942–7;
    hereinafter *FRUS*), vol. 3, pp. 795–6.

2 'The League of Nations Mandate for Palestine' (confirmed by the Council of the
    League of Nations on 24 July 1922), Preamble, Articles 2, 4–6.

3 Palestine Royal Commission, *Report. Presented to the Secretary of State for the Colonies in
    Parliament by Command of His Majesty, July 1937* (London: HMSO; rep. 1946), pp. 271–5.

4   General Staff H.Q., Jerusalem, 'History of the Disturbances in Palestine 1936–1939', Dec. 1939, WO 191/88; *A Survey of Palestine. Prepared in December 1945 and January 1946 for the information of the Anglo-American Committee of Enquiry* (reprinted 1991 in full with permission from Her Majesty's Stationery Office by the Institute for Palestine Studies, Washington D.C.), vol. 1, pp. 38, 46, 49; Yuval Arnon-Ohana, *Herev Mibait: Hamaavak Hapnimi Batnuah Haleumit Hafalestinit* (Tel Aviv: Yariv-Hadar, 1981), pp. 278–86; Hillel Cohen, *Army of Shadows: Palestinian Collaboration with Zionism, 1917–1948* (Berkeley: University of California Press, 2008), Chapter 5.

5   For the full text of the White Paper see: 'Cmd. 6019: Palestine, Statement of Policy', May 1939.

6   'Palestine Jews to Protest', *The Times*, 16 May 1939; Weizmann to Mr Justice Louis D. Brandeis, 8 May 1939, *FRUS*, The Far East, Near East and Africa, 1939, vol. 4, p. 749; Rabbi Stephen S. Wise to the Secretary of State, 22 May 1939, *ibid.*, p. 761; CZA, 'Political Report of the London Office of the Executive of the Jewish Agency', submitted to the Twenty-Second Zionist Congress at Basle, December 1946, pp. 9–10.

7   D. Gurewitz to Political Department, 'Figures on Jewish-Owned Lands at the Beginning of 1940', 4 April 1944, Ben-Gurion Archive (BGA), Sde Boker.

8   Reader Bullard, *Two Kings in Arabia. Letters from Jeddah 1923–5 and 1936–9* (Reading: Ithaca Press, 1993), p. 266 (diary entry for 19 May 1939).

9   Minister in Iran to the Foreign Ministry, 15 April 1941, *Documents on German Foreign Policy 1918–1945* (London: HMSO, 1949; hereinafter DGFP), ser. D, vol. 12, pp. 558–60; Minutes of JAE Meeting, 21 May 1941, BGA.

10   Elias Sasson, 'Why and How the Mufti Moved to Iraq', 2 November 1939, CZA, S25/3750; Majid Khadduri, 'General Nuri's Flirtations with the Axis Powers', *Middle East Journal*, Summer 1962, pp. 328–9.

11   'The Mufti', 30 November 1939, PRO, KV2/2085; 'Palestine. The Mufti's Intention to Keep the Revolt Simmering; Propaganda in Favor of his Return to Palestine, Etc.', 7 December 1939, *ibid.*; 'The Mufti's Activities and Interests', 5 February 1940, *ibid.*; 'Palestine. Miscellaneous Arab Information', 15 March 1940, *ibid.*; 'The Mufti's Propaganda at Nabi Musa', 10 May 1940, *ibid.*; 'Palestine. Revival of Pro-Mufti Activities', 11 June 1940, *ibid.*

12   'Activities of the Mufti. Possibility of Intrigue in the Middle Euphrates', 18 January 1940, KV2/2085; 'The Mufti's Activities', 21 February 1940, *ibid.*; 'The Mufti. Summoning of Followers to Baghdad to Discuss Plans, Etc.', 15 May 1940, *ibid.*

13   The Ambassador in Turkey to the Foreign Ministry (Enclosure), 6 July 1940, DGFP, ser. D, vol. 10, pp. 143–4; The Grand Mufti to Adolf Hitler, 20 January 1941, *ibid.*, ser. D, vol. 11, pp. 1151–5; Record of the Conversation between the Führer and the Grand Mufti of Jerusalem on Nov. 28, 1941, in the Presence of Reich Foreign Minister and Minister Grobba in Berlin, Nov. 30, 1941, *ibid.*, pp. 881–5.

14   G.3/D. (C. & D.), 'Intelligence report on the Mufti', 16 December 1943, KV 2/2085.

15   Minutes of Jewish Agency Executive (JAE) Meeting, 4 October 1942 & 7 November 1943.

16 Telegram from the prime minister to the deputy prime minister, 29 April 1944, FO 371/40135.

17 See memorandum on 'Developments in Palestine During Recent Months', n.d., 1942, FO 371/35034; memorandum 'Dr Weizmann's Policies', British Embassy, Washington to Eastern Department, FO, 9 July 1942, FO 371/31379; MacMichael to Malcolm MacDonald, 23 November 1938, CO 753/387/5; Colonial Office memorandum, 'Control of Jewish Land Transfers in Palestine', 5 January 1939, CO 753/387/15; Washington Embassy to Foreign Office, 6 January 1943, FO 371/35031; Efraim Karsh and Rory Miller, 'Freya Stark in America: Orientalism, Anti-Semitism, and Political Propaganda', *Journal of Contemporary History*, July 2004, pp. 315–32.

18 Minutes of JAE Meeting, 13 February 1944; Minutes attached to 'Information about the Jews for Miss Freya Stark', FO 371/35039. See also: Halifax to Eden, 9 June 1944, FO 371/40131; Washington Embassy to Foreign Office, 15 May 1944, FO 371/40131.

19 'A Policy for Palestine', in the report on 'International Post-war Settlement', *Manchester Guardian*, 24 April 1944.

20 See, for example, minutes of the JAE meeting of 7 May 1944, and Mapai central committee meeting the next day, BGA

21 Alan Bullock, *Ernest Bevin: Foreign Secretary, 1945–1951* (London: Heinemann, 1983), pp. 181–2; Weizmann's address to the Convention of the Zionist organization of America at Atlantic City, 19 November 1945, FO 371/51128. For the Foreign Office's attitude to the Jewish refugee problem see H. Henderson, 'Memorandum on Jewish Refugees', 19 October 1946, FO 371/52646.

22 CAB 128/1, 38th Conclusions, 4 October 1945; Bevin to Halifax, 12 October 1945, FO 371/45381/E7757; 'Future of Palestine', *The Times*, 14 November 1945; 'Short Minutes of Meeting Held at 77 Great Russell Street, London, WC1, on Friday, 2 November 1945', BGA.

23 Bevin to Halifax, 12 October 1945. See also: 'Report by Mr. Ben-Gurion on his visit to the Camps given at a meeting at 77 Gt. Russell St., London, WC1, on Tuesday, 6 November 1945', BGA.

24 'Future of Palestine'; Walter Laqueur (ed.), *The Israel-Arab Reader* (Harmondsworth: Penguin, 1970), pp. 54–5.

25 'Short Minutes of Meeting Held at 77 Great Russell Street, London, WC1, on Tuesday, 23 October 1945', BGA; 'Jews' Prospects in Europe', *The Times*, 14 November 1945; Eliahu Elath, *Hamaavak al Hamedina, Washington 1945–1948* (Tel Aviv: Am Oved & The Zionist Library, 1979), vol. 1, pp. 368, 400.

26 'Palestine: Future Policy', Secret Memorandum by the Secretary of State for the Colonies, 16 January 1947, Annex I, CAB 129/16, C.P. (47) 31.

27 Richard Crossman, *Palestine Mission: A Personal Record* (New York: Harper, 1947), p. 131. Even the venomously anti-Zionist and anti-Semitic head of the Cairo Middle East Office, Sir John Troutbeck, condescended to the Arabs as 'silly, feckless people … of medieval outlook' incapable of 'the same kind of loyalty to each other that one expects but does not always get from Europeans'. Troutbeck to Wright, 18 May 1948, 371/68386/E8738; Troutbeck to Bevin, 24 January 1949, FO 371/75054/E3518; Troutbeck to Wright, 3 March 1949, FO 371/75064.

28 CAB 128/6, C.M. (46), 71st Conclusions, 22 July 1946; CAB 128/11 C.M. (47), 6th Conclusions, Minute 3, 15 January 1947; 'An Analysis of the Palestine Situation, April 1948', Cunningham Papers, Middle East Centre, St Antony's College, Oxford University.

29 From Cairo (BMEO) to Foreign Office, 11 June 1948, FO 371/68650.

30 CAB 128/12, C.M. (48), 12th Conclusions, 5 February 1948.

31 Judith Tydor Baumel, 'Bridging Myth and Reality: the Absorption of She'erit Hapletah in Eretz Yisrael, 1945–48', *Middle Eastern Studies*, April 1997, p.362.

32 Bevin to Lord Inverchapel, PREM 8/859, Part II, telegram 5459 of 20 May 1948.

33 Thus, for example, Bevin told the US ambassador to London that 'the inclusion of Gaza and the Negeb [*sic*] in the Jewish State had been a terrible mistake as there were no Jews there, and this must be righted'. 'Record of Meeting with the US Ambassador to Discuss the Palestine Situation', 25 May 1948, FO 800/487.

34 On 11 September 1948 the British *chargé d'affaires* in Beirut cabled the Foreign Office: 'Of course if Syria could also be given a share albeit small in the spoils Abdullah's position would be stronger'. Two days later the Foreign Office relayed this idea to Sir John Troutbeck, head of the British Middle East Office (BMEO) in Cairo, which acted as London's main liaison with Bernadotte: 'I have been considering the suggestion that Syrian acquiescence in the aggrandisement of Transjordan would be more easily obtained if there could be some cession of territory in Northern Palestine to Syria'. Evans to Foreign Office, 11 September 1948, FO 371/68861/E11891; Foreign Office to Rhodes, 13 September 1948, FO 800/487.

35 For British plans for reducing Israel's size, see, for example: 'Palestine: Memorandum by the Secretary of State for Foreign Affairs', CAB 129/29, C.P. (48) 207, 24 August 1948; CAB 128/13, C.M. (48), 57th Conclusions, 26 August 1948; Foreign Office to BMEO in Cairo, 28 August 1948 & 11 September 1948, 800/487.

36 Bernard Burrows, 'Conversation with Musa el-Alami', 6 December 1947, FO 371/61585/E11764.

37 See, for example, Michael Wright, 'Palestine', 15 June 1948, FO 371/68650/E8409; Foreign Office to the British ambassador in Washington, 18 June 1948, FO 371/68650/E8626.

38 United Nations General Assembly, 'Progress Report of the United Nations Mediator on Palestine to the Secretary-General for Transmission to the Members of the United Nations. In pursuance of paragraph 2, part II, of resolution 186 (S-2) of the General Assembly of 14 May 1948', S/648, 16 September 1948.

39 Foreign Office to Amman, 6 July 1948, FO 800/487.

40 Washington to Foreign Office, 24 and 28 May 1948, FO 371/68650.

41   CAB 128/12, C.M. (48), 33rd Conclusions, 27 May 1948; 'Palestine – British Aid to Arab States', British Embassy, Washington, D.C., 25 May 1948, FO 371/68651.

42   'Record of Conversation between the Secretary of State and Edgar Gallad Bey at 11.30 a.m. on May 26th, 1948', FO 800/487.

43   Foreign Office to Cairo, 22 July 1948, FO 371/68641.

44   Anthony Parsons, *From Cold War to Hot Peace: UN Interventions 1947–1994* (London: Michael Joseph, 1995), p. 3.

Chapter 3

1   For a different view see Andrew Bacevich, *American Empire: the Realities and Consequences of U.S. Diplomacy* (Cambridge: Harvard University Press, 2002).

2   Yale Law School, The Avalon Project, 'Washington's Farewell Address 1796'.

3   David Fromkin, *A Peace to End All Peace: The Fall of the Ottoman Empire and the Creation of the Modern Middle East* (New York: Avon, 1990), p. 257.

4   *Lord Riddell's Intimate Diary of the Peace Conference and After 1918–1923* (London: Victor Gollancz, 1933), entry for 27 April 1919, p. 60; David Lloyd George, *Memoirs of the Peace Conference* (New Haven: Yale University Press, 1939), vol. 2, p. 818.

5   'American Commissioners Plenipotentiary', 27 March 1919, in *Papers Related to the Foreign Relations of the United States – The Paris Peace Conference 1919* (Washington, D.C.: US Government Printing Office, 1919), vol. 11, pp. 133–4.

6   Walter Laqueur (ed.), *The Israel-Arab Reader* (Harmondsworth: Penguin, 1970), pp. 37–9.

7   Zeine N. Zeine, *The Struggle for Arab Independence* (Beirut: Khayat's, 1960), p. 50; 'Report by British Liaison Officer on Political Situation in Arabia', Damascus, 16 May 1919, in E.L. Woodward & R. Butler (eds), *Documents on British Foreign Policy 1919–1939*, First Series (London: Her Majesty's Stationery Office, 1960), vol. 4, p. 264. For the complete memorandum submitted by the Congress to the Commission see Abu Khaldun Sati Husri, *Yawm Maisalun: Safha min Tarikh al-Arab al-Hadith* (Beirut: Dar al-Ittihad, 1964), pp. 261–4.

8   Eliezer Tauber, *The Formation of Modern Syria and Iraq* (London: Cass, 1995), p. 15; Khairiyya Qasmiyya, *al-Hukuma al-Arabiyya fi Dimashq bayna 1918–1920* (Cairo: Dar al-Ma'arif, 1971), p. 67, fn 2.

9   'Report of the American Section of the International Commission on Mandates in Turkey, Submitted by the Commissioners Charles R. King and Henry Churchill Crane, Paris, August 28, 1919, "Confidential Appendix – The Interference of the Occupying Governments with the Commission's Inquiry"', *Papers Related to the Foreign Relations of the United States – The Paris Peace Conference*, vol. 12, pp. 780–1, 848–50.

10 Elie Kedourie, 'The Transition from a British to an American Era in the Middle East', in Haim Shaked and Itamar Rabinovich (eds), *The Middle East and the United States: Perceptions and Policies* (New Brunswick: Transaction Books, 1980), p. 4.

11 Wm Roger Louis, *Imperialism at Bay: the United States and the Decolonization of the British Empire 1941–1945* (New York: Oxford University Press, 1978), chapter 1.

12 'Palestine – Strategic Appreciation', prepared by Bevin for Attlee, 24 May 1948, FO 371/68650/E7032.

13 Philip J. Baram, *The Department of State in the Middle East 1919–1945* (Philadelphia: University of Pennsylvania Press, 1978), pp. 50–5, 82–7, 246–7; 'Attitude of the United States toward Zionist and Arab Agitation Regarding British Policy in the Middle East and the Future Status of Palestine', *Foreign Relations of the United States*, 1942, *The Near East and Africa* (Washington, D.C.: US Government Printing Office, 1942; hereinafter *FRUS*), vol. 4, pp. 538–51; 'Memorandum by the Deputy Director of the Office of Near Eastern and African Affairs (Alling) to the Assistant Secretary of State (Dunn)', 5 April 1945, *FRUS*, 1945, vol. 8, p. 698.

14 See, for example, 'Excerpts from the Minutes of the Sixth Meeting of the United States Delegation to the Second Session of the General Assembly, New York, September 15, 1947, 10am', *FRUS*, 1947, vol. 5, pp. 1147–51.

15 Even Truman was sufficiently alarmed by this patently false claim as to dispatch a special envoy to Prime Minister Ben-Gurion to enquire whether the newly established state of Israel was going to become a 'red state', only to hear back that all fears in this respect were groundless and that there was no 'immediate Soviet danger'. David Ben-Gurion, *Yoman Hamilhama* (Tel Aviv: Ministry of Defence Press, 1982), vol. 3 pp. 846–7.

16 See, for example, 'Memorandum Prepared for the Department of State', 30 September 1947, *FRUS*, 1947, pp. 1166–70.

17 David McCullough, *Truman* (New York: Simon & Schuster, 1992), pp. 597, 604.

18 Peter Grose, *Israel in the Mind of America* (New York: Knopf, 1983), pp. 67, 134, 138–41, 300.

19 Memorandum by the President's Special Counsel (Clifford) to President Truman, 8 March 1948, *FRUS*, 1948, vol. 5, part 2, pp. 690–1; Nadav Safran, *The United States and Israel* (Cambridge: Harvard University Press, 1963), pp. 38–9.

20 President Truman to King of Saudi Arabia (Abdul Aziz ibn Saud), 25 October 1946, *FRUS*, 1946, pp. 714–16; Truman to Ibn Saud, 27 January 1947, *FRUS*, 1947, vol. 5, p. 1012.

21 Washington Embassy to Foreign Office, 28 November 1947, FO 371/61891.

22 Lord Inverchapel to Bevin, 21 May 1948, FO 371/68649.

23 Baram, *The Department of State in the Middle East*, p. 5.

24 'Casualties in Palestine since the United Nations Decision, Period 30th November, 1947 to 3rd April, 1948', CO 733/483/5, p. 19.

25 'An Analysis of the Palestine Situation, Apr. 1948', Cunningham Papers, St Antony's College, Oxford University, IV/5/33.

26 Report by the Policy Planning Staff on Position of the United States With Respect to Palestine, 19 January 1948, *FRUS*, NEA, vol. 5, part 2, p. 554; Memorandum by the Director of the Office of Near Eastern and African Affairs (Henderson) to the Director of the Office of United Nations Affairs (Rusk), 6 February 1948, *ibid.*, p. 601. See also: Memorandum by Mr. Dean Rusk to the Under Secretary of State (Lovett), 26 January 1948, *ibid.*, pp. 556–62; Memorandum by Mr. Samuel K.C. Kopper of the Office of Near Eastern and African Affairs, 27 January 1948, *ibid.*, pp. 563–66; Personal Comments by Mr. Kennan on Mr. Rusk's Memorandum of 26 January 1948, *ibid.*, pp. 574–81.

27 First Special Report of the United Nations Palestine Commission to the Security Council: The Problem of Security in Palestine, 16 February 1948 & Draft Report Prepared by the Staff of the National Security Council, 17 February 1948, *ibid*, pp. 631–2; The Department of State to President Truman, 23 February 1948.

28 Statement Made by the United States Representative at the United Nations (Austin) Before the Security Council on 19 March 1948, *ibid.*, pp. 742–3.

29 Grose, *Israel*, p. 276; Margaret Truman, *Harry S. Truman* (New York: William Morrow, 1973), pp. 387–9.

30 President Truman to Secretary of State, 22 February 1948, *FRUS*, 1948, vol. 5, part 2, p. 645; McCullough, *Truman*, p. 611; John Snetsinger, *Truman, the Jewish Vote, and the Creation of Israel* (Stanford: Hoover Institution Press, 1974), pp. 86–7.

31 Trygve Lie, *In the Cause of Peace* (New York: Macmillan, 1954), p. 171; The Consul General at Jerusalem (Macatee) to the Secretary of State, 22 March 1948, *FRUS*, 1948, vol. 5, part 2, p. 753.

32 Secretary of State to the Embassy in Egypt: Following statement was released by President today, 25 March 1948, *ibid.*, pp. 759–60.

33 Resolutions of the Zionist General Council, adopted at the Session preceding the establishment of the State of Israel, April 1948, Ben-Gurion Archives (BGA), Sde Boker; Dr. Chaim Weizmann to President Truman, 9 April 1948, *ibid.*, pp. 807–9; Text of declaration adopted by General Zionist Council in Tel Aviv, 12 April 1948, *FRUS*, 1948, vol. 5, part 2, pp. 842–3.

34 Taha Hashemi, *Mudhakkirat Taha al-Hashemi, vol. 2 – 1942–1955* (Beirut: Dar al-Tali'a li-l-Taba'a wa-l-Nashr, 1978), pp. 214–16 (diary entries for 17 and 22 April 1948); Tzuri to Golani, 'News Summary: Tiberias', 21 April 1948, Hagana Archive (HA), 105/143, p. 275; Hagana Operational Directorate, 'Logbook of the War of Independence', p. 260; Nahum Ab (Abu), *Hamaavak al Tveria* (Tel Aviv: Ministry of Defence Publishing House, 1991), pp. 199–217.

35 Efraim Karsh, 'Nakbat Haifa: the Collapse and Dispersion of a Major Palestinian Community', *Middle Eastern Studies*, October 2001, pp. 25–70.

36 Efraim Karsh, *Palestine Betrayed* (New Haven: Yale University Press, 2010), pp. 2, 264–72.

37 Memorandum by the Director of the Office of Near Eastern and African Affairs (Henderson) to the Under Secretary of State (Lovett), 22 April 1948, *FRUS*, 1948, vol. 5, part 2, pp. 840–2.

38 Memorandum of Conversation, by the Secretary of State, 4 May 1948, *ibid.*, pp. 901–4; Grose, *Israel*, pp. 284–6.

39 Memorandum of Conversation by Mr. Henderson, 29 April 1948, *FRUS*, 1948, vol. 5, part 2, p, 876.

40 The Consul in Jerusalem (Wasson) to the Secretary of State, 3 May 1948, *ibid.*, p. 889.

41 Austin to the Secretary of State, 4 May 1948, *ibid.*, p. 897; Draft Memorandum by the Director of the Office of United Nations Affairs (Rusk) to the Under Secretary of State (Lovett), 4 May 1948, *ibid.*, p. 895.

42 Memorandum of Conversation by Secretary of State, 12 May 1948, *ibid.*, pp. 973–4.

43 Transcript of Remarks Made by Mr. Dean Rusk in Conversation by Telephone with Mr. Jessup and Mr. Ross, 11 May 1948, *ibid.*, 965–9; Memorandum by the Legal Advisor (Gross) to the Under Secretary of State (Lovett), 11 May 1948, *ibid.*, pp. 959–65.

44 Memorandum of Conversation by Secretary of State, 12 May 1948, *ibid.*, pp. 974–5.

45 Memorandum of Conversations, by Under Secretary of State (Lovett), 17 May 1948, *ibid.*, pp. 1005–7; The Agent of the Provisional Government of Israel (Epstein) to President Truman, 14 May 1948, p. 989; The Secretary of State to Mr. Eliahu Epstein, at Washington, 14 May 1948, *ibid.*, p. 992; Rusk's letter to the Historical Office, 13 June 1974, *ibid.*, p. 993; McCullough, *Truman*, pp. 615–18.

Chapter 4

1 Stephen McFarland, 'A Peripheral View of the Origins of the Cold War: The Crises in Iran, 1941–47', *Diplomatic History*, October 1980, pp. 339–40.

2 Habib Ladjevardi, 'The Origins of U.S. Support for an Autocratic Iran', *International Journal of Middle Eastern Studies*, 15 (1983), pp. 225–9; The Ambassador in Iran (Murray) to the Secretary of State, 26 June 1945, *Foreign Relations of the United States* (hereinafter *FRUS*), 1945, vol. 8, pp. 385–86.

3 The Ambassador in Iran (Allen) to Secretary of State, 26 May 1946, *ibid.*, p. 486; Secretary of State to the Ambassador in Iran (Allen), 4 June 1946, *ibid.*, pp. 491–3.

4 Ladjevardi, 'The Origins of U.S. Support', p. 232; Memorandum by the Director of the Office of Near Eastern and African Affairs (Henderson) to the Under Secretary of State (Acheson), 18 October 1946, *FRUS*, 1946, vol. 7, p. 534. See also: The Ambassador in Iran (Allen) to Secretary of State, 10 and 17 June; 30 September; 6 October 1946, *ibid.*, pp. 496–7, 501, 518–20, 522–3.

5 The Ambassador in Iran (Allen) to Secretary of State, 25 July 1947 & The Secretary of State to the Embassy in Iran, 21 June 1947, *FRUS*, 1947, vol. 5, pp. 918, 922.

6   The Acting Secretary of State to the Embassy in Iran, 26 September 1947, *ibid.*, p. 961.

7   The Ambassador in Iran (Allen) to the Secretary of State, 3 June, 9 September, 2, 11 and 23 October 1947, *ibid.*, pp. 913, 949, 965, 967, 969–72; The Ambassador in Iran (Allen) to the Acting Chief of the Division of Greek, Turkish, and Iranian Affairs (Jernegan), 26 December 1947, *ibid.*, p. 998. See also: Ladjevardi, 'The Origins of U.S. Support', pp. 233–6; Louise L'Estrange Facett, *Iran and the Cold War: The Azerbaijan Crisis of 1946* (Cambridge: Cambridge University Press, 1992), Chapter 3; Richard W. Cottam, *Iran and the United States: A Cold War Case Study* (Pittsburgh: University of Pittsburgh Press, 1988), pp. 66–75.

8   'Memorandum by the Secretary of State: Interview between the President and the Shah of Iran', 18 November 1949, *FRUS*, 1949, vol. 6, p. 572.

9   The Secretary of State to the Embassy in Iran, 8 January 1948 & The Ambassador in Iran (Allen) to the Secretary of State, 16 January 1948, *FRUS*, 1948, vol. 5, pp. 92, 96.

10 The Secretary of State to the Embassy in Iran, 22 February 1949 & The Ambassador in Iran (Wiley) to the Secretary of State, 21 April 1949, *FRUS*, 1949, vol. 6, pp. 484, 507.

11 Memorandum by the Deputy Director of Mutual Defense Assistance (Ohly) to Major General L.L. Lemnitzer, 14 December 1949, *ibid.*, pp. 484, 507, 590.

12 For this episode see: Kermit Roosevelt, *Countercoup: the Struggle for the Control of Iran* (New York: McGraw Hill, 1979); Stephen Kinzer, *All the Shah's Men: The Hidden Story of the CIA's Coup in Iran* (New York: Wiley, 2003); Darioush Bayandor, *Iran and the CIA: The Fall of Mosaddeq Revisited* (New York: Palgrave Mcmillan, 2010).

13 Letter from the Shah of Iran to President Johnson, 7 January 1964, *FRUS*, 1964–8, vol. 22, Iran, doc. 2.

14 Letter from President Johnson to the Shah of Iran, 19 March 1964, *ibid.*, doc. 8; Memorandum from Secretary of State Rusk to President Johnson, 3 June 1964, *ibid.*, doc. 31.

15 Thus, for example, the deal included 176 M-60A1 tanks rather than the more obsolete M-47s (supplied to Israel) as suggested by the Pentagon. For the text of the agreement see: Telegram from the Department of State to the Embassy in Iran, Washington, 2 July 1964, *ibid.*, doc. 47.

16 'National Intelligence Estimate 34–69, 10 January 1969', *FRUS*, 1969–76, vol. E-4, doc. 1; Tehran Embassy to Department of State, 'Country Policy Appraisal – Iran', 17 October 1968, p. 2, *Digital National Security Archive* (hereinafter DNSA); Central Intelligence Agency, 'Intelligence Memorandum: The Shah of Iran and his Policies', 5 June 1967, p. 6, *ibid.*

17 Department of State, 'Visit of the Shah of Iran June 11–12, 1968: Background Paper. Iran's Relations with Communist Countries', 8 June 1968, DNSA; *idem*, 'Iran–U.S. Relationships', August 1972, *ibid.*; 'Memorandum from the Executive Secretary of the Department of State (Read) to the President's Assistant for National Security Affairs (Kissinger)', Washington, 30 January 1969, *FRUS*, 1969–76, vol. E-4, doc. 2.

18   Central Intelligence Agency, 'Special Memorandum: The Shah's Increasing Assurance', pp. 1–2, DNSA.

19   *Guardian*, 9 October 1971; *AFP*, 24 June 1974; *DPA*, 10 June 1976; Amin Saikal, *The Rise and Fall of the Shah* (Princeton: Princeton University Press, 1980), pp. 146–7.

20   Henry Kissinger, *White House Years* (Boston: Little Brown, 1979), p. 224.

21   National Security Council Memorandum 92, 'U.S. Policy toward the Persian Gulf', 7 November 1970 (sent to the Secretary of State, Secretary of Defense, Director of Central Intelligence, Director of U.S. Information Agency), DNSA.

22   See, for example, phone conversations between Nixon and Kissinger, and between Kissinger and the Iranian ambassador to Washington, both on 12 April 1971, Kissinger Telephone Conversations, DNSA.

23   Secret memorandum from Henry A. Kissinger to the Secretary of State and Secretary of Defense, 'Follow Up on the President's Talk with the Shah of Iran', 25 July 1972, DNSA; Secret memorandum from Kissinger to the Secretary of State and Secretary of Defense, 'Follow Up on the President's Talk with the Shah of Iran', 15 June 1972, *ibid.*; White House, 'Memorandum on Conversation' (between Mohammed Reza Pahlavi, Shahanshah of Iran and the President), 30 May 1972, Saadabad Palace, Tehran, *ibid.*

24   'Iran Study' (interagency report submitted to Congress), 28 February 1978, pp. 2–3, DNSA; Jimmy Carter, *Keeping Faith: Memoirs of a President* (Toronto: Bantam Books, 1982), p. 448; John D. Stempel, *Inside the Iranian Revolution* (Bloomington: Indiana University Press, 1981), pp. 72–4; James A. Bill, *The Eagle and the Lion: The Tragedy of American-Iranian Relations* (New Haven: Yale University Press, 1988), pp. 202–9.

25   'Iran Study', pp. 2–4.

26   Kissinger, *White House Years*, p. 1262.

27   Office of the Inspector General, Foreign Service, 'Inspection Report: the Conduct of Relations with Iran', September 1976, p. 2, DNSA.

28   *Ibid.*; Bill, *Eagle and Lion*, pp. 178–80, 204; Daniel Yergin, *The Prize* (New York: Simon & Schuster, 1991), pp. 533–5, 582.

29   House Select Committee of Intelligence Report (The Pike Report) on American involvement in the Kurdish insurrection, as reprinted in *Village Voice* (New York), 26 January 1976. The main findings of the report also formed the basis for two indicting articles by William Safire: 'Mr. Ford's Secret Sell-out', *New York Times*, 5 February 1976; 'Son of Secret Sell-out', *New York Times*, 12 February 1976.

30   Department of State to Tehran Embassy, 'Letter from President Carter to the Shah', 15 July 1977, *The National Archive – Access to Archival Databases* (AAD).

31   Carter, *Keeping Faith*, pp. 434–5; Richard Sale, 'Carter and Iran: from Idealism to Disaster', *Washington Quarterly*, autumn 1980, p. 80.

32   Admiral Stansfield Turner, *Secrecy and Democracy: the CIA in Transition* (New York: Perennial Library, 1985), p. 115. See also: Central Intelligence Agency, Office of

National Estimates, 'Nothing Succeeds like a Successful Shah', 8 October 1971; CIA, 'Iran: An Overview of the Shah's Economy', 16 October 1974; 'Iran's Modernizing Monarchy: A Political Assessment', secret aerogram from Richard Helms to Department of State, 8 July 1976 – all in DNSA.

33 John D. Stempel (Tehran Embassy), 'Confidential Report', 28 February 1977, p. 1, DNSA.

34 'The Future of Iran: Implications for the U.S.', Department of State, Bureau of Intelligence and Research, drafted by Franklin P. Huddle, 28 January 1977, DNSA.

35 See, for example, 'Iran in the 1980s', Secret Report, CIA, 5 October 1977; William Showcross, *The Shah's Last Ride* (New York: Simon and Schuster, 1988), pp. 230–9; William H. Sullivan, *Mission to Iran* (New York: Norton, 1981), p. 155.

36 Tehran Embassy to Secretary of State, 'Rumors Re Health of Shah', 26 July 1978, p. 2, DNSA.

37 'Your Appearance before the House International Relations Committee, Thursday, July 28, 10am on the Sale of AWACS to Iran', Memorandum to Cyrus Vance from Alfred Roy Atherton, 27 July 1977, p. 13, DNSA.

38 Central Intelligence Agency, 'Iran in the 1980s', August 1977, pp. 1–2; 'Iran in the 1980s', 5 October 1977, p. 8, both in DNSA.

39 See, for example, Embassy to Secretary of State, 'Qom Aftermath and other Events', 16 January 1978; Embassy to Secretary of State, 'Religion and Politics: Qom and its Aftermath', 26 January 1978; Embassy to Department of State, 'The Iranian Opposition', 1 February 1978; Embassy to Department of State, 'Understanding the Shiite Islamic Movement', 3 February 1978; Embassy to Department of State, 'Disturbances in Isfahan', 6 May 1978; Shiraz Consulate to Department of State, 'Social Unrest in Iran', 14 May 1978, all in DNSA.

40 Tehran Embassy to Secretary of State, 'Iran's Internal Problems: Need for Information', 7 June 1978, DNSA.

41 Charles Naas (acting head of mission) to Department of State, 'Uncertain Political Mood: Religious Developments, Tougher Royal Line on Demonstrations', 1 August 1978, DNSA; Carter, *Keeping Faith*, p. 438.

42 Sullivan to Vance, 'Recommendation for President to Shah Letter', 29 August 1978, DNSA.

43 Sullivan to Department of State, 'Situation in Iran', 10 September 1978, pp. 3–5, DNSA.

44 Tehran Embassy to Department of State, 'Political Attitudes in Southern Iran', 9 September1978, Summary and Introduction, DNSA.

45 Defense Intelligence Agency, 'Assessment of the Political situation in Iran', 1 September 1978; Central Intelligence Agency, 'Iran National Intelligence Estimate', *c.* September 1978, pp. 6, 27, both in DNSA.

46   Sullivan to Department of State, 'Looking Ahead', 22 October 1978; Embassy to Secretary of State, 'Opposition on the Move: Deal in the Wind?' 22 October 1978, both in DNSA.

47   Sullivan to Department of State, 'Looking Ahead: Shifting Iranian Public Attitudes', 31 October 1978, DNSA.

48   Gary Sick, *All Fall Down: America's Tragic Encounter with Iran* (New York: Penguin, 1985), p. 4; Zachary Karabell, '"Inside the US Espionage Den": the US Embassy and the Fall of the Shah', *Intelligence and National Security*, January 1993, p. 56; David E. Mark (INR acting director) to Secretary of State, 'The Gathering Crisis in Iran', 2 November 1978.

49   Sullivan to Department of State, 'Thinking the Unthinkable', 9 November 1978. See also: Cyrus R. Vance, *Hard Choices: Critical Years in America's Foreign Policy* (New York: Simon and Schuster, 1983), pp. 325, 329.

50   Department of State, Bureau of Near Eastern and South Asian Affairs, 'Iran Scope Paper', p. 1, 18 November 1978, DNSA.

51   The Director of Central Intelligence, 'Alert Memorandum', pp. 6, 8, 29 November 1978, DNSA.

52   Turner, *Secrecy and Democracy*, p. 114; U.S. House of Representatives, Permanent Select Committee on Intelligence, Subcommittee on Evaluation, Staff Report, 'Iran: Evaluation of U.S. Intelligence Performance Prior to November 1978', January 1979, DNSA.

53   Zbigniew Brzezinski, *Power and Principle: Memoirs of the National Security Advisor 1977–1981* (London: Weidenfeld and Nicolson, 1983), p. 397.

54   Carter, *Keeping Faith*, p. 446; Bill, *The Eagle and the Lion*, p. 259.

55   'Conversation among President Nixon, Ambassador Douglas MacArthur II, and General Alexander Haig, Washington, April 8, 1971', *FRUS*, vol. E-4, *Documents on Iran and Iraq, 1969–72*, doc. 122.

56   Brzezinski, *Power and Principle*, p. 355. See also Precht's 'eyes only' letter to Sullivan on 19 December 1978, lamenting Brzezinski's underhand tactics (DNSA).

57   Cottam, *Iran and the United States*, pp. 175, 285 fn 27.

58   Brzezinski, *Power and Principle*, pp. 368–9.

59   As early as October 1977, Professor Richard Cottam of the University of Pittsburgh, a leading Iran expert, warned a congressional hearing of the possible adverse consequences of the administration's pressure on the shah to improve his human rights records. See: House of Representatives, 'Human Rights in Iran: Hearing before the Subcommittee on International Organizations', 26 October 1977, pp. 8–15. See also John Stempel (Tehran embassy), 'Straws in the Wind: Intellectual and Religious Opposition in Iran', 25 July 1977, DNSA.

60   *Ibid.*, pp. 376–82; Turner, *Secrecy and Democracy*, p. 88; Carter, *Keeping Faith*, p. 443.

61   Efraim Karsh, 'Iran: Anatomia shel Mahapecha', *Maarachot*, April 1979, pp. 24–5.

Chapter 5

1   The only other Third World area in close proximity to Russia is Southeast Asia. Yet unlike the Middle East, this area is not directly contiguous to Russian territory but buffered from it by China.

2   Surprisingly enough, this last point has eluded most Western analysts. See, for example: Robert O. Freedman, *Soviet Policy toward the Middle East since 1970* (New York: Praeger, 1982); Alvin Z. Rubinstein, *Red Star on the Nile* (Princeton: Princeton University Press, 1977); Galia Golan, *Yom Kippur and After* (Cambridge: Cambridge University Press, 1977); Adam Ulam, *Dangerous Relations: The Soviet Union in World Politics* (New York: Oxford University Press, 1983), pp. 40, 114–15, 182–3; Walter Z. Laqueur, 'Soviet Dilemmas in the Middle East' & Roman Kolkowitz, 'Soviet Policy in the Middle East', in Michael Confino and Shimon Shamir (eds), *The USSR and the Middle East* (New Brunswick: Transaction Books, 1973), pp. 77–89; Henry A. Kissinger, *White House Years* (Boston: Little, Brown, 1979), chapters 10, 14, 15, 30. A slightly dissenting view is presented by Adeed and Karen Dawisha, 'Perspectives on Soviet Policy in the Middle East' & Adeed Dawisha, 'The Soviet Union and the Arab World', in their edited volume, *The Soviet Union in the Middle East* (London: Macmillan, 1982).

3   E.H. Carr, *The Bolshevik Revolution* (Harmondsworth: Penguin, 1973), vol. 3, p. 464.

4   Richard W. Cottam, *Iran and the United States: A Cold War Case Study* (Pittsburgh: University of Pittsburgh Press, 1988), pp. 80–1.

5   Y. Primakov, *Anatomy of the Middle East Conflict* (Moscow: Nauka, 1979), p. 145.

6   Central Intelligence Agency, *Communist Aid Activities in Non-Communist Less Developed Countries, 1979 and 1954–79* (Washington, DC, October 1980), pp. 14, 20.

7   See, for example, Walter Laqueur, *The Struggle for the Middle East: the Soviet Union and the Middle East 1958–1970* (London: Penguin, 1972); *idem, Confrontation: The Middle East and World Politics* (New York: Bantam, 1974); Uri Ra'anan, 'The USSR and the Middle East: Some Reflections on the Soviet Decision-Making Process', *Orbis*, vol. 17 (1973).

8   See, for example, Marshall A.A. Grechko, *The Armed Forces of the Soviet Union* (Moscow, 1975; translated and published under the auspices of the United States Air Force); Mark Katz, *The Third World in Soviet Military Thought* (London: Croom Helm, 1982).

9   For various collusion theories regarding the Soviet role in the run-up to the 1967 war see, for example: Laqueur, *The Struggle for the Middle East*; Judith A. Klinghoffer, *Vietnam, Jews and the Middle East: Unintended Consequences* (New York: St Martin's Press, 1999); Avigdor Dagan, *Moscow and Jerusalem: Twenty Years of Relations Between Israel and the Soviet Union* (London: Abelard-Schuman, 1970), p. 208; Theodore Draper, *Israel and World Politics: Roots of the Third Arab-Israeli War* (London: Secker & Warburg, 1968), p. 130; Raymond Aron, *De Gaulle, Israel & the Jews* (London: André Deutsch, 1969), p. 71; Michael B. Oren, *Six Days of War: June*

1967 and the Making of the Modern Middle East (New York: Presidio Press, 2003), p. 55; Isabella Ginor and Gideon Remez, *Foxbats over Dimona: The Soviets' Nuclear Gamble during the Six Day War* (New Haven: Yale University Press, 2007).

10   Mahmoud Riad, *The Struggle for Peace in the Middle East* (London: Quartet, 1981), p. 102; Muhammad Heikal, *The Sphinx and the Commissar: The Rise and Fall of Soviet Influence in the Middle East* (New York: Harper & Row: 1978), ch. 11; Jean Lacouture, *Nasser: A Biography* (London: Secker & Warburg, 1973), pp. 330–1.

11   Muhammad Heikal, *The Road to Ramadan* (London: Fontana, 1976), pp. 87–8.

12   Lt Gen. Saad Shazly, *The Crossing of Suez* (London: Third World Centre for Research and Publication, 1980), p. 114.

13   Henry A. Kissinger, *Years of Upheaval* (Boston: Little, Brown, 1982), pp. 209–10, 296.

14   Yoel Ben-Porat, 'The Yom Kippur War: A Mistake in May and a Surprise in October', *Maarachot*, July–August 1985, pp. 2, 6 (Hebrew). The article draws on hitherto unclassified intelligence reports.

15   Kissinger, *Years of Upheaval*, pp. 297–9, 461; Richard Nixon, *RN: The Memoirs of Richard Nixon* (New York: Simon & Schuster, 1990), pp. 884–5; 'Memorandum for the President's Files by the President's Assistant for National Security Affairs (Kissinger), 23 June 1973, *Foreign Relations of the United States (FRUS), 1969–1976*, vol. 25, doc. 73 (internet edition).

16   *Pravda*, 26 September 1973. For further Soviet public warnings see, for example: *Sovyetskaya Rossiya*, 13 September 1973; *Izvestiya*, 5 October 1973; TASS, 4 September and 4 October 1973.

17   Kissinger, *Years of Upheaval*, p. 463.

18   'The Performance of the Intelligence Community before the Arab-Israeli War of October 1973: A Preliminary Post-Mortem Report', December 1973, Submitted by the Director of Central Intelligence following Review by the United States Intelligence Board, Digital National Security Archive (DNSA). See also: 'Middle East Developments and the Prospects for an Arab-Israeli Settlement', paper prepared by the National Security Council's Staff, 24 September 1973; 'Briefing Memorandum from the Director of the Bureau of Intelligence and Research (Cline) to Secretary of State Kissinger', 30 September 1973, *FRUS*, 1969–76, vol. 25, docs. 91, 93.

19   Victor Israelyan, *Inside the Kremlin during the Yom Kippur War* (University Park: Pennsylvania State University Press, 1995), pp. 14–15.

20   See, for example, Hanoch Bartov, *Dado*, vol. 1 (Tel Aviv: Maariv, 1978), p. 314; Chaim Herzog, *The War of Atonement* (London: Weidenfeld & Nicolson, 1975), pp. 48–50.

21   For the Egyptian account of the incident see: Heikal, *The Road to Ramadan*, pp. 207–9, 212–14; Sadat's interviews with the *Observer* (19 March 1978) and with the Lebanese newspapers *an-Nahar* (1 March 1974) and *al-Anwar*, 28 March 1974. For the Soviet version see: Vinogradov's account to *as-Safir* (Beirut), 17 April 1974; Israelyan, *Inside the Kremlin*, chapter 2.

22 See, for example, *Pravda*, 18 February, 6 and 21 June, and 19 August 1968; *Izvestiya*, 2 February 1968.

23 *Jerusalem Post*, 17 February 1989.

24 United Nations, Security Council, Resolution 242 (1967) of 22 November 1967, S/RES/242, http://unispal.un.org/unispal.nsf/0/7D35E1F729DF491C85256 EE700686136.

25 Efraim Karsh, *Soviet Policy towards Syria since the 1970s* (London: Macmillan, 1991), chapter 1.

26 See, for example, *Pravda*, 21 July 1988; *Izvestiya*, 8 September 1989; *Literaturnaya Gazeta*, 31 May 1989; TASS, 5 September 1988; Radio Peace and Progress in Hebrew, 31 May 1988. See also interview with Vladimir Polyakov (Head of the Near East Department in the Soviet Foreign Office), in *Le Quotidien de Paris*, 13 October 1988, and in *Izvestiya*, 8 September 1989; Deputy Foreign Minister Petrovsky's speech at the UN General Assembly as reported by TASS, 14 December 1988, and his interviews with *al-Hawadith* (London), 21 October 1988, and *al-Qabas* (Kuwait), 14 October 1988.

27 TASS, 19 June 1985, 29 October and 1 November 1988; *Pravda*, 20 June 1985; *Krasnaya Zvezda*, 1 and 3 November 1988; Moscow Radio, 24 April 1987; *al-Anba* (Kuwait), interview with Konstantin Geyvendov (*Izvestiya*'s Middle Eastern commentator), 12 September 1987.

28 *Damascus Radio*, 16 December 1988.

29 For Soviet pressures on the PLO to recognize Israel see, for example: *Pravda*, 10 April and 12 October 1988; V. Petrovsky's interview with *al-Qabas* (Kuwait), 14 October 1988; K. Brutents's interview with *al-Ittihad* (Abu Dhabi), 23 August 1988; *Krasnaya Zvezda*, 13 October 1988. See also: *Hadashot* (Tel Aviv), 29 August, 14 September and 14 October 1988; *Haaretz*, 8 and 14 October 1988.

30 *Damascus Radio*, 8 March 1989. For further Syrian criticism of the decision see: *Ibid.*, 19 and 20 November and 30 December 1988.

31 See, for example, *Radio Moscow in Arabic*, 10 and 11 October 1975.

32 *Radio Peace and Progress in Arabic*, 28 May 1976.

33 For the text of the communiqué see: *Damascus Radio*, 4 June 1976. See also: Karen Dawisha, *Soviet Foreign Policy towards Egypt* (London: Macmillan, 1979), p. 78; TASS, 5–7 June 1976; *Pravda*, 6–8 June 1976.

34 TASS, 6–8 July 1976; *Radio Moscow*, 28 August 1976; *Le Monde*, 20 July 1976; *Egyptian Gazette*, 13 June 1976; *Radio Beirut*, 25 July 1976; *Financial Times*, 9 and 10 August 1976.

35 *Damascus Radio*, 10, 18 and 20 June 1976.

36 *Ibid.*, 12 August and 12 October 1976.

37 *Pravda*, 27 and 29 December 1985; *Radio Moscow*, 27 and 28 December 1985.

38 Jimmy Carter, *Keeping Faith: Memoirs of a President* (Toronto: Bantam Books, 1982), pp. 471–2.

39 US Embassy in Afghanistan to Department of State, 'Afghan-Soviet Relations on the Eve of Taraki's Trip to Moscow', 6 December 1978, DNSA; David Gibbs, 'Reassessing Soviet motives for invading Afghanistan: A declassified history', *Critical Asian Studies*, 38/2 (2006), pp. 246–9; *idem*, 'Does the USSR Have a "Grand Strategy"? Reinterpreting the Invasion of Afghanistan', *Journal of Peace Research*, 24/4 (1987), pp. 372–4; P.R. Chari, 'Continuing turmoil in Afghanistan', *Strategic Analysis*, 3/3 (1979), pp. 85–8.

40 Wilson Center Digital Archive, 'Transcript of CPSU Politburo discussions on Afghanistan', 17 March 1979 (emphasis added).

41 *Ibid.*, 'Transcript of telephone conversation between Soviet Premier Alexei Kosygin and Afghan Prime Minister Nur Mohamed Taraki', 17 March 1979.

42 *Ibid.*, 'Transcript of CPSU Politburo discussions on Afghanistan', 18 and 19 March 1979 (text in direct contiguity to the 17 March meeting); *ibid.*, 'CPSU CC Politburo Decisions on Afghanistan', 18 March 1979.

43 *Ibid.*, 'Record of Conversation between L.I. Brezhnev and N.M. Taraki', 20 March 1979; 'Meeting of Kosygin, Gromyko, Ustinov, and Ponomarev with Taraki in Moscow', 20 March 1979.

44 *Ibid.*, 'Memo on Protocol #149 of the Politburo, "Our future policy in connection with the situation in Afghanistan", April 1, 1979'.

45 *Ibid.*, 'Protocol #150 of the CC CPSU Politburo Session, April 21, 1979'; 'CPSU CC Protocol #152/159, May 24, 1979, and Instructions to Soviet Ambassador in Afghanistan', 24 May 1979; Boris Ponomarev, 'Reports from Kabul (excerpts)', 19/20 July 1979; 'Record of Conversation between Soviet Ambassador to Afghanistan A.M. Puzanov and H. Amin', 21 July 1979; 'Conversation of the chief of the Soviet military advisory group in Afghanistan, Lt. Gen. Gorelov, with H. Amin', 11 August 1979; 'Report from Soviet Deputy Defense Minister Army Gen. Ivan Pavlovskii, during visit to Afghanistan, 25 August 1979'.

46 US Embassy in Afghanistan to Department of State, 'GDR Ambassador Reports that Soviets Hope to Replace Prime Minister Amin with a Broader Based Government', 18 July 1979, DNSA. See also: *idem*, 'Further Comments by East German Ambassador about Soviet efforts to Alter Afghan Regime', 29 July 1979.

47 'New Afghan Head Called Survivor of a Rebel Ambush Over Weekend', *New York Times*, 20 September 1979; Michael Kaufman, 'No Light at End of the Tunnel For Russians in Afghanistan', *ibid.*, 23 September 1979.

48 Wilson Center Digital Archive, 'Excerpt from transcript, CPSU CC Politburo meeting', 20 September 1979.

49 *Ibid.*, 'Transcript of Brezhnev–Honecker summit in East Berlin (excerpt on Iran and Afghanistan', 4 October 1979.

50 *Ibid.*, 'Report on the Situation in Afghanistan, Gromyko, Andropov, Ustinov, and Ponomarev to CPSU CC', 29 November 1979; 'Personal Memorandum [from] Andropov to Brezhnev', 1 December 1979; Secretary of State Vance to Kabul Embassy, 'Excerpts from Noon Briefing: Afghanistan', 5 December 1979, DNSA.

51 Anthony Arnold, *Afghanistan: The Soviet Invasion in Perspective* (Stanford: Hoover Institution Press, 1985), pp. 92–3; A.Z. Hilali, 'The Soviet decision-making for intervention in Afghanistan and its motives', *Journal of Slavic Military Studies*, 16/2 (2003), pp. 115–17.

52 For Amin's requests for Soviet troops see: Wilson Center Digital Archive, 'Telegram from Chief Soviet Military Adviser, "Report from Kabul"', 2 and 4 December 1979. For the Politburo's decision see: 'To Comrades Brezhnev, Andropov, Gromyko, Suslov, Ustinov: Extract From Protocol No. 176 of the Meeting of the CC CPSU Politburo of 6 December 1979'.

53 Alexander Lyakhovskiy, *Plamya Afgana* (Moscow: Iskon 1995), pp. 109–12 (translated by Svetlana Savranskaya for the National Security Archive); 'Summary of a meeting on Afghanistan', 10 December 1979, *ibid.*, p. 121 (translated for the Wilson Center Digital Archive by Gary Goldberg).

54 Wilson Center Digital Archive, 'CC CPSU Politburo Resolution #176/125, Concerning the Situation in 'A' [Afghanistan]', 12 December 1979; Lyakhovskiy, *Plamya Afgan*, pp. 109–12.

55 Wilson Center Digital Archive, 'Declaration of the CC CPSU to the Party Leadership concerning the Situation in Afghanistan, Attachment to CPSU Politburo Protocol #177', 27 December 1979.

Chapter 6

1 Lawrence Freedman and Efraim Karsh, *The Gulf Conflict 1990–1991: Diplomacy and War in the New World Order* (Princeton: Princeton University Press, 1993), pp. 5–7.

2 Gary Sick, *The October Surprise: America's Hostages in Iran and the Election of Ronald Reagan* (New York: Random House, 1991). This conspiracy theory was thoroughly discredited by two congressional hearings: 'The "October Surprise" Allegations and the Circumstances Surrounding the Release of the American Hostages Held in Iran', United States Senate Committee on Foreign Relations (Washington, D.C.: Government Printing Office, 1992); Joint Report of the Task Force to Investigate Certain Allegations Concerning the Holding of American Hostages by Iran in 1980, Committee of the Whole House on the State of the Union (Washington, D.C.: Government Printing Office, 1993).

3 See, for example, Thomas L. McNaugher, 'Walking tightropes in the Gulf', in Efraim Karsh (ed.), *The Iran–Iraq War: Impact and Implications* (London: Macmillan, 1987), pp. 171–200; Theodore Draper, *A Very Thin Line: The Iran–Contra Affairs* (New York: Hill and Wang, 1991).

4   Francis Fukuyama, 'The End of History?' *National Interest*, summer 1989.

5   *Observer* (London), 21 October 1990.

6   For Iraqi criticism of Kuwaiti and UAE oil policies see: *Iraqi News Agency (INA)*, 17 and 20 February and 1 May 1990; *Baghdad Radio*, 20 February 1990; *al-Sharq al-Awsat* (London), 18 May 1990.

7   *Baghdad Radio*, 18 July 1990.

8   J. Miller and L. Mylroie, *Saddam Hussein and the Crisis in the Gulf* (New York: Times Books, 1990), p. 15.

9   *Baghdad Radio*, 17 July 1990.

10   *Ibid.*, 16 July 1990.

11   *Ibid.*, 17 July 1990.

12   *Al-Qabas* (Kuwait), 20 July 1990; *al-Rai al-Amm* (Jordan), 26 July 1990.

13   Freedman and Karsh, *The Gulf Conflict*, pp. 50–4.

14   Glaspie admitted to having told Saddam that Washington had no opinion about Iraq's border dispute with Kuwait but argued that such aloofness had been the main trait of US policy in the Middle East, where all Arab countries were beset by border disputes of one kind or another.

15   This was in the ambassador's report back to Washington. *International Herald Tribune*, 13–14 July 1991.

16   *Ibid.*

17   For the Iraqi version of the meeting see: *International Herald Tribune*, 17 September 1990; *Economist*, 29 September 1990; *Observer*, 21 October 1990; Pierre Salinger and Eric Laurent, *Secret Dossier: The Hidden Agenda Behind the Gulf War* (London: Penguin, 1991), pp. 47–63. Glaspie claimed the Iraqi text to be only 80 per cent correct and has given her own version of the meeting. Senate Foreign Relations Committee, 20 March 1991; House Foreign Affairs Subcommittee on Europe and the Middle East, 21 March 1991.

18   Freedman and Karsh, *The Gulf Conflict*, p. 54.

19   Bob Woodward, *The Commanders* (New York: Simon & Schuster, 1991), p. 212.

20   *New York Times*, 23 September 1990; *International Herald Tribune*, 13–14 July 1991; *Financial Times*, 27 July 1990.

21   Eric Laurent, *Tempête du desert: les secrets de la Maison Blanche* (Pars: Olivier Orban, 1991), p. 27.

22   For further discussion of the US military options at the time of the Iraqi invasion see Freedman and Karsh, *The Gulf Conflict*, chapter 5.

23   Fred Halliday, 'The Gulf War 1990–1991 and the Study of International Relations', *Review of International Studies*, 20 (1994), pp. 115–16.

24   *INA*, 20 August 1990; *Radio Moscow in English*, 5 September 1990; *Independent* and *Financial Times*, 5 September 1990; *Guardian*, 25 September 1990.

25   US News and World Report, *Triumph without Victory: The History of the Persian Gulf War* (New York: Three Rivers Press, 1992), p. 195.

26   *Daily Telegraph*, 15 January 1991.

27   *The Times*, 2 October 1990; *Financial Times*, 5 October 1990.

28   *Observer*, 8 September 2002.

29   Robert M. Gates, *Duty: Memoirs of a Secretary at War* (New York: W. H. Allen, 2014), p. 26.

30   See, for example: 'Secret Weapon', *Newsweek*, 4 September 1995; *Sunday Times*, 27 August 1995; *Yediot Aharonot* (Tel Aviv), 27 and 28 August 1995.

31   See, for example, *Baghdad Television*, 12 September and 3 December 2001.

32   United Nations Security Council, 'Resolution 1441 (2002). Adopted by the Security Council at its 4644th meeting, on 8 November 2002'.

33   CNN.com, 'U.S. Secretary of State Colin Powell's presentation to the U.N. Security Council on the U.S. case against Iraq', 6 February 2003.

34   Efraim Karsh and Inari Rautsi, *Saddam Hussein: A Political Biography* (New York: Free Press, 1991), p. 1.

35   The White House, Office of the Press Secretary, 'President Bush Announces Major Combat Operations in Iraq Have Ended. Remarks by the President from the USS Abraham Lincoln At Sea Off the Coast of San Diego, California', 1 May 2003.

36   Ibrahim to Muhammad Ali, Ramadan 13, 1248 (10 August 1832), Abd. case 243, doc. 85, in Asad J. Rustum, *The Royal Archives of Egypt and the Origins of the Egyptian Expedition to Syria* (Beirut: American University of Beirut, 1936), p. 59; H. Batatu, *The Old Social Classes and the Revolutionary Movements of Iraq* (Princeton: Princeton University Press, 1978), p. 25.

37   Mark Wilbanks and Efraim Karsh, 'How the "Sons of Iraq" Stabilized Iraq', *Middle East Quarterly*, fall 2010, p. 58.

38   Amatzia Baram, 'Who Are the Insurgents? Sunni Arab Rebels in Iraq', United States Institute of Peace, Special Report 134, April 2005, p. 6.

39   James A. Baker, et al., *The Iraq Study Group Report* (New York: Vintage, 2006); Mahan Abedin, 'Anbar Province and Emerging Trends in the Iraqi Insurgency', Jamestown Foundation, Terrorism Monitor, 15 July 2005.

40   Lt Gen. Peter Chiarelli, teleconference news briefing, Iraq, US Department of Defense, Washington, D.C., 15 September 2006.

41 David H. Petraeus, 'How We Won in Iraq', *Foreign Policy*, 29 October 2013. See also his testimony before the Senate Armed Services Committee, *Associated Press*, 8 April 2008.

42 Wilbanks and Karsh, 'How the "Sons of Iraq" Stabilized Iraq', pp. 62–3. See also: Stephen Biddle, Jeffery Friedman and Jacob Shapiro, 'Testing the Surge: Why did Violence Decline in Iraq in 2007', *International Security*, summer 2012, pp. 7–40; Steve Simon, 'The Price of the Surge', *Foreign Affairs*, May/June 2008; Marc Lynch, 'Explaining the Awakening: Engagement, Publicity, and the Transformation of Iraqi Sunni Political Attitudes', *Security Studies*, vol. 20 (2011), pp. 36–72.

43 Petraeus, 'How We Won in Iraq'; Special Inspector General for Iraq Reconstruction (SIGIR), 'Information on Government of Iraq Contributions to Reconstruction Costs', 29 April 2009, p. 6.

44 SIGIR, 'Quarterly Report and Semiannual Report to the United States Congress', 30 July 2010, pp. 9–10.

45 Cullen Dirner, 'A Brief History of President Obama and the 2007 Surge of Troops in Iraq', *ABC News*, 23 August 2010.

46 The White House, Office of the Press Secretary, 'Remarks of President Barack Obama – As Prepared for Delivery Responsibly Ending the War in Iraq', Camp Lejeune, North Carolina, 13–14 February 2009.

47 Ernesto Londofi, 'Iraqis don't expect political impasse to be resolved by fall', *Washington Post*, 1 August 2010.

48 Michael D. Shear and William Branigin, 'Obama speaks with vets on Iraq drawdown', and Peter Baker, 'In Speech on Iraq, Obama Reaffirms Drawdown', *ibid.*, 2 August 2010.

49 The White House, Office of the Press Secretary, 'Weekly Address: Renewing America's Global Leadership', 22 October 2011.

50 *Ibid.*, 'Remarks by the President and First Lady on the End of the War in Iraq', 14 December 2011. See also: 'Remarks by the President on Ending the War in Iraq', 21 October 2011'; 'Remarks by President Obama and Prime Minister al-Maliki of Iraq in a Joint Press Conference', 12 December 2011.

51 Gates, *Duty*, pp. 554–5; 'Iraq must decide on US presence in coming weeks', *Telegraph*, 21 April 2011.

52 SIGIR, 'Quarterly Report and Semiannual Report to the United States Congress', 30 July 2012, pp. 6–7.

53 *Ibid.*, pp. 8–10 and 'Quarterly Report to the United States Congress', 30 October 2012, pp. 9, 61.

54 Meir Amit Intelligence and Terrorism Information Center at the Israeli Intelligence & Heritage Commemoration Center, 'ISIS: Portraits of a Jihadist Terrorist Organization', November 2014, pp. 20–30; Erin Marie Saltman and Jonathan Russell, 'Islamic State: the Changing Face of Modern Jihadism' (London: Quilliam Foundation, 4 November

2014), pp. 27–30; Kenneth Katzman, 'Iraq: Politics, Governance, and Human Rights' (Washington, D.C.: Congressional Research Service, 29 October 2014), pp. 8–9; Jessica D. Lewis, 'Al-Qaeda in Iraq Resurgent: The Breaking the Walls Campaign Part I' (Washington, D.C.: Institute for the Study of War, September 2013).

55 SIGIR, 'Quarterly Report to the United States Congress', 30 April 2013, pp. 5–6, and 'Final Report to the United States Congress', 9 September 2013, pp. 66–7; United Nations Iraq, 'Civilian Casualties', http://www.uniraq.org/index.php?option=com_k2 &view=itemlist&layout=category&task=category&id=159&Itemid=633&lang=en; Toby Dodge, 'Iraq's renewed political violence – Is the country heading back into civil war?' International Institute for Strategic Studies: Manama Voices, 7 December 2013; Zachary Laub and Jonathan Masters, 'Islamic State in Iraq and Syria' (New York: Council on Foreign Relations, updated 8 August 2014).

56 International Crisis Group, 'Déjà vu all over again? Iraq's escalating political crisis', *Middle East Report*, no. 126, 30 July 2012, pp. 14–15; 'Iraq PM warns of Syria crisis spillover', Al Jazeera, 28 February 2013.

57 Liz Sly, 'Al-Qaeda disavows any ties with radical Islamist ISIS group in Syria, Iraq', *Washington Post,* 3 February 2014; 'Al-Zawahiri calls on ISIS leader to return to Iraq', *alakhbar English* (Beirut), 3 May 2014.

58 'Sunni rebels declare "Islamic caliphate"', Al Jazeera, 30 June 2014; Abdelwahed al-Ansari, 'How did "Islamic State" proclaim caliphate?', *Al Monitor*, 7 July 2014; Damien McElroy, 'Rome will be conquered next, says leader of "Islamic State"', *Telegraph*, 1 July 2014.

59 'How foreign fighters are swelling ISIS ranks in startling numbers', CNN, 14 September 2014.

60 The White House, Office of the Press Secretary, 'Statement by the President on ISIL', 10 September 2014 (emphasis added); NBC News, 'Obama administration says U.S. is "at war" with ISIS', 12 September 2014.

61 'US says ISIS made "substantial gains in Iraq"', *al-Arabiya News*, 15 October 2014; 'US-led airstrikes kill several ISIS leaders', *ibid.*, 18 December 2014; 'Reports of US Fighters Emerge as ISIS Gains in Iraq', *Fiscal Times*, 17 December 2014.

Chapter 7

1 Trygve Lie, *In the Cause of Peace* (New York: Macmillan, 1954), pp. 172–3.

2 Circular Telegram from the Department of State to Certain Posts, 18 May 1967, *Foreign Relations of the United States* (hereinafter *FRUS*; internet edition), 1964–8, vol. 19, doc. 16. See also Information Memorandum from the Deputy Assistant Secretary of State for International Organizations Affairs (Popper) to Secretary of State Rusk, 19 May 1967, *ibid.*, doc. 19; Letter from Premier Kosygin to President Johnson, 27 May 1967, *ibid.*, doc. 84.

3 Richard B. Parker, *The Politics of Miscalculation in the Middle East* (Bloomington and Indianapolis: Indiana University Press, 1993), p. 8.

4   Muhammad Fawzi, *Harb al-Thalath Sanawat, 1967–1970* (Cairo: Dar al-Mustaqbal al-Arabi, 1980), pp. 71–2. Fawzi's reassuring findings were corroborated by both Egyptian military intelligence and a special UN inspection. Moreover, on three occasions the Soviet ambassador to Israel was invited by the Israeli authorities to visit the border area but declined to go. See: Abdel Muhsin Kamel Murtagi, *al-Fariq Murtagi Yarwi al-Haqa'iq: Qaid Jabhat Sinai fi Harb 1967* (Cairo: Dar al-Watan al-Arabi, 1976), p. 64; Indar Jit Rikhye, *The Sinai Blunder* (London: Cass, 1980), pp. 11–12.

5   Anwar Sadat, *In Search of Identity: An Autobiography* (New York: Harper & Row, 1978), p. 172; Muhammad Hassanein Heikal, *1967: al-Infijar* (Cairo: al-Ahram, 1990), pp. 514–19; Richard B. Parker, 'The June War: Some Mysteries Explored', *Middle East Journal*, Spring 1992, p. 192.

6   Nasser's speech on the anniversary of the Egyptian revolution, 23 July 1967 in Walter Laqueuer (ed.), *The Israel-Arab Reader* (Harmondsworth: Penguin, 1970), p. 248; Intelligence Memorandum Prepared in the Central Intelligence Agency, 3 June 1967, *FRUS*, 1964–8, vol. 19, doc. 143.

7   Nasser's speech of 23 July 1967; Intelligence Memorandum Prepared in the Central Intelligence Agency, 3 June 1967; Robert Stephens, *Nasser: A Political Biography* (London: Allen Lane, 1971), p. 489.

8   Israel Defence Forces, Southern Command, 'The Four-Day War, 1967' (an internal IDF document, June 1967; Hebrew). The existence of operational plans to occupy Israeli territory was also confirmed by Egyptian military sources. See, for example, Muhammad Abdel Ghani Gamasy, *Mudhakirat al-Gamasy: Harb October 1973* (Paris: al-Manshurat al-Sharqiya, 1990), pp. 70–1, 73–4.

9   Telegram from the Embassy in the United Arab Republic to the Department of State, 21 May 1967, *FRUS*, 1964–8, vol. 19, doc. 28.

10   Telegrams from the Embassy in Syria to the Department of State, 1 June 1967, and The Embassy in the United Arab Republic to the Department of State, 30 May and 1 and 2 June 1967, *ibid.*, docs. 100, 117, 119, 128; Minutes of the Ninth Meeting of the Middle East Control Group, 4 June 1967, *ibid.*, doc. 148; Lyndon B. Johnson, *The Vantage Point: Perspectives of the Presidency, 1963–1969* (New York: Holt, Rinehart, and Wilson, 1971), p. 293.

11   Telegram from the Embassy in the United Arab Republic to the Department of State, 2 June 1967, *FRUS*, 1964–8, vol. 19, doc. 134; Nasser's speech to Arab trade unionists, 26 May 1967, in Laqueuer, *The Israel-Arab Reader*, pp. 215–18.

12   Mahmoud Riad, *The Struggle for Peace in the Middle East* (London: Quartet Books, 1981), p. 48.

13   P. J. Vatikiotis, *Nasser and His Generation* (London: Croom Helm, 1978), p. 245.

14   Abdel Magid Farid, *Nasser: The Final Years* (Reading: Ithaca Press, 1994), p. 202. Farid served as secretary-general of the Egyptian presidency for 11 years until 1970.

15   *New York Times*, 28 December 1970.

16 Arab Republic of Egypt, *White Paper on the Peace Initiatives Undertaken by President Anwar Sadat [1971–77]* (Cairo: Ministry of Foreign Affairs, n.d.), pp. 5–16; 'UN Document S/10070/Add. 2', 5 March 1971; Yitzhak Rabin, *The Rabin Memoirs* (London: Weidenfeld & Nicolson, 1979), p. 157.

17 For the text of the 1975 agreement, and its secret annexes, see Edward Sheehan, *The Arabs, Israelis, and Kissinger* (New York: Readers' Digest, 1976), pp. 245–57.

18 Tawfiq Hakim, *The Return of Consciousness* (London: Macmillan, 1985), pp. 24–5, 34, 37, 43, 44, 50. See also: Jalal al-Din Hamamsi, *Hiwar Wara'a al-Aswar* (Cairo: al-Maktab al-Misri al-Hadith, 1976); Sami Jawhar, *al-Samitun Yatakalamun: Abdel Nasser wa-Madhbahat al-Ikhwan* (Cairo: al-Maktab al-Masri al-Hadith, 1976).

19 Abraham Ben-Zvi, *The United States and Israel: The Limits of the Special Relationship* (New York: Columbia University Press, 1993), pp. 99–100.

20 Moshe Dayan, *Halanetzah Tochal Herev?* (Jerusalem: Yediot Aharonot, 1981), p. 45.

21 Cyrus Vance, *Hard Choices: Critical Years in America's Foreign Policy* (New York: Simon & Schuster, 1983), p. 163. For the text of the joint statement see: Telegram from Secretary of State Vance's Delegation to Certain Diplomatic Posts, 1 October 1977, *FRUS*, 1977–80, vol. 8, pp. 634–6.

22 Jimmy Carter, *Keeping Faith: Memoirs of a President* (Toronto: Bantam, 1982), pp. 290–1; idem, *The Blood of Abraham* (Boston: Houghton Mifflin, 1985), p. 42. See also: Zbigniew Brzezinski, *Power and Principle: Memoirs of the National Security Advisor 1977–1981* (London: Weidenfeld & Nicolson, 1983), p. 99; Vance, *Hard Choices*, pp. 180–4.

23 Memorandum of Conversation, 30 September 1977, *FRUS*, 1977–80, vol. 8, pp. 624–9.

24 Telegram from the Embassy in Egypt to the Department of State, 3 November 1977 & Telegram from the Department of State to the Embassy in Egypt, 5 November 1977, *ibid.*, pp. 741–6; Brzezinski, *Power and Principle*, p. 111.

25 Telegram from the Embassy in Egypt to the Department of State, 10 and 23 November 1977, *FRUS*, 1977–80, vol. 8, pp. 750–3, 773; Telegram from the Department of State to the Embassy in Egypt, 12 and 18 November 1977 & Telegram from the Department of State to the White House, 18 November 1977 & Telegram from the Department of State to the Consulate in Jerusalem, 18 November 1977, *ibid.*, pp. 753–4, 756–61.

26 'The Palestinian National Charter', Resolutions of the Palestine National Council, 1–17 July 1968, http://www.un.int/wcm/content/site/palestine/pid/12362.

27 Brzezinski, *Power and Principle*, pp. 94, 100, 102–5; Yitzhak Rabin, *Pinkas Sherut* (Tel Aviv: Maariv, 1979), vol. 2, pp. 507–15; Memorandum of Conversation, Washington, 23 November 1977, *FRUS*, 1977–80, vol. 8, pp. 765–9; Edward Said, *The Pen and the Sword: Conversations with David Barsamian* (Edinburgh: AK Press, 1994), p. 137.

28 *Al-Anba* (Kuwait), 5 and 13 December 1988. For other Palestinian statements in the same vein see, for example, interview by Khaled Hassan, head of the PNC's committee for external and parliamentary relations, with *al-Musawar* (Cairo), 20 January 1989; interview with Salim Zaanun (aka Abu Adib), the PNC's deputy chairman, with *al-Anba* (Kuwait), 21 November 1988; interview by Rafiq Natsha (Abu Shakir), a member of the PLO's central committee, with *al-Sharq al-Awsat* (London), 9 December 1988, and with *al-Jazira (Saudi Arabia)*, 1 January 1989.

29 *Baghdad Voice of the PLO*, 8 January 1991.

30 *Al-Hayat al-Jadida*, 15 November 1997.

31 Thus according to Palestinian accounts. See, for example: *al-Quds*, 18 and 30 August 2000; *Palestinian Authority Television*, 28 July 2000; *al-Hayat al-Jadida*, 28 July 2000; *al-Musawwar* (Cairo), 18 August 2000.

32 Hussein Agha and Robert Malley, 'Camp David: the Tragedy of Errors', *New York Review of Books*, 9 August 2001.

33 *Jerusalem Post*, 26 and 30 July 2000; *New York Times*, 26 July 2000.

34 *Economist*, 14 October 2000, p. 57.

35 *Jerusalem Post*, 29 December 2000; Dennis Ross on *Fox News*, 21 April 2002. Ross's account was confirmed by Arafat's longtime confidante Mamduh Nawfal. See, *al-Ayyam* (PA official newspaper), 19 January 2001.

36 Ehud Ya'ari, 'Wait and Fire', *Jerusalem Report*, 26 March 2001, p. 21; Leslie Susser, 'Where's Uncle Sam?' *ibid.*, 2 July 2001, p. 14; *Maariv*, 15 March 2001.

37 *Ibid.*, 11 September 2001.

38 Bob Woodward, *Bush at War* (New York: Simon & Schuster, 2002), p. 297.

39 *Jerusalem Post*, 28 and 29 January, 15 February, and 12 and 24 March 2002; Douglas Frantz & James Risen, 'A Secret Iran–Arafat Connection is Seen Fueling the Mideast Fire', *New York Times*, 24 March 2002; Akiva Eldar's interview with Arafat, *Haaretz*, 23 June 2002.

40 Woodward, *Bush At War*, pp. 323–4.

41 *Jerusalem Post*, 19 April and 6 May 2002.

42 www.ABCNews.com, 24 June 2002.

43 www.palestine-pmc.com/details.asp?cat=1&id=888; http://english.wafa.ps/body .asp?field=Enews&id=2658 (both are PA official sites).

44 Jackson Diehl, 'Abbas's Waiting Game', *Washington Post*, 29 May 2009; 'Chief Palestinian Negotiator Saeb Erekat: Abu Mazen Rejected the Israeli proposal in Annapolis Like Arafat Rejected the Camp David 2000 Proposal', MEMRI, TV Clip 2074, 27 March 2007; Palestinian Media Watch Bulletin, 28 November 2007 (pmw .org.il/bulletins_nov2007.htm#b2811070); Aluf Ben, 'Olmert Almost Made History', *Haaretz*, 26 June 2009.

45 'Abbas Won't Recognize Israel as a Jewish State', *Ynet.news.com*, 27 April 2009.

Chapter 8

1   'When Barry Became Barack', *Newsweek*, 22 March 2008.

2   The White House, Office of the Press Secretary, 'Remarks by the President on a New Beginning', Cairo University, Cairo, Egypt, 4 June 2009.

3   'Obama administration pulls references to Islam from terror training materials, official says', *Daily Caller*, 21 October 2011; 'Obama bans terms "Islam" and "Jihad" from US security document', *Haaretz*, 7 April 2010; 'NASA Chief Bolden's Muslim Remarks to Aljazeera Causes Stir', *Space.com*, 7 July 2010.

4   'Fort Hood army officer shouted "Allahu Akbar" before shooting rampage', *Guardian* (London), 6 November 2009; 'Fort Hood shooting: the meaning of "Allahu Akbar"', *Telegraph* (London), 6 November 2009.

5   'Protecting the Force: Lessons from Fort Hood', DoD Independent Review Related to Fort Hood, January 2010, D-2. For a much more considered report see: 'A Ticking Time Bomb: Counterterrorism Lessons from the US Government's Failure to Prevent the Fort Hood Attack', A Special Report by Joseph I. Lieberman, Chairman, Susan M. Collins, Ranking Member (Washington, DC.: United States Senate Committee on Homeland Security and Governmental Affairs, 3 February 2011).

6   Chelsea J. Carter, 'Fort Hood shooter writes to ISIS leader, asks to become "citizen" of Islamic state', CNN, 29 August 2014.

7   'Obama – The Vox Conversation. Part Two: Foreign Policy', 9 February 2015.

8   The White House, Office of the Press Secretary, 'Press Briefing by Press Secretary Josh Earnest', 10 February 2015.

9   *Ibid.*, 'Press Briefing by Press Secretary Josh Earnest', 13 January 2015.

10 The White House Blog, 'Osama Bin Laden Dead', 2 May 2011; CNN, 'Transcript: President Obama's speech on Combating ISIS and Terrorism', 11 September 2014.

11 'Director of National Intelligence James Clapper: Muslim Brotherhood "Largely Secular"', *ABC News*, 10 February 2011.

12 'Remarks by the President on a New Beginning'.

13 The White House, Office of the Press Secretary, 'Remarks by the President on the Middle East and North Africa', 19 May 2011.

14 'Reactions: Bin Laden's death', Al Jazeera (Doha), 2 May 2011.

15 Human Rights Watch, 'Saudi Arabia: Surge in Executions', 21 August 2014.

16 As cited in James Poniewozik, 'The Banality of Bin Laden', *Time*, 13 December 2001.

17 Pew Research Global Attitudes Project, 'Global Opinion of Obama Slips, International Policies Faulted', 13 June 2012.

18   As cited in Fouad Ajami, 'The Arabs Have Stopped Applauding Obama', *Wall Street Journal*, 29 November 2009.

19   UN Security Council Resolutions 1696 (31 July 2006); 1737 (23 December 2006); 1747 (24 March 2007); 1803 (3 March 2008); 1835 (27 September 2008).

20   'Obama's Tone in Iran Message Differs Sharply from Bush's', *Washington Post*, 21 March 2009.

21   'Obama to Iran – "A New Day, a New Beginning"', *The Times* (London), 21 March 2009.

22   'Remarks by the President on a New Beginning'.

23   'Text of Barack Obama's Inaugural Address', *New York Times*, 20 January 2009; 'Remarks by the President on a New Beginning.'

24   'Ayatollah mocks U.S. Pre-election Overture', CBS, 24 June 2009.

25   David Sanger and Thom Shanker, 'Gates Says US Lacks A Policy to Thwart Iran', *New York Times*, 18 April 2010.

26   Robert M. Gates, *Duty: Memoirs of a Secretary at War* (New York: W.H. Allen, 2014), pp. 391–3.

27   International Crisis Group, 'In Heavy Water: Iran's Nuclear Program, the Risk of War and Lessons from Turkey', Middle East and Europe Report no. 116, 23 February 2012, p. 12.

28   The White House, Office of the Press Secretary, 'Remarks by the President in a News Conference', 14 November 2012.

29   Farhad Rajaee, *Islamic Values and World View: Khomeini on Man, the State and International Politics* (Lanham: University of America Press, 1983), pp. 82 –3.

30   International Atomic Energy Agency, 'Iran–EU Agreement on Nuclear Programme', 14 November 2004; 'Iran agrees to suspend uranium enrichment', CNN.com, 15 November 2004; 'Rouhani, on Iranian TV in May, detailed how he broke nuclear pledge', *Times of Israel*, 6 October 2013.

31   'Full Text of Iran's Hassan Rouhani at UN', *Times of Israel*, 25 September 2013.

32   Jay Solomon and Carole E. Lee, 'Historic Call for Obama, Rouhani', *Wall Street Journal*, 27 September 2013; Jeff Mason and Louis Charbonneau, 'Obama, Iran's Rouhani hold historic phone call', Reuters, 28 September 2013.

33   IAEA, 'Communication dated 27 November 2013 received from the EU High Representative concerning the text of the Joint Plan of Action', INFCIRC/855.

34   Saeed Kamali Dehgan, 'Iran's leaders and public celebrate Geneva deal', *Guardian*, 24 November 2013; BBC News, 'Iran agrees to curb nuclear activity in Geneva talks', 24 November 2013; Y. Mansharof et al., 'The Geneva Joint Plan of Action: How Iran Sees It (1)', MEMRI – Inquiry & Analysis Series Report, no. 1050, 13 January 2014.

35 Paul D. Shinkman, 'Iranian President Hassan Rouhani Says Nuclear Deal Marks U.S. "Surrender"', U.S. News & World Report, 14 January 2014.

36 See, for example, United States Institute of Peace – The Iran Primer, 'Western Countries Flood Tehran', 29 April 2014; Kenneth Katzman, 'Iran Sanction', Congressional Research Service, 23 October 2014, pp. 57–8, http://www.cbsnews.com/news/ayatollah-mocks-us-pre-election-overture/; Lee Smith, 'The Collapse of Sanctions on Iran', Weekly Standard, 3 March 2013.

37 Olli Heinonen, 'The Iranian Nuclear Programme: Practical Parameters for a Credible Long-Term Agreement' (London: Henry Jackson Society, November 2014), pp, 6–7, 17–18.

38 Jeffrey Goldberg, 'The Crisis in U.S.–Israel Relations Is Officially Here', Atlantic, October 2014.

39 'U.S. proposes Iran keep nuclear infrastructure but reduce ability to make bomb', Haaretz, 16 October 2014.

40 Jay Solomon and Carole E. Lee, 'Obama Wrote Secret Letter to Iran's Khamenei About fighting Islamic State', Wall Street Journal, 6 November 2014; IAEA Director General Yukiya Amano, 'Challenges in Nuclear Verification: The IAEA's Role on the Iranian Nuclear Issue', address at the Brookings Institution, Washington, D.C., 31 October 2014, p. 4 (emphasis in original).

41 Patrick Goodenough, 'Iran: "Hypocritical" Obama Adopts Friendly Tone in Secret Letters, Tough Tone in Public', cnsnnws.com, 13 November 2014; A. Savyon and Y. Mansharof, 'Iran's Pragmatic Camp Calls for Exploiting Obama's Weakness to Attain Comprehensive Nuclear Agreement on Tehran's Terms', MEMRI – Inquiry & Analysis Series Report, no. 1127, 26 October 2014.

42 The White House, Office of the Press Secretary, 'Remarks by President Obama to the Turkish Parliament', Ankara, Turkey, 6 April 2009.

43 Ibid.

44 Hannibal Travis, 'Did the Armenian Genocide Inspire Hitler?' Middle East Quarterly, winter 2013, p. 27.

45 Taner Akçam, The Young Turks' Crime against Humanity: The Armenian Genocide and Ethnic Cleansing in the Ottoman Empire (Princeton: Princeton University Press, 2012), p. xi.

46 'Barack Obama emphasizes the importance of U.S.–Armenia relations', Armenian Reporter, 2 October 2008.

47 'Remarks by President Obama to the Turkish Parliament.'

48 'Armenian genocide resolution passes US Congress Committee', Voice of America, 3 March 2010.

49 The White House, Office of the Press Secretary, 'Statement by the President on Armenian Remembrance Day', 24 April 2014.

50 Armenian National Committee of America, 'President Bush Breaks Pledge to Recognize Armenian Genocide', 24 April 2001.

51 Samantha Power, *A Problem from Hell: America and the Age of Genocide* (New York: Basic Books, 2002).

52 Daniel Pipes, 'How Turkey Went Bad', *Weekly Standard*, 13 October 2014; Michael Rubin, 'Turkey, from Ally to Enemy', *Commentary*, July/August 2010; Dani Rodrik, 'The Death of Turkey's Democracy', *Wall Street Journal*, 23 June 2010; 'Time to get tough on Turkey's Erdogan, US foreign policy experts tell Obama', *Jerusalem Post*, 23 February 2014.

53 Cited in Svante E. Cornell, 'What Drives Turkey's Foreign Policy?' *Middle East Quarterly*, winter 2012, p. 18. See also: Suat Kiniklioglu, 'The Return of Ottomanism', *Zaman* (Istanbul), 20 March 2007; Omer Taspinar, 'Neo-Ottomanism and Kemalist Foreign Policy', *Zaman* (Istanbul), 22 September 2008; Tariq Alhomayed, 'Turkey: Searching for a Role', *al-Sharq al-Awsat* (London), 19 May 2010.

54 'Turkey's Prime Minister Surprises Merkel: Erdoğan Proposes Turkish Medium High Schools for Germany', *Spiegel Online International*, 8 February 2008; 'Cologne's Turkish Spectacle: Erdoğan's One-Man Show', *ibid.*, 11 February 2008.

55 Nimrod Raphaeli, 'Turkey Throws Iran a Safety Net', MEMRI – Inquiry & Analysis Series Report, No. 629, 3 August 2010.

56 'Erdoğan's Davos Outburst is Nothing New', *Forbes*, 30 January 2009.

57 Neil MacFarquhar and Ethan Bronner, 'Report Finds Naval Blockade by Israel Legal but Faults Raid', *New York Times*, 1 September 2011.

58 Cornell, 'What Drives Turkey's Foreign Policy?', pp. 15–16; Ilias I. Kouskouvelis, 'The Problem with Turkey's "Zero Problems"', *Middle East Quarterly*, winter 2013, pp. 47–56.

59 'Turkish Prime Minister Erdogan Compares Israel To Hitler, Says: They Will Drown In The Blood That They Shed', MEMRI, Special Dispatch No. 5842, 16 September 2014.

60 See, for example, Tulin Dloglu, 'AKP Reacts to US Criticism of Turkey', *Al Monitor*, 8 February 2013; 'Davutoğlu: US Senate debate is "operation against AKP"', *Daily News* (Ankara), 17 July 2014.

61 Fareed Zakaria, 'Inside Obama's World: The President Talks to TIME About the Changing Nature of American Power', *Time*, 19 January 2012; Jonathan Schanzer, 'An Unhelpful Ally', *Wall Street Journal*, 25 June 2014.

62 Damla Aras, 'Turkish-Syrian Relations Go Downhill', *Middle East Quarterly*, spring 2012, pp. 41–50; 'Erdogan criticizes U.S. for airdropping weapons to Kurdish fighters', *al-Arabiya*, 22 October 2014.

63 'Joe Biden Apologizes For Saying Turkey Admitted To Border Security Failures In ISIS Fight', *Huffington Post*, 4 October 2014.

64 Andrea Elliott, 'Muslim Voters Detect a Snub from Obama', *New York Times*, 24 June 2008.

65   Scott Wilson, 'Obama Searches for Middle East Peace', *Washington Post*, 14 July 2012.

66   'Obama snubbed Netanyahu for dinner with Michelle and the girls, Israelis claim', *Daily Telegraph*, 25 March 2010.

67   'Netanyahu declares 10-month settlement freeze "to restart peace talks"', *Haaretz*, 25 November 2009.

68   'Palestinians Reject Netanyahu Speech', *Independent* online, 14 June 2009; MEMRI, 'Fatah's Sixth General Conference Resolutions: Pursuing Peace Options without Relinquishing Resistance or Right to Armed Struggle', 13 August 2009.

69   'At Knesset winter session opening Netanyahu says Palestinian state may be a source of continued conflict if irresponsibly handled', *Jerusalem Post*, 10 November 2010; 'Both sides must take steps for negotiations to continue' and 'Abbas to Arab League: Israel has violated all agreements', *ibid.*, 10 December 2010.

70   'UN General Assembly Votes to Recognize Palestinian State', CBS News, 30 November 2012.

71   'Kerry: Two-year window is maximum for two states', *JTA*, 18 April 2013.

72   'Arab League rejects Israel as Jewish State', *Haaretz*, 26 March 2014; Raphael Ahren, 'Kerry focuses blame on Israel for collapse of talks', *Times of Israel*, 8 April 2014; Ben Birnbaum and Amir Tibon, 'The Explosive, Inside Story of How John Kerry Built an Israel–Palestine Peace Plan – and Watched It Crumble', *New Republic*, 20 July 2014.

73   'Obama: FAA took "prudent action" in Israel', *USA Today*, 25 July 2014; 'In deaths of civilians in Gaza, US weapons sales to Israel come under scrutiny', *Washington Post*, 23 August 2014; Goldberg, 'The Crisis in U.S.–Israel Relations'.

74   Wanda Carruthers, 'Lindsey Graham: Allies Say Obama Respects Enemies More than Friends', *Newsmax*, 23 January 2015

75   'Only 16% of Israeli public believe US president's administration is more pro-Israel than pro-Palestinian', *Jerusalem Post*, 30 October 2014.

76   Birnbaum and Tibon, 'The Explosive, Inside Story of How John Kerry Built an Israel-Palestine Peace Plan – and Watched It Crumble.'

77   Palestinian Centre for Policy and Survey Research (Ramallah), 'Palestinian Public Opinion Poll no. 45', 13–15 September 2012; Pew Research Global Attitudes Project, 'America's Global Image Remains More Positive than China's. Chapter 1: Attitudes toward the United States', 18 May 2013; *idem*, 'Global Opposition to U.S. Surveillance and Drones, but Limited Harm to America's Image', 14 May 2014.

Chapter 9

1   The White House, Office of the Press Secretary, 'Remarks by the President on the Middle East and North Africa', 19 May 2011.

2 'Interview with Syrian President Bashar al-Assad', *Wall Street Journal*, 31 January 2011; Robert M. Gates, *Duty: Memoirs of a Secretary at War* (New York: W.H. Allen, 2014), p. 523.

3 The White House, Office of the Press Secretary, 'Statement by the President on Events in Tunisia', 14 January 2011.

4 Gates, *Duty*, pp. 504–5.

5 Mahmoud Abbas's interview with *Akhbar al-Yawm* (Cairo), 30 November 2014, as brought by MEMRI, Special Dispatch 5898, 5 December 2014.

6 The White House Blog, 'President Obama on the Situation in Egypt: "All Governments Must Maintain Power through Consent, Not Coercion"', 28 January 2011.

7 The White House, Office of the Press Secretary, 'President Obama on Transition in Egypt', 1 February 2011.

8 Ryan Lizza, 'The Consequentialist: How the Arab Spring Remade Obama's Foreign Policy', *The New Yorker*, 2 May 2011, p. 34.

9 The White House, Office of the Press Secretary, 'Remarks by the President on the Middle East and North Africa', 19 May 2011.

10 See, for example, 'Remarks by the President to the White House Press Corps', The White House, Office of the Press Secretary, 20 August 2012.

11 The White House, Office of the Press Secretary, 'Statement by the President on Syria', 31 August 2013.

12 Yoav Limor, 'Turbulence Expected to Continue in 2015' (interview with Brig. Gen. Itai Baron, outgoing head of the IDF's intelligence research department), *Israel Hayom*, 15 January 2015 (Hebrew); 'Kerry willing to talk with Syria's Assad', *Wall Street Journal*, 15 March 2015.

13 The White House Blog, 'The President on Libya: "The Violence Must Stop; Muammar Gaddafi Has Lost the Legitimacy to Lead and He Must Leave"', 3 March 2011.

14 United Nations Security Council, Resolution 1970 (2011), adopted by the Security Council at its 6491st Meeting, 26 February 2011; Resolution 1973 (2011), adopted by the Security Council at its 6498th Meeting, on 17 March 2011.

15 Barack Obama, David Cameron and Nicolas Sarkozy, 'Libya's Pathway to Peace', *New York Times*, 14 April 2011.

16 Gates, *Duty*, pp. 511–12, 522.

17 Amnesty International, 'Detention Abuses Staining the New Libya' (London, 2011); US State Department, '2011 Human Rights reports: Libya', 24 May 2012; Seumas Milne, 'If the Libyan war was about saving lives, it was a catastrophic failure', *Guardian*, 26 October 2011; Human Rights Watch (HRW), 'Libya: Militias Terrorizing Residents of "Loyalist" Town', 30 October 2011; HRW, 'Libya: Bolster Security at Tawergha Camps', 5 March 2012; HRW, 'Libya: Stop Arbitrary Arrests of Black Africans', 4 September 2011; HRW, 'Death of a Dictator', 17 October 2012; Alex Newman, 'Libyan Rebels Accused of "Ethnic Cleansing", Black Genocide', *New American*, 15 September 2011.

18 '"Funny" Anti-Gaddafi Cartoons Reveal Rebels' Racism, Anti-Semitism', *PJ Media*, 1 May 2011; Sarah Schlesinger, 'Libya Fails an Important Test', *National Review* online, 11 October 2011.

19 Con Coughlin, 'West's fears over spectre of al-Qaeda among rebels', *Daily Telegraph*, 29 March 2011; Gary Gambill, 'The Libyan Islamic Fighting Group (LIFG)', *Jamestown Foundation*, 24 March 2005; Ian Black, 'Libya rebels reject Gaddafi's al-Qaida spin', *Guardian*, 1 March 2011; *idem*, 'The Libyan Islamic Fighting Group – from al-Qai'da to the Arab spring', *ibid.*, 5 September 2011.

20 'Energized Muslim Brotherhood in Libya eyes a prize', CNN, 25 March 2011.

21 Dana Ford et al., 'Egypt's president calls for a "religious revolution"', CNN, 6 January 2015; Daniel Pipes, 'What Egypt's President Sisi Really Thinks', *Middle East Quarterly*, autumn 2014; Cynthia Farahat, 'The Arab Upheavals: Egypt's Islamist Shadow', *ibid.*, summer 2011, pp. 19–24.

22 The White House, Office of the Press Secretary, 'Statement by President Barack Obama on Egypt', 3 July 2013.

23 'Director of National Intelligence James Clapper: Muslim Brotherhood "Largely Secular"', ABC News, 10 February 2011.

24 See, for example, National Endowment for Democracy, 'Democratic Transition in the Middle East: Between Authoritarianism and Islamism', 12 July 2012; Samuel Tadros, 'Egypt's Elections: Why the Islamists Won', *World Affairs Journal* (March/April 2012); Marc Lynch, 'Islamists in a Changing Middle East', *Foreign Policy*, 8 July 2012; Gregory Gause III, 'The Year the Arab Spring Went Bad', *Foreign Policy*, 31 December 2012.

25 'Remarks by the President on the Middle East and North Africa', 19 May 2011.

26 'Libya: We gave US three-day warning of Benghazi attack', *Independent* (London), 18 September 2012.

27 'Face the Nation', CBS, 16 September 2012; The White House, Office of the Press Secretary, 'Press Briefing by Press Secretary Jay Carney 9/18/2012'; 'As Carney labels Libya strike terrorism, Obama continues to cite anti-Islam film', Fox News, 21 September 2012; US Department of State, 'President Obama on Death of U.S. Embassy Staff in Libya', 12 September 2012; 'Transcript: President Obama Talks to the U.N. about Mideast Peace, Iran', ABC News, 25 September 2012.

28 Bernard-Henry Lévy, 'Libya, Sharia, and Us', *Huffington Post*, 3 November 2011. For Abdel Jalil's proclamation see: 'Sharia law declaration raises concerns in new Libya', *Egypt Independent*, 26 October 2011; 'Hinting at an End to a Curb on Polygamy, Interim Libyan Leader Stirs Anger', *New York Times*, 29 October 2011.

29 See, for example: Patrick Goodenough, 'Al-Qaeda Tries to Link Itself to Libyan Rebellion', cnsnews.com, 30 March 2011; 'Transcript: President Obama Talks to the

U.N. about Mideast Peace, Iran'; US Department of State, Office of the Spokesperson, 'Clinton on Support for Emerging Democracies', 26 September 2012.

30   General Nuri al-Said, *Arab Independence and Unity: A Note on the Arab Cause With Particular Reference to Palestine, and Suggestions for a Permanent Settlement to Which Are Attached Texts of all the Relevant Documents* (Baghdad: Government Press, 1943), p. 8

31   'Constitution of Palestine (2003)', Wikisource, http://en.wikisource.org/wiki/Constitution_of_Palestine_(2003).

32   'Full Text of Iraqi Constitution', *Washington Post*, 12 October 2005.

33   Bernard Lewis, *The Emergence of Modern Turkey* (New York: Oxford University Press, 3rd ed. 2002), p. 15.

34   'Religious Freedom in Turkey: Situation of Religious Minorities', European Parliament, Directorate General External Policies of the Union, Policy Department External Policies, Luxembourg, February 2008, pp. 2, 10; European Commission, 'Turkey 2010 Progress Report', Brussels, 10 November 2010.

35   See, for example, Omer Taspiner, 'Neo-Ottomanism and Kemalist Foreign Policy', *Zaman*, 22 September 2008; John Eibner, 'Turkey's Christians under Siege', *Middle East Quarterly*, vol. 18, no. 2 (spring 2011), pp. 41–52; Diana Muir Appelbaum, 'Islamic Supremacy Alive and Well in Ankara', *Middle East Quarterly*, winter 2013, pp. 3–15.

36   'Muslim Brotherhood Operatives in Turkey Call For Killing Egyptian Officials, Threaten Egypt; Turkish MP: Turkey Shelters "Many MB And Hamas Members"', MEMRI, Special Dispatch 5959, 6 February 2015.

37   See, for example: Yvette Talhamy, 'The Muslim Brotherhood Reborn: The Syrian Uprising', *Middle East Quarterly*, spring 2012, pp. 33–40; Hilal Khashan, 'Bandar bin Sultan's Botched Syrian Intervention', *ibid.*, winter 2014; Burak Bekdil, 'Turkey's Boomerang War in Syria', *Gatestone Institute*, 16 October 2014; Meir Amit Intelligence and Terrorism Information Center, 'ISIS: Portrait of a Jihadi Terrorist Organization', Tel Aviv, November 2014.

38   See, for example, Eric Schmitt, 'With Arms for Yemen Rebels, Iran Seeks Wider Mideast Role', *New York Times*, 15 March 2012; 'Houthis Take Over', *Economist*, 27 September 2014; Martin Reardon, 'Saudi Arabia, Iran, and the "Great Game" in Yemen', Al Jazeera, 30 September 2014; Greg Zoroya, 'Rebels capture Yemen presidential palace, shell residence', *USA Today*, 20 January 2015; Mohammed Ghobari, 'Yemen's Houthis dissolve parliament, assume power: televised statement', Reuters, 6 February 2015.

39   Chris Stephen, 'War in Libya: the *Guardian* Briefing', *Guardian*, 29 August 2014; *idem*, 'Libyan PM says Tripoli bombing will stop when extremists surrender', *ibid.*, 26 November 2014.

40   'ISIS-linked Camps in Libya Fan Concerns about Growing Militant Threat', *Time*, 5 December 2014; 'ISIS could expand to Libya: EU anti-terrorism chief', *al-Arabiya*, 5 December 2014.

41 C. Norris-Trent, 'Who Are Libya's Liberals?' France 24, 11 July 2012.

42 'Prime Minister's First Speech to the UN General Assembly', GOV.UK, 22 September 2011.

Epilogue

1 The White House, Office of the Press Secretary, 'Remarks by the President at National Prayer Breakfast', Washington Hilton, 5 February 2015.

2 Muhammad ibn Umar al-Waqidi, *Kitab al-Maghazi* (London: Oxford University Press, 1966), vol. 3, p. 1113.

3 Translated by the Middle East Media Research Institute (MEMRI), 'Special Dispatch Series, No. 447', 6 December 2002. See also: Gilles Kepel, *Jihad: The Trail of Political Islam* (Cambridge: Harvard University Press, 2002), p. 306; Michel Gurfinkiel, 'Islam in France: The French Way of Life Is in Danger', *Middle East Quarterly*, March 1997 (internet edition); Lorenzo Vidino, 'The Muslim Brotherhood's Conquest of Europe', *Middle East Quarterly*, winter 2005 (internet edition), Anthony Browne, 'The Triumph of the East', *Spectator* (London), 24 July 2004.

4 The White House, Office of the Press Secretary, 'Remarks by the President in Closing the Summit on Countering Violent Extremism', 18 February 2015.

5 *Ibid.*

INDEX